THE BRITISH CIVIL SERVICE

Current Issues and Future Challenges

Janice Morphet

First published in Great Britain in 2025 by

Bristol University Press
University of Bristol
1–9 Old Park Hill
Bristol
BS2 8BB
UK
t: +44 (0)117 374 6645
e: bup-info@bristol.ac.uk

Details of international sales and distribution partners are available at bristoluniversitypress.co.uk

© Bristol University Press 2025

British Library Cataloguing in Publication Data
A catalogue record for this book is available from the British Library

ISBN 978-1-5292-3491-6 hardcover
ISBN 978-1-5292-3492-3 paperback
ISBN 978-1-5292-3493-0 ePub
ISBN 978-1-5292-3494-7 ePdf

The right of Janice Morphet to be identified as author of this work has been asserted by her in accordance with the Copyright, Designs and Patents Act 1988.

All rights reserved: no part of this publication may be reproduced, stored in a retrieval system, or transmitted in any form or by any means, electronic, mechanical, photocopying, recording, or otherwise without the prior permission of Bristol University Press.

Every reasonable effort has been made to obtain permission to reproduce copyrighted material. If, however, anyone knows of an oversight, please contact the publisher.

The statements and opinions contained within this publication are solely those of the author and not of the University of Bristol or Bristol University Press. The University of Bristol and Bristol University Press disclaim responsibility for any injury to persons or property resulting from any material published in this publication.

Bristol University Press works to counter discrimination on grounds of gender, race, disability, age and sexuality.

Cover design: Nicky Borowiec
Front cover image: Getty/Adrienne Bresnahan

Contents

List of abbreviations		vi
Preface		viii
1	**Introduction: What is the Civil Service For?**	1
	Introduction	1
	The role of the civil service: an international context	2
	The civil service in the UK	8
	Conclusions	19
2	**What Kind of Civil Service Do We Have? The Structure of the Home Civil Service in England**	21
	Introduction	21
	How many civil servants?	22
	Tripartite structure of the civil service	23
	Issues for the civil service as an employer	36
3	**How Does the Civil Service Develop Policy?**	40
	Introduction	40
	What is policy?	41
	What stimulates policy development?	42
	Who makes policy – ministers or civil servants?	52
	How are policies constructed?	56
	Conclusions	59
4	**How Does the Civil Service Administer Policy?**	60
	Introduction	60
	The context for the administration of policy	63
	Administration vs implementation and delivery	66
	Issues to be considered when designing the administration of policy	70
	Determining the mechanism for delivery	72
	Agents of delivery	75

5	**Relationships with Ministers**		79
	Introduction		79
	The view of civil servants by ministers		81
	The view of ministers by civil servants		85
	Has the civil service become more politicised?		89
	Unwelcome intermediaries		91
	Events		95
6	**Devolution and the Role of Civil Service in the Union**		98
	Introduction		98
	What is the case for devolution of decision making?		102
	Relationships between Whitehall, Scotland and Wales before 1999		103
	Policy differentiation after the Devolution Settlement 1999–2010		104
	Recentralising the state and muscular unionism after 2010		106
	Civil servants in the DAs		109
	Devolution in England		112
	The future role of the civil service in drawing together the Union		113
	Conclusions		113
7	**Policy Formation after Brexit**		115
	Introduction		115
	The role of the EU in shaping UK domestic policy 1972–2020		119
	International sources of UK government policy post-Brexit		120
	What was the role of the civil service in developing policy and administration when the UK was in the EU?		123
	The challenges after Brexit		124
	What are the policy implementation challenges post-Brexit?		127
	Conclusions		128
8	**Civil Service: Weaknesses and Failures**		130
	Introduction		130
	The context for decision making		131
	What is the role of civil service in the failure to successfully administer government policy?		134
	Corruption		146
	Conclusions		148

9	**How Does the Civil Service Survive Change?** **The Persistence of Power**	**150**
	Introduction	150
	The Westminster Model	151
	Multiple Government reforms but no change?	153
	The UK civil service as a persistent political elite	153
	Methods of maintaining power: operating the Core Executive	155
	Methods of maintaining power: recruitment and promotion	159
	Maintaining power: creating a lattice of leverage	162
	Managing ministers	165
	Managing outside Whitehall	166
10	**The Civil Service – Forwards or Back?**	**168**
	What is the need for change?	168
	Can the WM accommodate devolution?	169
	Can the WM accommodate SpADs?	170
	What will be the long-term consequences for the civil service of Brexit?	171
	How can the civil service be focused on administration within the contractual state?	171
	What are the possible tools for change?	172
	Civil servants accepting the need for change in the civil service	172
References		175
Index		217

List of abbreviations

APPG	All Party Parliamentary Group
BIC	British Irish Council
CA	Combined Authority
CPO	Compulsory Purchase Order
CPRS	Central Policy Review Staff
CSC	Civil Service Commission
DA	Devolved Administration
DEA	Department of Economic Affairs
DExEU	Department for Exiting the EU
DfID	Department for International Development
EC	European Commission
EIB	European Investment Bank
ESRC	Economic and Social Research Council
EU	European Union
FCO	Foreign and Commonwealth Office
FMI	Financial Management Initiative
GATT	General Agreement on Tariffs and Trade
GPA	Government Procurement Agreement
HMT	His Majesty's Treasury
IfG	Institute for Government
IFRS	International Financial Reporting Standard
IfS	Institute of Fiscal Studies
IMF	International Monetary Fund
JUG	Joined-up Government
LURA	Levelling Up and Regeneration Act
LUWP	Levelling Up White Paper
MCA	Mayoral Combined Authority
MoG	Machinery of Government
MP	Member of Parliament
NAO	National Audit Office
NED	Non-Executive Director
NIC	National Infrastructure Commission
NICE	National Institute for Health and Care Excellence

LIST OF ABBREVIATIONS

NPM	New Public Management
OBR	Office of Budget Responsibility
OECD	Organisation for Economic Co-operation and Development
OfLog	Office for Local Government
PAC	Public Accounts Committee
PM	Prime Minister
PMDU	Prime Minister's Delivery Unit
PMSU	Prime Minister's Strategy Unit
PRP	Performance Related Pay
PSA	Public Service Agreement
RAS	Recruitment and Assessment Service
RBS	Royal Bank of Scotland
REUL	Retained EU Law
SCS	Senior Civil Service
SpADs	Special Advisers
SR	Spending Review
SRO	Senior Responsible Owner
UK	United Kingdom
UKFI	UK Financial Investments
WGA	Whole Government Accounts
WM	Westminster Model
WTO	World Trade Organization

Preface

There is a large literature on the civil service, particularly on how it has related to successive Prime Ministers and governments including the various challenges of proposed reforms. The mantra of the civil servant's role is anchored by the Northcote Trevelyan reforms (1854) which provide foundational protection in any debate about change. Subsequent 'heroes' of the civil service – Haldane, Fisher, Bridges and their more recent counterparts – Armstrong, O'Donnell and Heywood, have stated that their main objectives in office have been to keep the civil service in the same place as when they started, to see any stretched elastic of reform return to its initial state. Some of these texts discuss how civil servants conduct their practices of advice to ministers and, to a lesser extent, how policies are administered once agreed. This literature mainly encourages the reader to view the civil service from its perspective, providing interviews and access by lifting its veil of secrecy to a few. Those more questioning of its practices and outcomes are frequently 'othered' as outsiders, who have insufficient calibre and experience to understand the civil servant's world. It is made clear to those who join after career experience in other spheres, that, once civil servants, their career paths are focused on their exit strategies rather than promotion.

This book is an attempt to view the civil servant's world in a way that considers its culture, learning and competitive instincts but also how it undertakes its work, demonstrating that the cerebral can also be mechanistic. It starts by considering the British civil service in the context of those elsewhere, finding it is not quite as different and distinctive as generally stated as systems have changed and UK exceptionalism has been reduced. It examines how policies are made beyond the visible expectations of Government manifestos to the other short- and long-term pressures that have to be accommodated in the daily policy advice process. It considers the senior civil service's antipathy to administration, or delivery as it would be called elsewhere, and the effect that the lower status of procurement and contract management has had on the quality of public service delivery. It examines the sources of different types of failure. It also considers the pressures for change – the devolution agenda, Brexit, the administration of the contractual state and the inexorable rise of special advisers – the elephants who remain in the room of the Westminster Model.

The book also poses a question for which there appears to be no answer – why have all the attempts at civil service reform failed apart from those coming from within? There are prescriptions for change and improvement from think tanks, ministers and international comparisons but no discussion on why reform proposals by successive governments do not stick and what would be necessary to embed the changes intended. The civil service response would be that their permanence is a safeguard against 'presidentialism' or 'sofa government' – that is against increased control by politicians whose time in office is only ever short-lived. This book raises some of the reasons why change in the civil service is needed and some indication of the strategies that will be used to deflect it. It is a contribution to a longstanding debate, not a prescription, but without more honest discussions by those who are courageous enough to raise them, the circle of civil service life will continue as we know it and at detriment to the state – an issue also raised by Freedman (2024a).

This book would not have been written without the positive suggestion and support from Stephen Wenham of Bristol University Press, to whom I give my thanks. The invitation to write this book came from conversations that Stephen and I have had at the Political Studies Association Annual Conference meetings although, as with my book on 'Outsourcing' (2021), I little expected our regular tours of the political horizon to result in these invitations. The book has been written at a time of some personal difficulties and the support and understanding of Stephen and Zoe Forbes has kept me going at times. I have also valued conversations with colleagues and Robin Morphet, who like me, has had a career in local and central government before turning to academia. While thanking the many others with whom I have discussed the issues in this book, over at least half a lifetime, the thoughts and views here remain my own.

Janice Morphet
November 2024

1

Introduction: What is the Civil Service For?

Introduction

The civil service represents the administrative interface between the government and civil society (Pierre 1995c; Raadschelders et al 2007) although the extent of powers to control this relationship vary in different countries depending on tradition, the constitution and the role of government. The civil service can propose and advise ministers on government policy and its administration. For less important or routine policy, civil servants are more likely to make decisions. The major change in the civil service in western states since the 1980s has been the extent to which agencies and other privatised systems of administration have entered into governments and, while this was expected to extend the distance between politicians and the administration of their policies, this has not been the case in practice (Hood 1995). There has also been an extension of the role of politicisation in decision making, including the way in which advice is provided to ministers from special advisers (SpADs) that have potentially created distance between the civil service and ministers. Lastly the news cycle has shortened with a potential shift to more short-termism in policy making.

When discussing the role of the civil service in the UK, there are a number of dimensions to be considered, including its purpose and what kind of civil service the country needs. In this chapter, the civil service is considered in an international context that frames a discussion of its purpose in the UK. Five dimensions are used which are drawn from a range of texts on comparative civil service systems, how they operate and the pressures on them for change (van der Meer 2011). The first is a consideration of how the civil service operates within the constitution of the state and whether it has protections and rights within the legal framework. The second is the extent to which there is politicisation of the civil service. Do the most senior civil servants change with the party in power even where they may be professionals? Next, does the civil service advise on public service obligations or public value, or is their advice expected to be neutral without this kind of assessment? This goes beyond their requirements to undertake their roles ethically (Chapman 1988) and extends it to a more pro-active consideration within the state as a whole. There is a review of the qualifications, skills and development, and the links between these and promotion of senior civil servants. Lastly, what are the pressures for reform? Following this, the same approach is used for the UK civil service.

The role of the civil service: an international context

How does the civil service relate to the constitution?

The formation of the civil service has been associated with the development of the state as it has expanded its role in society. The civil service role has been increasingly codified, including for recruitment, the extent of its powers and its neutrality (van der Meer and Dijkstra 2011). However, the development of the civil service into a public-orientated and outward-facing institution took longer (Raadschelders and Rutgers 1999) as welfare states developed. The civil service has increasingly been regarded as more professionalised in providing policy advice while there is an expectation that civil servants should have greater skills for leadership and effective policy implementation (van der Meer and Dijkstra 2011; Gerson 2020).

In Organisation for Economic Co-operation and Development (OECD) states, other than the UK, constitutions are written and interpreted through the legal system – whether codified, in Europe, or common law. In the United States, the Supreme Court has a role in interpreting the constitution, whereas in France there is a constitutional council (Peters 1995). In France, the civil service is at the heart of the constitution, embedded in political culture, where it has a role in defining legal requirements when governments have been fractured (Rouban 1995). It is defined as having a social rather than legal position but has a mediation function in political crises (Rouban 1999). The *grands corps* hold the most senior roles and, since the nineteenth century, the civil service has been largely self-regulated and controlled, with any suggestion of interference being politically sensitive. In the United States, there is no tradition of a strong independent civil service but in a federal state structure, it has been seen as one of the mechanisms for coherence. The civil service is organised into different types of institutions and agencies both at the centre and in direct delivery such as AMTRAK which is part publicly and part privately owned (Peters 1995).

Is the senior civil service politically aligned?

The work of the civil service is a political construct, and while there is a Weberian expectation that civil servants should be neutral, relationships vary in different states, with some more formalised than others. As states have expanded, civil servants have become more important. Politicians are concerned about this growing bureaucratic power (van der Meer and Dijkstra 2011). As Putnam (1973) states, all bureaucracies are political and those serving in them understand the extent to which policy choices and advice are scoped and shaped by the ideology of politicians in control. Nevertheless, a key issue is the extent to which these boundaries on their advice are imposed by bureaucrats. Should a neutral view be maintained, and where should the balance be set and by whom? Civil servants may adopt the programmes of governments and be regarded as partisan by oppositions although their prompt switch in priorities after a change in government suggests otherwise. Civil servants may understand and seek to operationalise political ideology in the policy advice to their ministers but this is understood to be in the context of government.

Any consideration of the role of the civil service in relation to politicians will depend on the national constitutional framework and the culture of the relationship. In Greece, ministerial political advisers can displace civil servants (Sotiropoulos 1999). Members of the Dutch civil service are expected to be neutral although the political affiliations of civil servants are known (Raadschelders and Meer 2014) with postholders being distributed between the main political parties. Here, 33 per cent of the members of the second chamber of Parliament have worked as senior civil servants (Raadschelders and Meer 2014) but 23 per cent came into a political role directly from the civil service. There have also been direct appointments of officials into political positions but only in this direction. In some countries, civil servants may be shielded or excluded from politicisation through political advisers around ministers (Putnam 1973). In Italy, the civil service keeps itself apart from politicians and takes an isolationist position which Cassese (1999) argues is to its detriment.

Where politicians and civil servants are educated together, this can influence how they work subsequently. In France, politicians and those likely to become top civil servants frequently attend the École Nationale d'Administration (ENA) and their careers can be intertwined. Their common education may give them shared perspectives on policy and administration (Pollitt and Bouckaert 2011). This relationship is best described as on a continuum (Rouban 1995), with a gradual increase in politicisation since the early 1980s.

The extent to which the civil service is politically aligned in the United States is greater than in some European countries, particularly for the top posts (Peters 1995). Civil servants in the US also have their own policy agendas as they regard themselves as experts in their own fields and entitled to have a view (Peters 1995).

In some cases the relationship between politicians and civil servants can be described as moderate politicisation (Pollitt and Bouckaert 2011). In Finland, where party political affiliation of the senior civil service is important, there is no major turnover of officials at general elections when political control changes, not least as there is a tradition of coalition government. In Germany, senior officials not sympathetic to an incoming government can request study leave or to be moved to a less high profile job (Goetz 2011).

Has the introduction of outsourcing increased the likelihood of politicisation (Pollitt and Bouckaert 2011)? Some arguments made in favour of agencification suggested that this would depoliticise services operated within contract specifications and regulatory frameworks. Politicians promoted the potential for more efficiency and customer focus, and less political engagement in delivery. Pollitt and Bouckaert (2011) argue that this is a confused position while no public service ethos has emerged to interpret these changes.

Civil servants may become politicised by seeking ministerial attention when SpADs are appointed (Dahl 1969). SpADs are tied to ministers, although there are controls on their appointment by the head of government. In France, ministers have the right to appoint senor officials but this is controlled by the top of government (Page 1985). The selection of most senior civil servants has a political component, with appointments determined by ministerial cabinets, and these roles can be subject to replacement although, when this occurs, post-holders are not dismissed from the service (Rouban 1999). There are also no political restrictions on the activities of civil servants in France, who can stand for office in elections at all levels of the state. French civil servants are also politicised through networks and clubs, while reluctant to discuss these affiliations more broadly. The senior civil service may also have more communication with the cabinets of their ministers and the prime minister than with colleagues in other departments.

In Germany, top civil servants are temporarily retired if there is a change in government, although the vacant posts are filled from those within the civil service and the majority of civil servants stay in post (Derlien 1995). In Sweden, while government ministers usually head departments, they may also be run by members of the ruling party, although a minister cannot instruct an agency on a particular issue (Pierre 1995b). In Greece, the senior civil service has a clientelist relationship with politicians who form governments, not holding such senior roles as their titles suggest. In order to operate within the civil service, they have to be focused on their political masters and favoured elites rather than the people (Sotiropoulos 1999). While focusing on the ways in which the civil service might bend itself towards ministers, Page (1985) asks the opposite question – how far politicians bend to the civil service.

Does the civil service have a public service or public value obligation?

Lost in the frequency of usage is the meaning of 'servant' in the civil servant's role. There might be a distinction between service and servant, but the title implies that the postholder is subservient in the role – but to whom or what? Their political 'masters'? The state? The people? The law? Being a public or civil servant was seen as important in post-1945 welfarist governments (Steinberg and Austern 1990). To be a public servant was to be engaged in the delivery of improvement of society in the public interest and regarded as the most important project. This lasted until the early 1970s, when neo-liberalism, competition and individualism emerged and has subsequently prevailed. In some states, the welfarist model has battled to maintain its public interest role, although this balance has been kept in Germany and France, where the civil service is obliged to work for the benefit of the state. In some countries, such as the United States, working in the public sector is frequently seen as one of failure (Peters 1995).

How far does the civil service have a role in representing public value? There are two models of the administrative role within the state (Pollitt and Bouckaert 2011). The first is *Rechtsstaat*, where the state is a unifying body and is focused on the administration of the law. In this model, civil servants have considerable power (Page and Wright 1999), and are trained in law with administrative law supporting their role. The application of this law is through precedents in a hierarchy of administrative courts. There is a focus on law as an integrating force which is applied equally. Pollitt and Bouckaert (2011) contrast this with the public interest model of administration, where the state is given less prominence and the government is the main focus. In these systems, as in New Zealand, Australia and the UK, civil servants are not trained in law and the legal system has traditionally remained in the background. Here, civil servants are regarded as general citizens employed in state organisations and not a separate cadre. Government is by public consent while public interest can compete for benefits in an adversarial way. Here, Pollitt and Bouckaert (2011) argue, the government's role is to be a fair referee, with pragmatism and flexibility prized beyond technical expertise. Some countries, such as the Netherlands, Sweden and Finland, fall into a third category – having a legal basis but with wider and more flexible approaches. Here their administrative courts have an increasing role in determining rights in the application of the law and removing this from flexible administrative discretion. In some countries there has been a tradition of smaller ministries with independent agencies administering for the state as in Finland and Sweden (Pollitt and Bouckaert 2011).

In any discussion about the public service obligation of senior civil servants in the preparation of their policy advice, can this ever be neutral or depoliticised when resources are limited? While civil servants may not have a public service obligation in advising politicians, the public places trust in them to provide neutral, fair and balanced advice. Where there are problems in delivery, this is attributed to a lack of political control (Houston et al 2016). In the United States, there is a clear distinction in the public's understanding in the attribution of blame for public services between politicians and civil servants (Pollitt and Bouckaert 2011). However, there is also a direct appeal by politicians to the electorate about the benefits of administrative reform in improving service delivery and lowering costs (Pollitt and Bouckaert 2011). In this, politicians are blaming the civil servants for wasting resources.

Has the introduction of the General Agreement on Tariffs and Trade (GATT) Government Procurement Agreement (GPA) for utilities (1980) and the World Trade Organization (WTO) GPA for services (1994) across the Organisation for Economic Co-operation and Development (OECD) and the European Union (EU) Single Market had any effect on the public service ethos in the administration of public policy (Morphet 2021)? Pollitt and Bouckaert (2011) argue that there was a change in focus to customers as contract specifications were prepared for the first time. However, the public service ethos has not been updated or recodified in those countries which rely on it and are extensive users of contractual models. Elsewhere, such as the Netherlands and Nordic countries, Pollitt and Bouckaert (2011) argue that civil servants have maintained their control and position when competition has been introduced. On the other hand, there is an assumption that greater public involvement improves public services. Here civil servants deploy public service ethos while using bureau-shaping techniques and budget maximisation to maintain and enhance their own powers (Smith 1988; Dunleavey 1991).

What qualifications, skills and training do civil servants have?

The selection of senior civil servants varies in different states but there is recognition that no matter what route these senior civil servants take to the top, once there, they will join an elite. In the Netherlands, a new category of the Top Management Group was created in 2000 where officials are appointed by the cabinet. They serve 7-year terms after which they move. If no post is available they remain in a pool until one becomes available (Raadschelders and Meer 2014). Ministers are given greater flexibility to remove civil servants in the case of political incompatibility.

For academic qualifications, in the Netherlands there had been a preponderance of those with legal training. This has now changed with the majority taking social and political sciences, law and economics and also completing specialist master's courses particularly in public administration (Raadschelders and Meer 2014). In France and Germany, those with legal training remain the majority (Pollitt and Bouckaert 2011). In Austria, government ministries have their own training schools. In the Netherlands, a few senior civil servants are appointed after having experience of the private sector (Raadschelders and Meer 2014).

Both training and experience contribute towards promotion. In Greece, all promotion for most senior posts is internal, depends on years in service and education but can also be highly politicised (Sotiropoulos 1999). It is possible to have a salary in the highest rank, but not occupy a senior post. In France, the most senior civil servants regard themselves as intellectuals rather than managers and take an individualistic view of their roles (Rouban 1999) that is based, in initial recruitment, on the rank order of final examination marks. External recruits can access senior roles, where they have political support, but have to meet basic standards of education or experience. In France, there is an antipathy to specialists and potential links to management functions, so many young civil servants manage their career to avoid this route (Rouban 1999; Bezes 2007). In Germany, where there is a federal structure, most of the civil servants at the centre have a common curriculum with the legal profession (Derlien 1995). Those with specialist training, such as engineers, are not found in the centre as they operate in more specialist institutions.

Pressures for reform

When considering how to improve public services, the pressure is on the civil service to reform rather than ministers. However, it is also the case that training ministers to prepare them for their roles is rarely discussed and appears to be 'off limits' (Pollitt and Bouckaert 2011; Andrews 2024). In the 1980s and 1990s there were significant pressures for reform, which van der Meer and Dijkstra (2011) describe as endemic (p 282). As Pierre (1995a) states, these pressures have come in a range of forms from the implementation of the GPA and its attendant introduction of the private sector into the mainstream provision of public services, financial crises, sluggish economies and local authorities seeking more decentralisation and devolution of power. Reform pressures can be located in neo-liberal ideology in relation to the public sector from the early 1970s onwards, associated with depoliticisation driven by separating political and administrative accountability (Rouban 1995). At the same time, politicians have been seeking ownership of policies to ensure that benefits of changes accrue to them. The introduction of the welfare state was seen as a positive force for change but as neo-liberalism took hold, the public sector was regarded as the problem and not the answer.

In Germany, a reform commission was focused on removing the distinction between civil servants and other public servants (Derlien 1995) but did not receive political support for the changes proposed. However, there was also less pressure to implement the GPA and introduce competition into the civil service. Public agencies in Germany were transferred to operate within private law but remained in the public sector. There was also a shift from the public to private ownership on the reunification of Germany in 1990 which was seen as a major contribution to meeting GPA obligations. In

France, a more secure political foundation focused on civil service operations (Rouban 1995). While the French system was regarded as highly centralised, closer examination of its operation demonstrated that it was fractured, with ministerial structures in constant turmoil and competition within ministries on policy matters. In the early 1970s, the autonomy of the civil service changed and those making policy had a greater role in its administration, with civil servants made more accountable (Rouban 1995). Before 1980, civil servants kept ministers detached from functional administration. After this, cabinets set political agendas, with external advisers appointed to create a 'shadow hierarchy' for the civil service (Rouban 1995: 49). The process of modernisation in the late 1980s and early 1990s was largely undertaken by civil service directly within departments and was received more positively than reforms in 1980. There were also reform pressures in Sweden in the early 1990s (Pierre 1995b).

In the United States, as the civil service is not held in high regard, it is subject to reform pressures. The Grace Commission (1984) comprised over 2,000 private sector executives giving views on how business methods should be applied in government with 2,500 recommendations (Peters 1995). The assumptions were that the civil service would not be well-managed if left to its own leadership and may also be corrupt. This view was not shared by President Bush, who instituted the Volcker Commission in 1990, intended to revitalise the civil service. This was followed by the Gore Commission and the proposed re-orientation of the civil service to 'steering not rowing' (Osborne and Gaebler 1992).

The civil service in the UK

How does the civil service relate to the constitution?

The UK does not have a written constitution. The role of the modern civil service is based on the Northcote Trevelyan reforms (1854) which provide an anchor for traditions used today:

> It may be safely asserted that, as matters now stand, the Government of the country could not be carried on without the aid of an efficient body of permanent officers, occupying position duly subordinate to that of Ministers who are directly responsible to the Crown and to parliament, yet possessing sufficient independence, character, ability, and experience to be able to advise, assist, and, to some extent, influence, those who are from time to time set over them. (Northcote Trevelyan 1854: 3)

Northcote Trevelyan has persisted to act as a measure against which all changes proposed by successive governments are assessed. Parliamentary sovereignty, as part of the constitutional convention that remains today, was developed by Dicey (1885), who was against codification of the constitution and the introduction of administrative law, as in France, as this would reduce the flexibility of the constitution and be at odds with the common law tradition of England (Kirby 2019). Lloyd George, when Prime Minister (PM), described the civil service as the 'establishment of a central machine for the effective exercise of political and administrative power' (quoted in Lowe 2011: 42). This analogy was extended through the 1918 Haldane Report on the Machinery of Government as being a primary purpose of the civil service. Haldane's report became the de facto foundation of the Westminster Model (WM) which is maintained today. Here, the responsibilities of the government, the civil service and Parliament are defined as separate but interdependent. Within the WM, Parliament is the only power that can make laws and dispose of them (Gamble 1990; Bevir 2008). In the absence of a written constitution, the WM is a convention that ministers are responsible to Parliament for policy and its administration advised by the civil service.

Ministers are answerable to Parliament and through Select Committees (Benton and Russell 2013). Civil servants, when appearing before Select Committees are required, by the Armstrong Memorandum (1985), to represent the minister's views and not give independent 'evidence' (Thompson 1987; Barberis 1996a). They may also regard MPs as adversaries (Theakston 1995) or irrelevant. The civil service role in the WM is to advise ministers but not to be responsible for decisions. If there are problems in policy administration, it is the minister who must resign. While Haldane (1918) stated that civil servants should speak truth to power, the civil service could be described as having power without responsibility. When Prime Ministers are considered to be too interfering in the civil service or seeking to bypass it, then the WM is cited as a means by which relationships should return to a perceived 'golden age', (Rhodes et al 2008; Foster-Gilbert 2018). However, is this a convenient myth (Bevir and Rhodes 2010), with 'constructed traditions now being used to justify current positions' (Weller and Haddon 2016: 483)?

The golden period for the civil service was disrupted by the introduction of the welfare state after 1945 and it was argued by the Head of the Home Civil Service, Bridges (1954), that the civil service was being asked to extend its activities beyond its brief. This also represented the view that the civil service was being asked to perform mechanical and not intellectual tasks which has been a continuing tension between the civil service and government. Bridges was regarded as an archetypal Victorian civil servant, still operating on the principles of a non-interventionist state (Chapman 1988).

There have been other pressures on the WM such as when changes in the balance of power have been attempted. In the Johnson premiership (2019–22), a more presidential model was introduced (Brown 2020; Levinson 2022) with the Prime Minister's decision making being more powerful than that of Parliament and the civil service. The review of the constitution undertaken by the Institute for Government (IfG) and the Bennett Institute (Urban and Thomas 2023) examined the extent to which an unwritten form of governance, without legislative support, can work when one of the three parts of the WM, in this case the executive, decides that it will push the relationship to its limits. In the Johnson case, the PM was restrained by the courts and Parliament (Gaussen 2019; Sanders 2023). However, the report indicates that there are other parts of the WM that could push their powers to a limit, including the House of Lords and Parliament. Russell and Serban (2021) argue that the term WM is now so degraded that it should not be used at all, although this has drawn a response from Flinders et al (2022) who argue that it is stretched but not snapped.

There have also been other initiatives designed to change the balance of power within the WM including external recruitment of those with specific skills and experience. Northcote Trevelyan was in favour of older civil servants joining later in their careers but this practice has been controlled since 1918 (Fry 2000). During the Second World War many of those recruited into the civil service were described as 'non-established' – that is not having a permanent role, entitled to a pension or other benefits (Fulton 1968; Mahmod 1995), having long-standing non-established contracts terminated at short notice. Further, for those recruited in this way opportunities to advance into management were small (Fulton 1968; Toynbee 2023; NAO 2024a). When George Brown recruited economic experts into the newly formed Department of Economic Affairs, he termed these appointees as 'irregulars' (Davis 2009). However, like all appointees brought in for their expertise, they were never absorbed into the mainstream and left after short contract periods.

The WM is one of power hoarding by the executive within a first-past-the-post electoral system (Lijphart 1984), described by Lord Hailsham as an 'electoral dictatorship' for the party in government. In this system, Rhodes et al (2006) state that civil servants can appropriate, frame and enhance the role of traditions in their own interests. Given the flexible position of the WM in underpinning the civil service (Bevir and Rhodes 2010) how far can the role of the civil service be codified without a constitution? More fundamental changes to the civil service role as principal adviser to ministers have come through the introduction of pluralism in the advice provided through the increasing use of SpADs (Chapman 1988; Bevir and Rhodes 2006).

Is the Senior Civil Service politically aligned?

Since 1979, the maintenance of the civil service's political neutrality and whether there has been a drift towards politicisation (Sausman and Locke

2004) has been questioned. The most direct understanding of politicisation – the appointment of partisans to top civil service posts – has not occurred in any systematic way, although when becoming Prime Minister, Liz Truss dismissed the permanent secretary of the Treasury, as she regarded him as a representative of an economic orthodoxy she did not wish to pursue (Marsh 2023). In other cases, specific civil servants who did not get on with their ministers were moved or sought other posts (Richards and Diamond 2023). As noted previously, in other countries, civil servants are politically aligned and can lose office when governments change. In the UK, it is the tradition to have a non-politicised Civil Service (Christoph 1975). Instead, politicisation is not related to political parties but to the interests of the civil service (Rhodes 2001). Civil servants can have strong views on the options that ministers should choose and spend time in making this known going beyond neutral advice (Christoph 1975; Barberis 1996a; Stokes 2016). Does this count as politicisation?

Civil service politicisation was raised in the popular press in the Thatcher administration 1979–90 (Hennessy 1989: 628–87). Thatcher was accused of appointing officials who were, in the phrase associated with her, 'one of us', making life uncomfortable for those who were not. There is evidence that Thatcher used her limited powers to help the careers of several officials of whom she approved, but there is more discussion about whether these were truly 'political' appointments (Horton 2006). Hennessey (1989) states that 'one of us' did not mean ideologically conservative, but rather enthusiastic and keen to solve problems with a 'can do' attitude. One official believed to have benefited in this way was Peter Middleton who became Permanent Secretary at the Treasury in 1983, but he also found favour under the previous Labour government (Hennessy 1989).

The 'politicisation' argument became more apparent after 1997. Some SpADs to Blair, such as Geoff Mulgan, went on to become civil servants, leaving shortly afterwards and this did not mark a strong, general or lasting trend (Richards 2007). In 2003, the Labour government suggested that it wanted to change the appointment of senior officials to give ministers greater involvement (Cabinet Office 2003: 6), but withdrew its proposal shortly afterwards.

While there has been a rise in discussion about the role of SpADs, these have been in existence for over 100 years (Page and Jenkins 2005). Within the Senior Civil Service (SCS), the generalist tradition has prevailed with the civil service never being the sole source of advice, although they have mechanisms for ensuring ministers are aware of their preferences, even in mouths of others. While civil servants are not public figures, SpADs such as Steve Hilton, adviser to David Cameron (Finlayson 2011; Rhodes 2022) and Dominic Cummings, adviser to Boris Johnson, have had public profiles and been critical of civil servants (Syal 2020), creating courts around their respective PMs. Cummings described the civil service as 'the blob' (Rutter 2022) and this has been used as a term used by Conservative MPs and commentators in the right wing press.

However, SpADs are not in the WM which has not been reformed to accommodate their continuing and growing presence. In the 1970s, a *Yes Minister* episode detailed the ways in which civil servants spent time keeping a SpAD out of the way of their minister by finding him an office in Walthamstow (Lynn and Jay 1988) but this was a short-term victory, with SpADs now being a central part of advice teams alongside civil servants (Corry 2024). Not all SpADs are focused on policy formulation – some are speech writers or provide political liaison within the party or between departments. Increasingly, civil servants have found that SpADs could provide access to ministers and their thinking was useful to them (Page and Jenkins 2005; Stokes 2016).

Does the civil service have a public service or public value obligation?

There are public expectations that public bodies should be helping to deliver public value, which cannot be provided through the private sector and goes beyond a simple financial focus on public service delivery (Parston 1989). Should the civil service be expected to provide public value? Public services exist to provide support to the population and institutions required for the maintenance of society, not funded by the private sector. These services are provided through taxation. Public value is concerned with additionality that stretches beyond public administration or the functions of a bureaucracy to positively use the benefits of public service provision to achieve better outcomes for individuals and society. They are framed by economic, cultural, social and political values (Coyle and Sensier 2019) which can be considered in relation to each other. When Joseph Chamberlain, the Mayor of Birmingham (1873–76), identified the needs of the local and national economy as requiring healthy, well housed, fed and educated people to support development and growth (Marsh 1994; Cawood 2016), he intervened to provide them. Government interventions are still required to secure the same ends. Moore (1995) identifies these as public value, necessary for the functioning of society although they need to be justified in the role that they play. These public services are expected to be provided fairly and across the whole of society in ways that meet needs and play positive roles in enhancing the outcomes to the nation's benefit (Kelly et al 2002). As Coats and Passmore (2008) state, it is analogous to the mission of the private sector to maximise the potential of the organisation in achieving the stated ends of the business or, here, the public sector. Coyle and Sensier (2019) indicates that an organisation has a responsibility to identify its purpose and whether it is being successful in undertaking this.

Overall, there is little discussion on the role of the UK civil service acting in the public interest although there are assumptions that this is the case (O'Toole 1989). The principle of public interest is more apparent in the codes of conduct of professional bodies such as accountants rather than in the civil service. As generalists, civil servants are said to be able to take in a wide range of evidence and positions in providing advice to ministers, although this does not include the principle of public interest. This position has been overtaken by SpADs. There have been growing expectations from ministers that, as they embody public will, then civil servants should obey their requirements and not offer other advice.

An increased focus on financial efficiency and effectiveness was Thatcher's priority for government with a more political purpose (Dowding 1995). Thatcher used the Rayner scrutinies and subsequent initiatives to change the way in which the civil service was accountable in its use of public money (Peters and Pierre 2004). The promotion of the principle of efficiency in the civil service was performative on the part of government and more important than issues such as the quality of the service (Stewart and Walsh 1992). The civil service had always been regarded as guardians of the public purse and this drove a wedge into the public acceptance of its role in supporting the state, to raise doubts and concerns about wasting public funds when the country was in recession. Those in charge of these efficiency reviews, including Lord Rayner, former head of Marks & Spencer, were focused on the potential for business practices to save resources in government (Dowding 1995). The later Financial Management Initiative in 1982 (Sharifi and Bovaird 1995) attempted to identify the objectives of government departments and then how management and financial resources achieved them, although progress on these reviews within departments was slow (Stewart and Walsh 1992). This was followed by the Ibbs report (1988) on improving management in the civil service to ensure that the government could achieve better value for money. It related to the preparation of the implementation of the second part of the GPA, this time for services, which was under negotiation and implemented in 1994 (Morphet 2021a). Ibbs proposed further agencification of internal services within departments. He also identified the need for greater financial and management skills in the SCS (Parston 1989) but in practice it was proposed these were to be met through the agencification rather than civil servants who remained focused on policy formulation rather than its delivery.

Those who disliked this approach, disagreeing that public service was like a business, considered that the civil service was being adversely compared to those in the private sector (Stewart and Walsh 1992). An early Rayner review on the welfare benefits distribution system was leaked, generating sufficient political antipathy against its proposals to be implemented. A reflection on the process and the subsequent effect of the leak was positive about the response of the civil service to review and change although, in practice, the scrutiny's recommendations were stymied (Warner 1984). There were no agreed meanings to efficiency and effectiveness (Chapman and O'Toole 1995), although reviews were conducted within the culture of each department (Warner 1984). This approach was continued by Major when, in a speech to the Engineering Employers' Federation, Jonathan Aitken, then Chief Secretary to the Treasury, said: 'We now have the smallest civil service since 1939. We want the public sector to match the private sector in efficiency' (Aitken 1995 quoted in Chapman and O'Toole 1995: 14). Since Thatcher, the notion of efficiency and effectiveness in the civil service as part of a public service ethos has been replaced by a focus on efficiency, particularly since the introduction of austerity in the 2010 Coalition government (Gamble 2015).

There have been other concerns that civil servants optimise their positions rather than operating within the public service ethos. The number of civil servants employed at the centre is small and a political elite, including Permanent Secretaries in the core executive and functional departments. They meet regularly (Barberis 1996b; Rhodes 2007; Bevir and Rhodes 2010) and have achieved these roles after moving between the core executive and functional departments, changing jobs on average every 18 months to 3 years. Permanent Secretaries are regarded as being more permanent that politicians but both may hold posts for similar periods. Critics of the operation of the public service ethos by the civil service include Slessor (2002) who argues that the civil service has:

> [an] 'infallibility syndrome'; this is a belief that to admit to errors would diminish the authority of the civil service. This includes challenging and dismissing anything that might erode Whitehall's credibility and this approach is learned 'from the day a recruit joins … one should never let the side down'. This means that once a decision has been made on 'the line to take', be it on BSE, Foot and Mouth Disease [etc.] … it is imperative to hold a solid and united front … And if a choice must be made, departmental loyalty will win over objective truth. (Slessor 2002: 288)

Has the role of the civil service diminished in being able to represent a view of the public interest to ministers, or has this never been the case? Is there an anti- or agnostic public interest position in the civil service? The culture of maintaining ministerial positions on policies rather than public discourse on civil servant accountability can be seen where it has been tested through civil servant whistleblowers, using a public interest defence (Chapman 1988; Hunt 2013). The most well-known whistleblower was Clive Ponting (1985), who spoke out about the sinking of the Belgrano during the Falklands War. He argued that, in limited cases, a civil servant has duties beyond those to ministers to Parliament and this was the basis of his acquittal after he was prosecuted under the Official Secrets Act. However, the response from the Cabinet Secretary, who was Head of the Home Civil Service, was to issue the Armstrong Memorandum (1985), which formally incorporated and reasserted the traditional principle of loyalty to the government in the role of the civil servant. This did not satisfy critics, who argued that the Memorandum did not address conflicts of public interest and demanded an official Code of Ethics for both civil servants and ministers. Civil servants are required to be advocates of government policy rather than policy advisers and Horton (2006) argues that this undermines the principle of political neutrality. This also arose in the Sunak government after 2023, where there were criticisms of social media posts made by government departments which had party political messages.

Public interest can also be examined in the ways in which government uses resources to achieve its ends through detailed reviews by the National Audit Office (NAO), which is independent of government and reports directly to Parliament through the Public Accounts Committee. Since 1979, Parliamentary Select Committees have increased scrutiny of the executive and the civil service (Benton and Russell 2013). Both make recommendations but neither are binding on government and, although the civil service must provide data to the NAO, they are not required to give evidence to Parliament or Select Committees. Both focus on what has been undertaken and how resources have been used rather than the way in which changes could be made in the future (King and Crewe 2014). In the Blair period, public interest was regarded as part of social value. It was argued that more uniform methods of service delivery, deriving from contracts, should be replaced by public preference, resulting from public deliberation (Kelly et al 2002).

The antipathy of the SCS towards management and delivery functions remains rooted in Northcote Trevelyan and its subsequent traditions (Bevir and Rhodes 2010), which have rejected 'mechanical' rather than intellectual functions. On the other hand, Northcote Trevelyan recognised and sought to address the already existing departmental rivalries in government, arguing that this could only be solved by the Treasury through the enforcement of a strategy of controlled collaboration (Lowe 2011). However, the actions of the Treasury were slow and only served to increase conflict between departments but, in practice, the Treasury exercised control over departmental spending and programmes (Beer 1955) which required strategies from civil servants rather than evidence of their expenditure and successful delivery to the public. This role has been increased and strengthened post-Brexit.

The focus on public value was regarded as a shift from the contractual mode of many public services epitomised through New Public Management (NPM) and away from a state vs market polarisation of public service provision (O'Flynn 2007). The Blair government 1997–2007 gave considerable focus to providing public value and the role of the civil service in this (Richards 2007). While Blair sought advice from the civil service, he considered its role was implementing the policies that his government had determined. Blair's principle of public value was a mechanism for evaluating the success of public policy and its associated investment (Kelly et al 2002). Blair did not rely on either a fully public or private model of service delivery but rather referred to Giddens's 'Third Way' (2013), using which was best in different situations and where public preference had a role in selection as part of delivery. Other aspects of public value included fairness and outcomes, rather than measuring inputs. The pursuit of social value was seen to be a challenge in the civil service:

> The civil service also needs to ensure that its values remain in line with those of society if it is to create public value. The traditional civil service ethos of impartiality and objectivity remains as important as ever (as shown by the reaction to any hint of it being undermined). However, as expectations of government expand to include customer service, and effective delivery, and as the complexity of policy challenges increases, traditional values need to be complemented with new ones. (Kelly et al 2002: para 64)

What qualifications, skills and training do civil servants have?

The UK SCS has been rooted in the generalist tradition since 1854 although this has been increasingly criticised since the 1950s (Hood 1995) when the social class of graduates who would be eligible for the fast stream widened. However, these changes in the expectation of governments of what the civil service should be concerned with and whether they had the skills to do so continued through successive reports and reviews.

Pressures for reform

Following Northcote Trevelyan (1854) and Haldane (1918) there have been numerous attempts to reform the civil service including by Fisher in the 1930s, who cemented the primacy of the role of the generalist. The role of the Cabinet Office together with the Treasury and the Prime Minister's Office evolved into the Core Executive (Dunleavy and Rhodes 1990) which was responsible for ensuring that governments met international and domestic commitments. These were then administered by the functional departments, where rivalry and competition continued accompanied by an inward focus. In 1952, it was reported that 'permanent secretaries showed little interest in problems which did not affect their departments, and had taken an extremely departmental line on those which did' (L. Petch, quoted in Lowe 2011: 50). Greenaway (1983), Chapman (1978), Balogh (1959), Edwin Plowden (1989) and George Brown all argued for experienced and specialist entrants before the Fulton Report (1968). These and later external appointees, including Rayner for Thatcher and Goodman for Wilson, were also regarded as 'fixers' able to work in ways not open to traditional civil servants (Smith and Young 1996) and to offer solutions that might be closer to ministerial intentions (Levitt and Solesbury 2013).

The attempt at reform undertaken by the Fulton Committee (1966–68), established by PM Harold Wilson following a critical Fabian Tract (1964), was because government had 'broadened in scope' (para 7) and was more active than passive in the state. There was a need for the 'modern' civil service to 'handle the social, economic and technical problems of our time in an international setting' (para 12). It was the view of the committee that the civil service had not kept up, remaining within the culture of the generalist and 'amateur'. The report sets out how the civil service should be fulfilling its role in supporting government through reforms of its employment practices including:

- having a longer commitment to the specific role assigned to ensure greater efficiency which is lost through the job rotation scheme;
- the efficient management of government through the appointment of more specialists in leadership roles;
- more developed management skills to support the delivery of government policy;
- a reduction in the separation between the civil service and the rest of society in order to ensure that civil servants have more contact with daily life;
- better career planning, encouragement of initiative and performance management.

There was opposition to the recommendations in Fulton, which would have changed the role of the civil service within the WM to a delivery role in government. As Horton (2006) states:

> Fulton was clearly a challenge to the functional competence, power and legitimacy of the administrative class. It was met, however, with an immediate counter attack by the civil service elite who rejected the accusation of amateurism and lack of professionalism and defended their record of incremental change. Although the government accepted all but one of Fulton's 158 recommendations, and acted quickly to set up a new Civil Service Department and Civil Service College, it then lost power. It fell to the civil service to implement the other recommendations. The elite generalists reacted with particular skill in

responding positively to those recommendations, which they accepted as necessary but allowed to lapse those that threatened their position. The result was one of both continuity and further evolutionary change and a clear example of self-reinforcing and positive feedback mechanisms. (Fry 1984: 37–8)

The post-Fulton period was characterised by civil service malaise (Painter 2008). Heath, after Wilson, introduced reforms following a White Paper, *The Reorganisation of Central Government* (HM Government 1970), which redistributed Whitehall functions into larger departments, particularly those that were likely to have an ongoing relationship with the EU. At the same time, the first spectres of rolling back the state, a move away from the post-war welfarist consensus started to emerge (Davis 2009), as neo-liberal rhetoric grew in the United States, under Reagan, which permeated emerging discussions on world trade, resulting in a move away from centralist welfarism to competition and outsourcing (Morphet 2021a).

In the 1980s, Hood (1995) argues that Thatcher's pressure for reform was to deprivilege the civil service in general and the senor civil service in particular. However, what did this deprivileging mean? While it suggests a reduction in the number, status and conditions of civil service employment, Thatcher appeared to be more concerned with reducing their access to power through the advice provided to ministers. However, Thatcher's changes became focused on more routine operations which could be susceptible to the introduction of 'business methods'. Despite the implementation of the GPA, change was designed to maintain the status quo control by the civil service of strategic and functional roles. The extension of the GPA into services and implemented as further agencification and the Citizens Charter by John Major, 1990–97 (Falconer and Ross 1999), had an effect on the overall number of civil servants and how the civil service was structured. However, there were assumptions that power could be retained, despite the creation of arm's length bodies and outsourcing functions. Blair's view was that administrative change should not relate entirely to efficiency but also effectiveness in meeting government objectives through the application of public value principles (Bryson et al 2014). Government departments were given targets with related expenditure incentives through public service agreements (James 2004). These were resisted by the SCS as a mechanism for changing their role and making them accountable in ways that had not been included in the WM. A change in government in 2010 saw these removed and they were referred to as the lowest point in the Blair government for the civil service subsequently (Heywood 2021).

Formal attempts at reform are commissioned by all PMs. However, the fluidity of the WM that frames the civil service perspective continues to be argued as a 'good thing' continuing its constructed ambiguity (Weller and Haddon 2016). Discussion on the role and beneficial characteristics of the WM appear when the civil service is most under threat – by the Blair government 1997–2007, Brexit 2016–20 and the COVID-19 pandemic. In the process of implementing Brexit after the Referendum in 2016, at times it was not clear who was in charge of decision making, with tensions between the Executive, Parliament and the Judiciary with further issues related to the role of the civil service and the position of the devolved administrations (Baldini et al 2018). Parliamentary power in the House of Commons was reasserted during the process of implementing the Brexit referendum with a Parliamentary majority forcing a 'meaningful vote' (Lynch et al 2019; Aidt et al 2021).

In the post-Brexit period, the WM was under pressure again in the management of COVID-19. Here the responsibilities of the UK state were distributed between the devolved administrations and the Westminster government responsible for actions in England. The WM has no place for sub-national government within it, with powers being delegated to the devolved administrations (DAs) (Rawlings 2001), yet these provided enough space for separate rules and advice to be applied by First Ministers and an unintended consequence. Also during this period, civil servants, ministers, including the Prime Minister, the Chancellor of the Exchequer and SpADs held social events in No 10 (the activities became known as 'Partygate'). These were denied as being beyond the rules by Prime Minister Johnson to Parliament. Here, the police and Parliament exerted their powers over the executive and the civil service in the conduct of its behaviour.

Conclusions

In considering civil service systems in OECD countries and the UK, it is possible to see a range of similarities and a few differences. Civil servants have different relationships with politicians including knowing them for some time, as in France and which had traditionally been the case in the UK when civil servants and politicians had the same educational route through a narrow range of schools and universities (Fulton 1968). What is less likely in the UK is that civil servants and ministers have been former colleagues as in the Netherlands. The training in law as a basic education for civil servants is now less common across Europe than immediately post-1945, although this is still the case in Germany and France, but never in the UK. The pressures arising from the implementation of the GPA have been felt by all civil services but have been used differently. In most EU states, public services now operate within private business legislation but remain in public ownership. In the UK, the state appears content for ownership to be in the private sector. All civil service systems are under pressure for reform by politicians who have growing concerns about the level of power in their hands and their performance (van der Meer 2011). Across European states including the UK, there has been uncertainty about the source of these common liberalising reforms without any discussion of the GPA (van der Meer and Dijkstra 2011; Morphet 2021a). However, in the UK as elsewhere, such as France, Germany and Scandinavia, the scale of the reforms and their implementation appears to rest primarily on the civil service rather than being led by politicians. In France and the UK, there remains an anti-managerialist culture which is not the case in the Netherlands and Scandinavia (Raadschelders et al 2007). Does being a smaller nation within the EU require a different kind of civil service professionalisation whereas larger members can rely on their scale to achieve their policy objectives? Now that the UK is no longer a member of the EU, does it belong in the group of larger or smaller nations when seeking to define its influencing strategies and internal management capabilities?

2

What Kind of Civil Service Do We Have? The Structure of the Home Civil Service in England

Introduction

The structure of the UK civil service can be considered in two ways. The first is by grade of employment – the Senior Civil Service (SCS), clerical and administrative grades and, in the past, those engaged in manual or service positions such as messengers, drivers or canteen staff. Another way of considering civil servants is by the part of government in which they serve. Here there are also three divisions. Firstly, civil servants who support the core executive – the Prime Minister's office, the Treasury and the Cabinet Office. Secondly, those in functional departments whose ministers comprise the Cabinet and thirdly agencies, which are part of the functional departments but include the provision of passports, managing borders or back office services. Some of these functions are in non-ministerial departments such as His Majesty's Revenue and Customs (HMRC) and others engage with citizens and companies such as the Department of Work and Pensions. Much of the research and discussion about the civil service is focused on the role of the SCS in the core executive and the appointment and role of Permanent Secretaries in the functional departments (Barberis 1996b; Rhodes 2001).

Civil servants in the functional and operational parts of government come to public attention when there have been problems including public spats with ministers in the cases of Derek Lewis and prisons (Polidano 1999). Members of the SCS in functional departments may also be involved in wider disputes about government policy and performance such as Sarah Munby (Rutter 2022) and the Post Office Horizon issue (Samuels 2022). Some appointed chairs or independent advisers such as Sir William Shawcross on the Reform programme, Henry Dimbleby on food (Coombes 2023) and

Boris Johnson's adviser on standards, Alex Allan (Durrant et al 2021) also make the headlines following publicly expressed views that the government has not acted on advice they have been invited to provide. However, within the context and framework of the Westminster Model (WM) members of the civil service remain anonymous.

In this chapter, the role of the civil service in England is considered. (The civil service structures within the devolved administrations are discussed in Chapter 6.) This includes the relationships between the SCS, mainstream staff and those outsourced to undertake routinised administrative and clerical tasks. The issues related to the civil service as an employer are also discussed, including recruitment and retention and expectations of a 'job for life'. It also considers who leads the civil service and whether this role can be separated from that of the Cabinet Secretary as in the short Kerslake/Heywood period or through the appointment of a politician as First Civil Service Commissioner in 2021.

How many civil servants?

In September 2023, 'there were 496,150 full-time equivalent (FTE) civil servants – 6,840 (1.4 per cent) more than in the previous quarter, which is the highest quarterly growth rate since Q3 2021. There were 15,400 (3.2 per cent) more civil servants than a year before' (IfG 2023a). Since the introduction of agencification in 1987, there have been fluctuations in the number of civil servants, particularly since the introduction of the austerity programme by the Coalition Government in 2010. The lowest number of civil servants was just before the 2016 Brexit referendum at 384,230, since when it has risen to higher than former levels. The largest departments have many of their staff working in agencies or in public facing roles such as prison and probation officers in the largest Department, the Ministry of Justice. Those departments which have little or no contact with the public are the smallest such as HM Treasury.

In the UK constitution, the Prime Minister does not have executive powers except under specific conditions and the post holder remains *primus inter pares* with other cabinet members. The Prime Minister can exert pressure on priorities and during the Blair and Johnson periods there were discussions about the swerve towards a presidential form of UK government (Foley 2004; Bennister 2009; Ward and Ward 2023). After the Prime Minister, the Treasury has significant traditional and now growing powers since Brexit, over the expenditure and, *inter alia*, the policy of the functional departments (Boys-Smith 1968). This dates from the memorandum issued by the Treasury in 1868 (Beer 1955) and subsequently updated (HMT 2023). While the Treasury has not had formal powers to control the spending of functional departments since 1964 (Thain and Wright 1995) it plays a determining role in all departmental activities and their responsibilities and this lack of formal control has made the Treasury more controlling than before (Thain 2010). In some governments, such as Blair's (1997–2007) and the Coalition Government (2010–15), the Chancellor has been given a more direct role in the management of domestic policy. In the Brown government (2007–10), the Chancellor was unusually outward facing in response to the international financial crisis. These relationships between members of the government, particularly the Prime Minister, the Chancellor and the Home Secretary, have a significant influence on the power of the civil service within other departments through their everyday relations, which are not transparent.

Tripartite structure of the civil service

Much of the literature and research on the UK civil service focuses on the SCS (Burnham and Pyper 2008; Lowe 2011; Lowe and Pemberton 2020) and within this, those who work within the core executive providing advice to senior ministers (Grube and Killick 2023), including effectively controlling other departments (Lowe 2011; Dommett and Flinders 2015). Those who reach top posts such as the Cabinet Secretary or Head of the Home Civil Service, will be drawn from these groups rather than being appointed from outside (Theakston and Connelly 2018). Next we have the cadre of Permanent Secretaries (Barberis 1989; Barberis 1996b; Theakston 2000; Cooper 2020), who become heads and accounting officers for their department's activities, including the expenditure of agencies and any other bodies included in the national accounts as part of their remit (HM Treasury 2023). For example, the Permanent Secretary for Ministry of Housing, Communities and Local Government has the accounting officer responsibility for local government expenditure, although local authorities are democratically elected bodies and generate income from sources other than through the government grants and allocations. Here it is argued that as local authorities are institutions created by the state and not part of the constitution, they have no separate and independent role in the Machinery of Government (MoG) and WM (Alder and Alder 1999; Bailey and Elliott 2009).

Within functional departments, members of the SCS will head different divisions into which the department is organised, responsible for smaller units that focus on ministerial objectives. Nothing within any department's structure is fixed and divisions can be changed without reference to other bodies (Majone 1997). MoG changes can be made by Prime Ministers which can favour some departments and peripheralise others (Jarman and Greer 2010; Apps 2022). Beyond the functional departments, the operational civil service includes agencies such as those for the Environment or Highways and providers of direct services such as HMRC and DVLA. Separate from these are regulators of services of public interest such as water, power and communications (Scott 2000), and the Office of Budget Responsibility (OBR) (Clift 2023) and the National Audit Office (NAO) (Talbot and Wiggan 2010), which both report directly to Parliament and are led by members of the SCS.

SCS recruitment and subsequent career management are internal and managed by the Cabinet Office (Lœgreid and Wise 2007). Promotion is mostly within departments but there is some movement with the core executive. Although the SCS in the core executive remains small, relative to the size of the civil service as a whole, it maintains its position as a political elite. Other members of the civil service are recruited to functional and operational grades that are universal across departments although this varies within agencies. Civil servants may spend their whole careers in employment offices or processing passports, driving licenses or benefits. Operational staff within agencies such as prisons or re-nationalised railways are also civil servants.

The overall structure of the civil service has been consistent since reforms were introduced after the Fulton Committee Report (1968) before which those in operational roles were defined as members of the 'industrial civil service' (Christoph 1984; Mackenzie and Grove 1957). After this, a unified grade structure across the whole of the civil service was created across all departments (Burnham and Pyper 2008; Dowding 2003). The intention was to simplify pay negotiations and potentially allow individual civil servants to move between departments more easily. The second major set of changes came as a result of the Labour government's decision in 1976 to join, by treaty, the General Agreement on Tariffs and Trade (GATT) Government Procurement Agreement (GPA). The GPA opened government funded services to competition by sector to be implemented over a period of time (Morphet 2021a). There is some debate about whether 1976 was a more important turning point than the subsequent Thatcher implementation period (Thain and Wright 1995) but there were sequential and consequential linkages between the two. The GPA was developed through negotiation in the GATT over a period that commenced in the early 1970s. It was influenced in its content and tone by the re-emergence of right wing economic thinking in the United States supported by the Presidency of Ronald Reagan (Friedman 1974; Peterson 1979). The argument was that, following post-1945 reconstruction and the creation of more welfare state policies, the private sector had reached the limits of its contribution to the global economy through existing markets open to it. The private sector argued that it needed access to public sector expenditure. Post-war government support for sectors in the economy such as construction and manufacturing was coming to an end. This transition was supported by opening access to domestic debt such as through hire purchase, credit cards and mortgages.

However, Friedman and von Hayek's arguments went beyond this. After a long period of international negotiation, the GPA that was concluded in principle in 1976, in the UK, the IMF crisis ensured agreement from the then Labour government (Hickson 2005). The implementation of the GPA in the UK commenced in 1980, after a change to a Prime Minister who was ideologically supportive of the move towards exposing public services to competition but who had not included this commitment in their 1979 election manifesto (Gamble 1989). During the 1970s, when in opposition, Conservatives, including Nicholas Ridley (Taylor 2014; Gallas 2016) and Keith Joseph, were fully aware of these pressures to open the state to the private sector. The implementation of the GPA, in the following 20 years, created a different type of state (Majone 1997) and widened differences within the structure of the civil service.

Implementing the GPA: competition in central government

The adoption of the GPA as an international treaty meant that it had a binding effect on the UK beyond Parliamentary terms and its status in international law gave the civil service confidence that it could propose reforms that ministers had to implement to meet the UK's obligations in successive governments (Morphet 2021a). These were that the UK should expose different parts of the public sector to competition. Each signatory state to the GPA could determine its own order of progress with most leaving public services that would be politically difficult to later stages. The requirement was to open construction, utilities and transport, and later, in the second round, services, to private sector competition. Apart from those sectors which were entirely publicly funded, there was no obligation to award contracts to external bidders and, after 2011, there were increased requirements to introduce social value into these procurement evaluations (Bovaird 2015; Craven 2020). Different countries have used a range of methods (Grandia and Meehan 2017) and the UK is the only country to have privatised water (Wackerbauer 2007). In some countries, social housing has been retained in the quasi-public sector as in France, Sweden and the Netherlands, and in others, such as Austria, the funding for social housing is available to any public or private provider if it meets the government's tenancy requirements (Czischke 2014). In Germany, services have remained in public ownership but subject to private company legislation (Derlien 1995). In the UK, during the first phase of the GPA, a public tenant's 'right to buy' their home was introduced, in an attempt to diversify the ownership of existing public housing. For bus privatisation introduced in 1985, there could be competition at the bus stop between providers such as in Manchester, or for routes, operated under common ticketing and livery, such as in Transport for London.

While the first round of GPA implementation for construction and utilities aligned with Mrs Thatcher's political ideology, she was initially cautious. The movement of utilities from the status of nationalised industries to privatised ownership, through the creation of a market, was a major project for this period. However, it did not have much effect on the operation and structure of the civil service (Parker 2009; Parker 2013). The implementation of the GPA provided opportunities for the government to generate income to use for tax cuts (Marsh 1991) and develop a new private sector for these businesses, within the context of some public share ownership opportunities – 'Tell Sid' – (Roscoe 2023). Further, there was an expectation from the Treasury that relationships might continue much as before. Utilities were classified by the European Union as services of general public interest (Sauter 2008) and the role of the private sector in their management and pricing was required to be subject to new regulators established by the government (Stead 2017). These were meant to be independent, setting regulations and prices using an evidence-based approach, led by members of the SCS. While the direct reporting relationships between the nationalised industries and Parliament ended as Permanent Secretaries ceased to be their accounting officers, other opportunities for influence remained including the appointment of former civil servants to senior management.

The implementation of the GPA was framed within the Thatcher ideology but also built on existing structures within the civil service using targeted government initiatives. These included the Rayner scrutinies (Warner 1984; Stewart and Walsh 1992), the creation of Next Steps agencies (Burcher 1995; Gains 1999) and the Competition Act 1998 (Scott 2009). The direct delivery of capital projects or running utilities, were more associated with the use of the Private Finance Initiative (PFI) (De Lemos et al 2000), another mechanism for injecting competition into public service delivery. However, unlike other countries such as the United States (Janik 1986), the reasons for the changes were set within a domestic ideological narrative. While GPA reforms were motivated by neo-liberal thinkers in the US, Thatcher and Major, and later Blair and Brown, advised by the SCS, were able to rely on a Treaty agreement to support longer term strategic change in the structure of the state, confident that this could not be challenged.

The GPA remit was expanded to include public services. This coincided with the development of a single market in the EU (Cockfield 1994) to allow member state economies to benefit from the new trading opportunities created through the introduction of the GPA (Koch and Koch 2020). Another objective and outcome of the creation of the single market was to introduce the role of the EU as the institution that would create a regulatory environment to implement these treaty commitments and establish a compliance mechanism to report on progress to reach obligatory objectives in each member state. This provided the EU with a reinforcement of its role

(De Bièvre 2013). This second part of the GPA for services was introduced in 1994, when the GATT became the World Trade Organization (WTO). In the UK, a customer-led rhetoric, supporting efficiency and effectiveness, was adopted through Major's Citizen's Charter. In the US, this was described as the state 'steering not rowing' (Osborne and Gaebler 1992) and was deployed by the Clinton administration, although not without criticism (Peters 1997). Without transparency on these changes, the public sector sought to understand how they would affect public service delivery. The introduction of New Public Management (NPM) (Hood 1990), postulated a range of drivers for these changes, including the neo-liberal marketisation of public services, but without reference to the UK's treaty obligations.

As the Core Executive prepared for implementation of the GPA, the SCS considered how it could safeguard its own positions as primary advisers to ministers. It did not wish this to be outsourced to think tanks and management consultants (Rhodes 2001). The strategy was consistent across all government departments. The first stage was to identify functions considered to be peripheral or non-core that could be turned into arm's length public bodies or agencies. These were routinised public-facing functions of the state such as rural payments, passports and driving licences. It was assumed they could be outsourced quickly and without any effect on policy making. The second stage was to identify central functions within departments such as payroll, recruitment, building and facilities management, security, procurement and payments which could be provided by private contractors. The third stage was to identify those parts of the civil service which had regulatory functions such as prisons or the probation service that could be subject to agencification or outsourcing. While these services might not all be subject to competition, staff numbers and percentages of departmental expenditure could score well in any assessment of government functions open to competition. For the SCS, these processes would divert attention away from central policy making. One way of managing this could be through the appointment of management consultants to government departments, preparing services for agencification, contributing to an increasing percentage of departmental budgets open to the market. The implementation of the first stage of the GPA for utilities, construction and nationalised industries was greeted with some enthusiasm by members of the SCS in the Treasury, who anticipated that it would relieve the UK of some of its larger national costs and create a new approach to poor and unionised employment relationships and strikes (Parker 2013). Similarly, local authority public facing services were considered to be routine and low status, easily opened to competition.

Significant agencification of central government services was underway by the time the second round of the GPA for services was implemented in 1994 (Christensen and Lægreid 2006). In addition to central government, there were other parts of public expenditure controlled and managed directly by the public sector including local government, health and education. Moving the NHS and education, at the heart of welfare state, to delivery by the private sector would be politically difficult, as recognised by the civil service, Thatcher and Major (Le Grand and Robinson 2018). Further, there was no market for directly delivered public services such as refuse collection or running schools. Thus, much of the Major period was associated with market making for public services through market testing exercises (Greer and Rauscher 2011) to prepare for competition.

The SCS did not want further competition beyond the Next Steps Agencies and sought a period of stability from Major (Willman 1994), switching focus to other parts of the public sector such as local government. The introduction of the Citizen's Charter in 1991 (Pollitt 1994) was met with scepticism and alarm as it included not only competition in public bodies but into Whitehall directly in the White Paper *Competing for Quality* (HM Treasury 1991; Butcher 1995), using the arguments of efficiency and effectiveness. This was followed by a White Paper on the Civil Service, *Continuity and Change* (1994), which included statements on how the civil service was to relinquish direct control and allow more freedom in delivery through the preparation of annual departmental delivery plans. The role of the welfare state in focusing on monopolistic provision was criticised as not offering citizens choice of service provider (Dunleavey and Rhodes 1990). The associated definition of services and their standards for delivery was created through specifications in preparation for competition. It also gave assurance to a public that had been accustomed to the certainties of the welfare state direct delivery model (Thain and Wright 1995) and preparing it for private sector services.

While NPM has been much discussed, would having had a better understanding and greater transparency of the drivers of its application been better for public service reform? As Pollitt and Bouckaert (2011) demonstrated, NPM was a phenomenon across Europe and beyond. Once established, it became a useful shorthand for change that focused more on the 'how' rather than the 'why' of public service reform. However, in some countries, there were discussions about the effects on public services and the selection of mechanisms to introduce competition such as public housing compacts in the Netherlands. There was also some policy transfer in using examples of methods in other countries within the UK, citing education examples from Sweden (Wiborg 2015) and e-government from Australia (Margetts 2006).

These changes in the structure of the civil service and its methods were described as the 'end of Whitehall' (Campbell and Wilson 1995). It was suggested that decision-making was, in effect, taken out of the hands of civil servants and made by the private sector. There were arguments about loss of accountability for services and control by ministers. However, this was to misunderstand the GPA system and the nature of contracting (Morphet

2021a). In any service which is run by the private sector as a contractor, the government retains responsibility as the client, setting specifications and managing contract delivery against these. As client, it can issue financial penalties for contract defaults. The main challenge for the civil service was that it had little experience of contract management. The services outsourced and contract processes were and, continue to be, low status activities within the SCS, relegated to the sidelines of interest. Even when these contracts show signs of failing such as the Horizon system in the Post Office, the hostile environment and its contextual effects on the Windrush generation in the Home Office and the failures of Carillion to complete construction projects for the DH and DfE, these could all have been addressed earlier by civil servants managing the contracts (see Chapter 8). Attempts by governments to focus the SCS on the quality of delivery of contracts have been met with disdain and elite dismissal.

One of the issues that was raised early in the debate about NPM was how states retreat from the GPA model (Foster and Plowden 1996). The New Labour government demonstrated that there were different ways in which competition could be introduced into public services but they did not retreat from the WTO treaty commitment (Richards 2007). Successive governments have moved away from initial targets and it is likely that an overcommitment to the percentage of each sector exposed to competition was made to ensure compliance. Moving away from competition commitments has been because contracts have failed and, in the case of UK railways, led to renationalisation. Secondly, failures in efficiency and effective service have led services to return to increased public direction, as in the bus industry. Contracts have also terminated when delivery failed, exemplified by the probation service which has been restructured and reformed multiple times since first proposed for privatisation (Robinson et al 2016). Another reason for returning contracts to the public sector has been a failure of the company awarded the contract such as Carillion, leaving the government with a number of half-completed hospitals. One of the biggest failures of contracts has been through the provision of PPE in the pandemic (NAO 2020) and the privatisation of track and trace both of which had been managed by public bodies in previous emergencies. Finally there is growing public pressure to re-nationalise the water companies which have taken profits from the businesses while performing badly including refusing to supply the regulator with data on their performance. Other market models have not proved successful, such as free schools.

The Senior Civil Service

Recruitment and entry to the SCS through the fast stream is the first stage of a civil service career that might reach the most senior level. Recruitment is through an open process which has been criticised as being too exclusively drawn from Oxbridge and from public schools (Fulton 1968; Foster-Gilbert 2018). As Burnham and Pyper (2008: 195) state, the civil service always defends its recruitment process as not to do so would undermine the existing members. While most Prime Ministers have favoured the need to appoint more specialists, their numbers have continued to reduce. Although professionals and specialists are recruited into the SCS, in practice the fast stream and those destined for the most senior roles are defined as generalist administrators. As generalists they are considered to be able to interpret specialist advice from other civil servants, professionals, think tanks, trade associations or special advisers (SpADs) in recommendations that will fit with ministerial and government objectives. While ministers may wish to directly appoint senior staff to specific roles based on their experience, contracts are limited to 5-year terms (Pyper 1995). This is the same route for SpADs.

For those reaching the most senior roles, based on biographical data, Heclo and Wildavksy (1974: 7) found that 'The civil service is run by small group of people who grew up together' but Theakston and Fry (1989) argue that more is known about entrants than who gets to the top group of between 70 and 80. While Fulton (1968) and others place emphasis on Permanent Secretaries attending the same universities and schools, Theakston and Fry (1989) consider post-entry socialisation and acculturation more important. Between 1965 and 1986, 30 per cent of Permanent Secretaries had spent 26–30 years in the civil service, with 40 per cent being in one department only in this period (Barberis 1996b).

There are specific career paths for those destined for the most senior roles. These are partly determined by the recruits and partly by those placing them in their first or subsequent posts. When considering Permanent Secretaries and their career paths, the majority started in the fast stream, spent some time in the Treasury, in a ministers' private office – probably the Prime Minister, the Chancellor of the Exchequer or Home Secretary for the most senior roles such as Cabinet Secretary – and on a bill team (Chapman 2000; Stokes 2016). Civil servants selected for the fast stream through competitive processes also meet early in their careers through their cohorts and networks that operate in Whitehall. These are important in understanding which opportunities are emerging and provide informal ranking of ministers and departments. There is an integrative pressure related to the culture of the administrative class (Self 1965) but it is also very competitive.

There are also pitfalls – snakes as well as ladders – for civil servants aiming for the top roles. Like some management consultants, the SCS fast stream over-recruits for its later needs – both to ensure a range of candidates available but also to create a cadre of potential chief executives and directors of other public, private and third sector organisations through a lattice of leverage, discussed further in Chapter 9. Former civil servants maintain links with colleagues, have opportunities for informal soundings and provide access to external bodies. The relationships can be through board appointments, chairing inquiries or commissions and the honours system. All this gives some hope of reinstatement into the SCS, although this rarely happens. While the 'revolving door' approach to the appointment of former senior members of the SCS is the subject of scrutiny (Andrews and Beynon 2024), the creation of this civil service diaspora through lower level appointments is less remarked upon or noticed (Michelson 2023) and yet plays a significant role in the maintenance of SCS soft power as part of a long-term Jesuitical strategy. It also provides access to the SCS for the employing organisations.

Most training for the SCS is undertaken on the job, 'sitting by Nellie' as it is known in some sectors (Al-Jamal and Cullingford 2016; Bevir and Rhodes 2016), where the culture of the civil service is transmitted (Christoph 1975: 32). Training in public policy making appears to be endured but not taken as seriously as close working relationships with named 'hero' civil servants (Bailey and Lloyd 2017). There appears to be no specific training in public values (Foster-Gilbert 2018). The most important task for a member of the SCS is policy formulation followed by its administration. There is no focus on management (Plowden 1989) which is thought to distract from the main focus of the SCS (Horton 1996).

All civil servants serve the Crown (Rohr 2002; Faulkner 2014) rather than their specific ministers, and Trollope (1865) reminds us that this has been a longstanding tradition. The notion of ministerial accountability arises from a time when Parliament had greater control and was able to scrutinise decision-making (Bogdanor 1997). Civil servants act in the name of their ministers, but while ministerial responsibility is regarded as more publicly accountable, Christoph states that the result was more control by civil servants (1975: 33). By taking decisions in the name of the minister, civil servants have been largely protected from scrutiny by Parliament. There is also a lack of transparency in who is advising on policy and, although ministers are required to keep a register of their meetings with outside bodies (McKay and Wozniak 2020), this is not the case for civil servants who advise them. MPs do not have access to civil servants other than through Select Committees when the civil servants can be called to give evidence (Lowe and Pemberton 2020) but they must reflect the minister's views (Armstrong 1985), nor provide MPs with information or assistance in their work other than when something is related to a constituent or a PQ is asked.

One important principle in the SCS is moving between posts every 18 months to 3 years. Bridges (1950) argued that, although individuals might resent learning afresh in each post, after having five posts in 15 years they would feel experienced enough to do anything. Bridges also argued later that members of the SCS are specialists in the issues that they have worked on and are best placed to advise ministers with this experience. However, he argues that the SCS is most skilled at administration, although none are held responsible for what they are being asked to administer. The view of Tribe (1949) remains part of high SCS culture:

> I am afraid that in many departments of the public service there is still a feeling that questions of cost are matters for the Finance branch and it's rather beneath the dignity of the administrative officer to descend from the Olympian heights of policy framing to mundane questions of cutting out unnecessary expenditure. (quoted in Chapman and Dunsire 1971: 159)

The separation between the core executive and functional and operational departments of government was set out by Cabinet Secretary Robert Armstrong (1970) when he described their responsibilities for policy, finance and personnel. He stated that the Cabinet Office is not in charge of policy but rather in charge of providing the secretariat for policy activities which are the responsibility of ministers. The role of the Head of the Civil Service is also located in this strategic group and usually recruited from SCS within a traditional career pathway, has no power over civil servants, except as a direct report and is not the chief executive of the government. A chief executive role was created in 2014 to support to the Cabinet Secretary and the Head of the Civil Service; it has an accounting officer role and is responsible for managing Permanent Secretaries across government.

While parts of the civil service have strategic advisory responsibilities, there is also a leading role exercised by the Treasury which has been the pre-eminent force inside the core executive since 1868 (Beer 1955). Subsequently there have been successive attempts to define Treasury's power or remove functions from it such as personnel which have been in and out of its control. However, the extent of Treasury control may overbalance government (Self 1965). This is further exacerbated by the extent of UK exceptionalism within international government accounting models (Hay 2003; Marsh 2023). In terms of expenditure on specific policies, this was mitigated when the UK was a member of the EU, when treaty commitments had to be implemented, but has subsequently been lost after Brexit (Morphet 2021b) leaving the Treasury fully in charge again.

While attempting to protect the most senior advice roles to ministers from any form of GPA competition, the SCS has increasingly used advice provided by the private sector, including management consultants. More recent pressures and crises, including Brexit, the COVID-19 pandemic and financial crisis of 2022 have led to a greater churn in the SCS (Gandon 2023). While these issues have made the SCS less attractive, responses to crises also provided opportunities for accelerated advancement. Members of the SCS are represented through the First Division Association, named after the First Division, which was the forerunner of the administrative class (Barberis 1996a). It has engaged publicly in debates where minsters have been critical of the civil service since 2016.

Functional departments

The core executive will interpret Government policy and treaty commitments into policy packages for functional departments (Morphet 2013), where the SCS also have policy development and advisory roles to ministers in pursuit of these objectives. The departments are all individual (William 1980; Hennesey 1989) and operate within a *primus inter pares* context, that means that there is no direct control over their activities by the Prime Minister who must work with ministers and the core executive to achieve their objectives through political pressure, preferment and funding through HM Treasury. There are no incentives to working in an integrated way towards a common end despite governments attempting this, for example Blair and the Joined Up Government initiative (Pollitt 2003). In addition to competition, there are arguments that working in this way undermines departmental and ministerial accountability, exercised through the accounting officer role of Permanent Secretaries (Wilkins 2002; HM Treasury 2023). Officials seldom move between departments unless the distribution of functions changes as part of MoG reforms. Civil servants within functional departments are expected to have a 'department view' or 'orthodoxy' (Barker and Wilson 1997) on policy which they provide to ministers as part of their options in relation to any policy. Departments do not have an institutional memory and are more focused on the present than the past or the future. They will reuse policies by giving them different names or slightly changing their rules and when acting, departments are generally relying on control (Bunbury 1928).

The functional 'spending' departments generate most activity. Their programmes are set in a variety of ways (see Chapter 3) with their finances in the administrative remit of the Chief Secretary to the Treasury. The financial settlement for each department is set in the Spring Budget and the Autumn Statement, the latter introduced to help the UK match its public expenditure financial year with the EU. These budgets reflect a range of activities including ongoing commitments for services, specific departmental initiatives set out in the Spending Review cycles (Tryggvadottir 2022) and some capital budgets set over longer periods such as for schools. However, budgeting processes for departments are short term and do not support longer-term financial stability for capital projects. There are no financial incentives for Departments to work together or to make savings either for their own or other departments. A reduction in departmental expenditure in one year, achieved through savings or reducing fraud, will lead to a budget reduction in the following year and regarded as weakness of the Permanent

Secretary if this occurs. There are examples where savings on housing costs through benefit payments could be achieved through more capital investment in housing or more savings in the NHS could be achieved with higher funding for public health, which is the responsibility of local not central government, but these actions do not occur.

The balance of expenditure within functional departments between the centre and their subordinate agencies or organisations can be in significant (Thain and Wright 1995). There were concerns when the Next Steps programme and wider agencification was introduced, that centres of these departments would lose control. Initially, functional Permanent Secretaries were pleased to see these activities on the periphery. However, post-Brexit, there has been a move to regain control of agencies and organisations, including local government, by re-taking their powers and/or their budgets in a re-centralisation process (Morphet 2021b). When the UK was part of the EU, much of the domestic policy and legislation framing functional activities and expenditure were pooled within it. The functional departments had a role in ensuring compliance and, in some cases, contributed to negotiations although much of this was undertaken by the core executive (Morphet 2013). After Brexit, there have been few MoG changes (Diamond 2023a) and the mandates for these former EU pooled activities and associated guaranteed funding were lost to the functional departments and retained by the Treasury. In order to maintain budget size, functional departments started to take more proactive roles in administering their peripheral organisations. There were also Departmental concerns about competition for new policy and programme space in government which would now be contested. Some departments had already experienced the loss of influence in government and the Treasury when they were privatised in the 1980s, such as the Department of Energy which lost its status as a standalone department (Thain and Wright 1995).

The staff of the functional departments comprise members of the SCS in the most senior roles, below which there will be clerical and executive officers and professionals who have advisory and not executive roles, even if members of the SCS. There is a head of profession and all the professionals in that group have a relationship with the head regardless of the department in which they work. There is also a scientific civil service (Rutter 2022).

The functional departments have been subject to the government's geographical dispersal policies, primarily to reduce costs, for regional development or levelling up policies. This is a recognition that their status is lower and they do not need to be near Whitehall. The functions that have been moved will have been selected on the same basis as those moved as part of UK regional policy in the 1950s and 1960s and the agencification process in the 1980s and 1990s. There appeared to be little assessment of how these moves might work best for the country and the receiving communities (Nickson et al 2020).

The appointment of civil servant staff for the functional departments in undertaken at departmental level. Since 1920, the Prime Minister's approval has been needed for the appointment of all Permanent Secretaries (Mackenzie and Grove 1957) and more recently there has been an increased role for ministers in their appointment (Smith and Richards 2020). It is argued that ministers need confidence in their Permanent Secretaries and, as they are accountable for their department, they should have influence in appointing these posts. However, more active ministerial engagement has raised questions over principles of civil service neutrality and whether senior officials seeking appointment at this level would continue to 'speak truth to power' for fear of promotional non-preferment. The introduction of performance objectives for individual Permanent Secretaries in 2012 challenged the conception of individual ministerial accountability. As the Cabinet Office Minister Francis Maude argued at their launch:

> Publishing the objectives of Permanent Secretaries is an important step towards reforming the Civil Service and sharpening its accountability to ministers and the public. Everyone can now judge how well the most senior civil servants are doing at getting best value for taxpayers' money and delivering the government's objectives. (Cabinet Office 2012)

Other staff are recruited directly by Departments, frequently using external contractors to advertise and sift applications. There has been an increasing focus on the diversity of the workforce which has been seen to be successful in mainstream grades in functional and operational activities (Andrews and Ashworth 2015).

Some parts of the functional civil service comprise regulators with the status of departments. Hogwood (2008) argues that while this is a 'messy' solution, it reflects whether it has led to a loss of civil servant control. As Freedland (2001) has pointed out, if the separated relationship between the agency and its parent department was to work in the manner initially intended, decision-making at agency level could not be part of a departmental structure. This initial quasi-independence did not reflect departmental unity, nor what the constitutional doctrine of ministerial responsibility demanded. While the proponents of agencification could claim, publicly at least, that they had no wish to alter existing constitutional practice, their proposals, framed by a set of assumptions about management that paid little heed to the context to which they were to be applied, had the effect of instituting significant constitutional changes: not least in enabling the convention of ministerial responsibility 'actually to be spirited off the stage' (Freedland 2001). However, that has changed over time, as services have returned to more direct departmental control, accelerating since Brexit.

Operational departments

The operational part of the of the civil service structure is both within mainstream departmental structures and in agencies. In 2024, there were 422 agencies that form part of the UK government all led by civil servants. These comprise executive agencies, executive non-departmental public bodies, non-executive agencies, tribunals and boards. The largest Department, the Ministry of Justice, has the largest number of operational staff through prison, probation and court services. The Department of Work and Pensions has the second largest including staff working on Universal Credit, tax credits and pensions and following this HMRC (IfG 2024). All these departments have direct contact with the public. Other departments such as the Home Office also have public facing roles in relation to asylum, borders and specific policy issues including the implementation of the 'hostile environment' policy that is central to the Windrush generation scandal (Gentleman 2019; Hewitt 2020).

The processes of agencification in the 1980s included targets and financial management that had already been introduced on a more modest scale (Barberis 1996a). However, although there were discussions about who would set targets in organisations that were privatised or subject to a regulator, the continuing role of the client function of government was overlooked. The issues of contract failure, poor performance and delays, as with the Rural Payments Agency (Ward and Lowe 2007), passports (Diamond 2023a), driving licences and tests as well as other regulated sectors such as telecoms, the media and energy, all required a strong client role supported by policy, operating within EU legislation and budgets. While the operational civil service has been largely outsourced, some services such as probation and rail services have moved in and out of the public sector. Some departments have learned to use the client function and set regulatory frameworks as political and financial tools to reinforce government policy more closely than had been the case before. The role of consultants in operating the 'hostile environment' policies of Theresa May while Home Secretary chose the easiest options in meeting their contract targets by focusing on citizens who had come to Britain but never needed documentary proof of citizenship while the Home Office destroyed proof of their arrival (Gentleman 2022).

Issues for the civil service as an employer

Recruitment and retention

Appointments in the civil service were the responsibility of the Civil Service Commission (CSC) between 1865 and 1990, when the Recruitment and Assessment Service (RAS) was established as part of the Next Steps initiative. While retaining oversight for recruitment, their direct role was reduced to approximately 5 per cent of all appointees (Chapman 1991), that is all fast stream and SCS appointment with the rest being undertaken directly by departments using RAS or other recruitment providers. The RAS was also appointed as a contractor to the CSC. As part of the Order in Council made to implement these changes, responsibilities were given to the Treasury, rather than to a minister, for matters such as deployment, qualifications, age and conditions of service (Chapman 1991).

One major consideration for the civil service is its diversity at all grades and the extent to which it reflects the UK population. It is argued that having a bureaucracy similar to the population makes it more likely that the nation's concerns are reflected in policy advice and administration (Andrews and Ashworth 2015). It is also said to make policy-making choices more acceptable if the civil service is seen to be 'representative' (Sowa and Seldon 2003). It may also be viewed as a better place to work (Andrews and Ashworth 2015) particularly where recruitment and management reinforce these representative practices. While these principles have been present in the civil service, pressures to change the number of civil servants and to reduce human resource functions can undermine them in practice (Andrews and Ashworth 2015).

The use of competency frameworks for recruitment and selection was introduced in the mid-1980s. However, Horton (2000) states that these frameworks have never been applied systematically in recruitment and development across the civil service, leaving departments to apply the requirements when appointing. In a review of the application of competency frameworks across all departments and agencies in 2000, it was found that while 80 per cent had competency frameworks these were not necessarily applied to all posts. The SCS applied their own framework. Despite their broad application, there was resistance and a lack of support for the use of these frameworks by managers (Horton 2000) and there is no evidence of the wider benefits of their application when in place (Bailey and Lloyd 2017). The modernising government programme launched in 1999 included the intention to widen open recruitment to SCS posts over a 10-year period and to increase diversity. There was also a proposal to redesign the SCS recruitment process. Overall, there is no systematic assessment of retention rates for civil servants at any grades nor the costs of recruitment (NAO 2023; NAO 2024a).

The size of the civil service has varied considerably since 2010. At the point of the Brexit referendum, the number civil servants was at its lowest and subsequently it has been increased to its highest. In 2023, the NAO undertook a review of the recruitment and performance in response to Brexit and COVID-19 challenges. In some government departments, staffing represents the highest cost. The NAO found that the proportion of lower to higher paid staff had reduced, while since 2013, the recruitment of specialist staff had increased. The RAS has now been replaced by the

Government Recruitment Service operated by the Cabinet Office but there are no central standards or costs models for recruitment undertaken within each department (NAO 2023). The application of pay to equivalent roles across the civil service also varies, as does the departmental approach to performance management.

Training and development

Training and development within the UK civil service has focused as much on core executive priorities to operational departments as on developing the skills of individuals. There have been attempts to improve both policy making (Bailey and Lloyd 2017) and leadership training and development. The implementation of the *Modernising Government* White Paper in 1999 included 3,000 SCS members who had a common pay structure and a central organisation for their appointment and progression (Dawson 2001). One of the features of modernisation was the role of leadership for delivery, and a programme was developed inside the civil service. This included providing experience working in other organisations, recognising that members of the SCS viewed their leadership responsibilities as associated with their job role and not beyond this. This programme focused on managing rather than leading teams (Dawson 2001). There was also a lack of conviction that improving leadership would make any difference in practice. This suspicion about the merits of leadership in the civil service has a long tail of tradition and was anathema to the focus on 'delivery' as the key civil service task. The apparatus introduced by the Blair government, including capability reviews, public service agreements and the Prime Minister's Strategy Unit (PMSU) and Prime Minister's Delivery Unit (PMDU) were not welcomed by the civil service and 'leadership' became associated with these unwelcome changes (Chapman and O'Toole 2010). While the then Cabinet Secretary, Gus O'Donnell, appeared to support a vision for change, in practice this focused on excellence rather than leadership and neglected the implied downgrading of the policy advice role of the civil service to ministers. In 2024, the NAO undertook a review of leadership capability in the Cabinet Office, which had established the Government's people group in 2023 combining HR functions together with Government Skills and Curriculum Unit, the Leadership College for government and the Senior Talent and Resourcing Team. The Cabinet Office has responsibility for appointing the SCS. In their review, following that of 2022, the NAO found that there was no coherent or system wide approach and while working with departments the Cabinet Office did not provide a common framework. The NAO demonstrated that leadership skills are not valued in the SCS and there is no central approach to understanding what is required or how they should be implemented. In the programme of the Leadership College, this was on the agenda for grades 3 and above but below it provided orientation on responsibilities of postholders at particular levels. There is also training available for accounting officers focusing primarily on their appearances before Parliamentary Select Committees.

In considering the challenges faced by the civil service after Brexit, the NAO reviewed training and development (NAO 2023) finding it more focused on transferring culture, values and core executive priorities. Hard skills for finance and project management have increasingly been provided by consultants and short-term external appointees, not generating a career path for these specialists. More focused training to prepare civil servants for appearances in front of select committees appears to be a rehearsal for the performance rather than more systematic training in public presentation.

A career for life?

There are several issues that relate to the closed tradition of civil service promotion and lack of external recruitment. Bunbury (1928) argued that making it a job for life would mean that incentives, such as those used in business, would not work to create a more management focused service. Rather, incentives would be part of socialisation. The Nolan Committee (1995) also commented on incentives, this time through the later introduction of performance related pay (PRP). The Committee argued that PRP may provide incentives for civil servants to conform to political preferences and not offer ministers or their more senior officers a range of solutions (Barberis 1996a). The pressures to introduce more external recruitment to the civil service remain with commitments given but not fulfilled (NAO 2024a). Of the 20 per cent of appointees to the SCS who came from outside, many appear to leave quickly after feeling isolated and not supported in the same way as those appointed internally, with their professional skills and external expertise not valued (NAO 2024a). It appears that the UK SCS remains inward focused, self-referential and resistant to leadership and management responsibilities.

3

How Does the Civil Service Develop Policy?

Introduction

A key role of the civil service is to develop policy advice to ministers (Dowding 1995) and then administer its implementation, frequently through others including local authorities and agencies. In the core function of policy making, training and development of civil servants has been less important than their initial recruitment into the Senior Civil Service (SCS) and subsequent acculturation. The civil servant's duty of 'investigation … as preliminary to action' (Haldane 1918 quoted in Hennessey 1989: 297) remains a guiding principle. Richards (1997) argues this was eroded during the 1979–97 Conservative governments, although he states that criticisms were made of individuals rather than the civil service as a whole. Blair, as an incoming Prime Minister in 1997, assumed that the civil service would find difficulty in changing focus from the previous administration (Blair 2010), not least as there had been legendary spats between Labour ministers and civil servants (Castle 1973; Crossman and Howard 1991).

While there have been many studies on improving policy making to support delivery (Brans and Vancoppenolle 2005), improve the use of evidence (Stevens 2011) and perform better in comparison with other countries, particularly within the EU (Hood et al 2002), the civil service has maintained that its central legitimacy is to provide advice to ministers (Polsby 2001). The role of the civil service in working with other EU member states in developing UK policy between 1972 and 2020 created a different style of negotiated and transactional policy expertise which may suggest a change in skills in the post-Brexit period (Richardson 2018; Diamond 2023a). There have also been divergent paths in policy making within the devolved administrations since 1999, which have been created within new integrated and non-departmental structures (see Chapter 6). There is very little analysis about the processes of policy making (Headey

1975; Morphet 2013) although more on influencers such as donors and think tanks (Pautz 2014).

This chapter considers the provenance of policy within government including international agreements, election manifestos, think tanks, lobbyists, special advisers (SpADs), donors, events and ministerial interests. It considers the reputation for the civil service's 'Rolls Royce' minds and its motivations in the framing and administration of policy. There is a strong culture within the civil service but this is accompanied by a lack of institutional memory in favour of new initiatives. There is also a lack of evidence-based policy making and consideration of risks of failure for implementation in a short-term approach, frequently illustrated through the reports of the National Audit Office (NAO). This reflects a lack of strategic planning culture or capability.

This chapter concludes with a consideration of the criticisms of civil service policy making and whether these are fair. These will include the continuing tension between the culture of generalists and the need for management training, understanding finance and the role of specialists (NAO 2024a; Urban et al 2024). There are also issues of constant staff churn produced by the career development process (what Michael Gove termed 'the whirligig of Civil Service transfers and promotions' quoted in Maude 2023), and the consequences of this for efficiency, the quality of advice, and standards of work performed. This also relates to the development of leadership and management skills within the SCS (NAO 2022, 2024a) with insufficient in-service training. The training that is offered is on soft rather than hard skills, and is focused on lower levels within the hierarchy. SCS members do not like to be considered as managers, with weekly meetings of management teams being termed 'round ups'. As part of this, is there also a failure to consider risk within the culture of a perceived controlled system where the law can always be changed or the government can always pay? There is also a continuing criticism of the effects of siloed policies within and between departments to the detriment of the country as a whole. Added to this, since 1999, there has been a failure to consider the legitimate roles of the devolved administrations within the UK and the conflation of policies for England and the UK in the advice to ministers. As Haldane stated in 1918, 'the elaboration of policy cannot be so readily distinguished from the business of administration' (quoted in Chapman and Dunsire 1971: 287)

What is policy?

Government policy is the position that government takes on any issue that affects individuals, organisations and institutions. Policy reflects political ideology as represented by ministers. Policy can be supported by legislation and through allocations of expenditure (Wright and Gamble 1998).

Policies can operate at different levels and are developed through specific bodies or individuals that advise government, with expectations that its administration will be at lower tiers. The priority of policy formulation over its administration is longstanding and derives from Northcote Trevelyan (1854), reinforced by Haldane (1918). However, much of what a civil servant does is in responding to ministers on problems that arise rather than flagship policies. The former adviser to Cameron when Prime Minister, Steve Hilton, observed that 70 per cent of the issues crossing ministers' desks were not in the 'Programme for Government' (Rutter 2015: 39).

What stimulates policy development?

While there is much consideration of specific policies, there is less discussion of the ways in which the interplay of pressures for policy positions come together. These are numerous and include the application of international treaties, legal judgements, election manifestos and circumstances. Policy development can also be influenced by lobbying, think tanks and policy communities (Thijs et al 2017). These are considered in turn.

International agreements and obligations

A main source of policy stimulation is the external commitments made by the UK state through international treaties. Treaties make binding commitments on the country and last longer than Parliamentary terms. The nature of these agreements and the commitments to action will vary from general to specific. This provenance of policy making is not discussed much in the public domain and is developed by the core executive before being passed on to functional departments for detailed policy development and administration. Policy development from the core executive can be anticipatory, not least as some international treaties take a long time to negotiate. Here, there may be first mover advantages for countries that apply anticipated treaty obligations earlier than required, even during negotiation. These initiatives may influence the final nature of the treaty agreement which would then also provide advantages for consultancy and influence, demonstrating political leadership within international political discussions.

The construction of treaty obligations may be important as, when the UK was part of the EU (1972–2020), the form of the agreement was fundamental to its implementation (Morphet 2013). While an EU member, treaty obligations were used to shape UK domestic policy. The primary and overarching principles were enshrined in the Treaty on Accession and subsequent changes to it – which are consolidated within the foundational treaty. These have included Maastricht 1992, Amsterdam 2002 and Lisbon 2009 treaties. These treaty changes have a significant role in extending the policy areas which are pooled by member states and the ways in which decisions are made on them. Some have had a direct effect on the internal policy of member states such as those for subsidiarity in the Maastricht 1992 and Lisbon 2009 treaties, where article 5 gave much greater requirements for central government to devolve funding and powers to lower tiers of the state (Arribas and Bourdin 2012).

The second way in which EU treaties influenced UK policies was in the legal form of the policy agreement. These are primarily constructed in two ways. The first is through a Directive which was initially more popular as a form of policy agreement (Zhelyazkova 2013). Here changes agreed have to be implemented by a specific date but the form and the timing can vary within each member state to suit internal political timetables. It is more convenient to implement policy changes when there is a general election or change in political leadership of the governing group. The second format used by the EU is through the provision of a Regulation which has to be implemented on a specific date in the wording used, giving member state governments no manoeuvrability in timing and framing the new policies that are being implemented. After enlargement started in 1992, there was a shift towards Regulations particularly where the changes had an impact on the single market or related to infrastructure investment. As Directives and Regulations were included in the overarching treaty, the government did not require approval by Parliament for their implementation. There was a reluctance to address the relationship between the UK and the EU throughout the period of membership, and Regulations and Directives were passed into domestic legislation, as though independent of the EU (Morphet 2013). As there were long periods of negotiation, the core executive was able to plan for their implementation and attach other public service reforms to them in the certain knowledge that they would be implemented. This 'gold plating' became a common civil service practice during the UK's membership of the EU (Morris 2011).

A second approach to developing policy to meet international agreements can be seen in the UN's climate change target timescale for reducing emissions. Each country can determine how to meet the target and variations are offered given that each country will have a different starting set of conditions, for example on the use and type of energy. The makeup of components to implement these treaty commitments may change and can be packaged in different ways from specific regulatory control of the use of plastic, car type and emissions levels, bans and fiscal incentives.

As international agreements are negotiated by the Foreign, Commonwealth and Development Office and the core executive, the consideration for UK civil servants will be on the effects of different forms of policy required to meet treaty obligations. In some cases the shifts in policy required may be considerable, requiring time and political space to bring them into effect, by shaping political and public narratives. The drive and thrust of these emerging policy requirements need to align with the government's political ideology, so while the Labour Party agreed the UK's membership of the Government Procurement Agreement (GPA) in 1976, it was much easier for the core executive to frame the reforms required for implementation around the ideologies of Margaret Thatcher. When John Major became Prime Minister, this coincided with the implementation of the services GPA and allowed him to develop a rhetoric of efficiency while serving the citizen, making new markets to ensure that these obligations could be met. An example of this longstanding preparation for implementation, both political and in the civil service, is shown by a Cabinet Minister in the Heath and Thatcher governments, David Howells:

> On the one hand I was very interested in privatisation, after all some of us had been working on the topic since the 1960s, contrary to the Lawson memoirs that imply that it was all him. We were getting these ideas from America in the 1960s. It's true they did not take off under Heath but we worked a lot of these things out and through the 1970s we developed them. So I was mad keen on privatisation and wider ownership and changes in the nature of the capital markets and oil was the prime candidate. I think I had hopes beyond that for electricity and gas, coal seemed out of reach in those days. (Richards and Smith 2002: 788)

Once the treaty has been agreed there will be further negotiation on implementation, compliance and domestic policy monitoring. This is important in the way the core executive presents the requirements to ministers and packaging to demonstrate that policies have been implemented by functional departments. In some cases, international treaty obligations have little preparation in domestic policy narratives and become 'orphan policies'. An example of the way in which the relationships in the Westminster Model (WM) were changed without much explanation was in the Blair government's creation of the Supreme Court. At the time this was seen as an unexplained but increasingly justified approach to the constitution following the introduction of administrative law and the increase in judicial reviews (Bevir 2008). However, there was never any explanation or preparation to discuss the application of EU treaty principles for the separation of power and the opportunity for administrative redress.

Political manifestos

Political manifestos represent the views of a party (Dolezal et al 2018). At national level, each political party will have its own way of developing manifesto policy through a range of grass roots processes, formal motions at party conferences or in other institutionalised settings. Manifestos are coalition documents intended to catch the attention of the electorate and reinforce policy priorities to a range of audiences, including within the party (Harmel et al 2018). Before a general election, parties in opposition are provided with 'facilitation' meetings where the shadow ministers spend time with civil servants providing a bridge into departments if they are elected. In 2023, the Prime Minister Rishi Sunak initially forbade these meetings, breaking the practices in place since 1960, finally allowing them in spring 2024. In these meetings, the SCS start their advisory process, become more familiar with the priorities and styles of their potential ministers and help to frame policies linked to the manifesto. This will also be the opportunity for the SCS to inject policies required to meet international obligations, determining how they can be interwoven into the priorities that the party has identified. It is also a time when departmental civil servants can introduce their own priorities (Barker and Wilson 1997). The same processes will be undertaken for the party in government, but here civil servants will have some understanding of the agenda. However, even here there are opportunities to reset policies such as through suggesting the appointment of a different Secretary of State or ministerial team in an election reshuffle.

Manifesto policy promises are important in a number of ways. Policy commitments are included in the annual King's speech (Jennings et al 2011). If a policy commitment is contained in the manifesto, then the Salisbury Convention is invoked and the House of Lords will not oppose it. These manifesto promises are also linked to success in a general election and for departmental policy commitments in the winning party's manifesto. These guarantee priority in Parliamentary time and Treasury funding. Here, civil servants may be acting as budget maximisers (Dunleavy 1991) both at times of government expansion and budget reduction, such as during austerity post-2010, and the financial crises in 2008, 2022 and post-Brexit. Finally, party manifestos are important as governments come towards the next general election. While being able to call a general election at a time of the Prime Minister's choosing may have political advantages, it also creates added pressure on assessments of the implementation of the party's manifesto (Bara 2005). In some elections, a dominant issue can take over and overshadow the wider range of policy commitments such as in 2019, the Brexit election (Allen and Bara 2021).

Sofa government

As well as these formal processes of policy development, there are a range of other methods through which policies can be developed and agreed. One method, sofa government, was said to be a characteristic of Blair 1997–2007.

This was criticised by Robin Butler, a former Head of the Home Civil Service and Cabinet Secretary:

> Of crucial import here is the evidence elicited by Hutton of the 'remarkable informality (to use no sharper term)' of how the business of government has been transacted under the Blair premiership, which … 'was surely an uncomfortable surprise, even to cognoscenti'. (2004: 125)

The Butler Report (2004) made much of sofa government operating in and around No 10, and voiced adverse comments on the relationship between civil servants, most especially those working in the intelligence services, and key policy-focused figures in the Prime Minister's inner circle (Hennessey 2005). The report was critical about the way in which the Prime Minister had organised and conducted the collective Cabinet dimension of his administration. Another former Cabinet Secretary criticised this approach (Wilson 2004: 85) as undermining good government and a civil service concern of a near exclusive focus on 'delivery' at the expense of attention to due process and bypassing existing Machinery of Government (MoG) in the WM.

External shocks – climate and humanitarian catastrophe, economic turbulence, war

Another major source of policy in government is that induced by external shocks such as war, humanitarian crises and economic turbulence. Examples here have included the COVID-19 pandemic (2020), the 2008 financial crisis and the Ukrainian war (2022). While there will be existing policies on all these matters, the swift development of new, more active policies for the UK's role and contribution can sideline other planned policy programmes in Parliament and for civil service priority attention in a 'government fog' (Du Gay 2006).

Royal Commissions and government committees

Royal Commissions have been used less frequently since 1979 than in the past. Royal Commissions take evidence and then make recommendations on a national issue. Their role has been overtaken by the enhanced powers of Parliamentary Select Committees introduced in 1979, which have the same powers to take evidence and make recommendations. Other committees of inquiry have been set up including on the press (Leveson 2011), the use of infected blood products (Langstaff 2024), COVID-19 (2023), the Post Office Horizon prosecutions (2024), the Iraq war (Chilcot 2009) and maternity services in specific hospital trusts (Ockenden 2014) all of which have made recommendations to government. While the government makes a formal response to all those forms of scrutiny, it is not required to make any policy or legislative change. The role of civil servants in relation to these forms of scrutiny is clear – they should not provide information without the specific direction of their ministers as the ultimate responsibilities lie with them (Armstrong 1985).

His Majesty's Inspectorates and coroners' reports

A range of formal processes make recommendations for action by government. These include reports of avoidable deaths by coroners such as those caused by air quality, the role of social media in child suicides, mould in housing and fire in tower blocks. His Majesty's Inspectorates also make proposals for legislative change following disasters or accidents where lives have been lost and endangered. Some of these reports attract media attention and public campaigns but the government is not required to act.

Domestic events: dangerous dogs, NHS failures

Action can be promoted in Parliament when there is national public outcry about an issue although the resulting legislation is often criticised as being faulty and poorly conceived (Hood et al 2000; Allcock and Campbell 2021). Ministers and their civil servants are asked to come forward with solutions to prevent re-occurrences of some tragic events or to right injustices such as in the Post Office Horizon issues where the government sought to change the constitution in an attempt to meet the public opinion.

Forthcoming elections – general and local

While the UK has been regarded as a state free from political corruption and pork barrel politics, the Johnson and Sunak administrations demonstrated different behaviours. The Prime Ministers were willing to use funds intended to meet local needs for economic regeneration after COVID-19 and other levelling up funds as mechanisms to attract votes in forthcoming elections (Hanretty 2021). Although this had some effect in the first by-election of the post-2019 Johnson government in Hartlepool, subsequently it had little impact on by-election results. Both Prime Ministers stated during their campaigns that a vote for their party candidate would be a certain way of ensuring government funding to their areas. There have been examples of this in the past when ministers have attempted to gain the support of the Prime Minister for a specific project which is expected to be significant in forthcoming election such as Barbara Castle and the Humber Bridge (Simon 1984).

While specific schemes may be the subject of political promises, there remains a question of what processes are used by the civil service to assess different funding bids where the results appear to produce a party political benefit. Is there intense internal pressure from SpADs to change the methodologies or do civil servants bow to the pressures of their ministers?

Ministerial entrepreneurialism

In addition to political priorities, there is also ministerial entrepreneurialism reflecting specific interests in addition or preference to the Prime Minister's priorities. This may be a product of enthusiasm, a long-held interest such as issues of disability or from self-interest. They may also represent an anti-bureaucratic approach by ministers who want to use the system in their own way (Du Gay 2000). In some cases this antibureaucratic approach has been the product a right wing government such as under Liz Truss (2022) or through the actions of specific ministers such as Jacob Rees-Mogg when he was minister for the civil service within this short lived Truss government.

Members' ballots and individual campaigns

Some policy and legislation is made through the ballot held between MPs at the beginning of each Parliament which allows them to introduce a bill of their choice. This is not specified at the time of the ballot and topics range from long held interests to the best case made to the MP by groups seeking legislative change. MPs do not receive support when they are successful in the ballot. When the system was reviewed by the House of Commons Procedures Committee in 2010, most of its proposals were rejected. Support from the Public Bills Office in Parliament has been frozen since 2016 (Moriue 2020). Some bills pursued through the ballot system can be 'handout bills' by government, given to MPs who gain a slot by party whips, where government wants small changes but does not wish to give time. MPs who take handout bills may regard it as a way to gain favour from the whips or to pay back for some previous misdemeanour. Many private members' bills are killed off by other MPs through filibustering (Marsh and Marsh 2002). The success of private members' bills can be influenced by whether the government gives extra time to their hearing and government can also remove a bill by asking one of its own side to shout 'object'. Some of those proposing these bills do not expect to be successful but use the opportunity to gain public attention for an issue (Hazell and Reid 2018; Cavari et al 2023). A number of important human rights acts were passed into law using this method in the 1960s including liberalising of laws on abortion, homosexuality and divorce and the abolition of capital punishment. This was considered to be the golden age of private members' bills.

Donors

The role of donors in influencing policy may be considerable, although it is difficult to track the direct relationship. Since 2000, donations to parties have increased by 250 per cent in the UK (Draca et al 2023) with over 60 per cent of donations made by individuals, including Transparency International's (2021) investigation of the influence of development donors on housing policy.

Lobbying by think tanks and APPG

Think tanks are established to promote interests through policy papers and research that attempt to influence decision making in government. They are funded by donors who may be wealthy individuals or a coalition of interests promoting an issue. They include a range of topics, some of which may be specific and others more general (Pautz 2014). Some will be politically aligned. Their influence on government policy is understood, although specific policy impacts cannot always be identified. While think tanks might be more frequently associated with influencing politicians and their SpADs, there is a growing understanding of the ways in which they can collaborate with civil servants less transparently.

Many MPs have a career in politics prior to entering Parliament including in think tanks, and this gives them a different approach from the civil service (Foster-Gilbert 2018). Civil servants may find think tanks convenient in promoting arguments to ministers in ways that they cannot, while ministers might signal a change in direction based on think tank research or a policy paper. Think tanks are regulated within national systems (Stone and Garnett 1998) including the extent to which they are subject to disclosure requirements by politicians. The increasing proliferation of think tanks may be a more externalised understanding of the forces of influence on government decision making. Up to the 1960s, influences on government and civil servants might have been through those who were educated at the same schools or universities, although this was less publicly apparent until the Fulton Report (1968). However, there is now a view that those seeking to gain policy influence need to mobilise public support for political traction on decision makers. Further, Stone and Garnett (1998) argue that lobbyists reflect the politicisation of knowledge and their role is now established in political networks and elites. While Denham and Garnett (1998) demonstrate US think tanks are better funded and more prolific, in the period since 2010 there has been a marked increase in the role of the US Right in funding think tanks in the UK, particularly those located in a building in Tufton Street which has become synonymous with these bodies including the IEA and the Centre for Policy Studies. While there were right-wing think tanks from the early 1970s, headed by those who eventually became members of

Thatcher's government, including Nicholas Ridley, the US funding model has been a more recent development. However, some think tanks such as the Institute of Fiscal Studies and the NIESR are regarded as being sources of objective analysis and quoted by media in this way. Think tanks seek to influence policy makers using a range of methods including publications, events such as round tables or through smaller discussions over private lunches or dinners.

The rise of All Party Parliamentary Groups (APPGs) provides another form of think tank which is unregulated. These are single issue groups, supported by MPs and members of the House of Lords, that focus on an issue which transcends party politics. APPGs may be funded through external organisations which help to organise events on the Parliamentary estate. There were 250 APPGs in 1996 and over 600 in 2015 (Thomas 2015). While there are some groups that are supported by the private sector, a large number are also supported by charities seeking to gain political traction on issues that are their primary concern. However, in some sectors such as the pharmaceutical industry, many health APPGs were in receipt of company funding (Rickard and Ozieranski 2021). Parliament publishes a register of all APPGs each year. Civil servants have no direct relationships with these groups.

Petitions and public demonstrations

When the public wishes to express its concerns to government and considers that it is not gaining any influence on an issue, public petitions or demonstrations may ensue. A petition can be launched and registered through Parliament and on the Parliamentary website there is an indication of which have been considered, debated or received a response from government. Some argue that they are an effective form of public engagement (Leston-Bandera 2019) although they are mostly against current government policy. However, Matthews (2021) shows that MPs can be antagonistic to these petitions and they do not have any priority within the Parliamentary system.

Deliberative assemblies

A deliberative assembly can take many forms and is sponsored by a public body with an independent chair. It can take the form of a citizen's jury or assembly and used to advise on policy or determine decisions in choice-based situations. They have been used in Canada on electoral reform (Fournier 2011), Ireland on a range of social and constitutional reforms (Walsh and Elknik 2021) and France on climate change (Galván and Zografos 2023). They have been suggested as a way of public decision-making by Gray (2024) who advised the Labour Party, stating that civil servants would not like them as they would have no control over the outcomes. Citizen's assemblies have been used in the UK at local and sub-regional levels (Davidson and Elstub 2014) and more recently for current issues at a national level – Citizens' Assembly on Brexit (Renwick et al 2018) and the Citizens' Assembly on Social Care (House of Commons 2018). The format used for the Citizen's Assemblies can vary in a number of ways including the length of time over which the deliberation is held, the contributions or experts and discussions between those participating. As Renwick (2017) states, the discussion at the assembly can vary according to the strength of feeling of the participants, which can range from agnostic to highly charged and polarised.

A major consideration in the use of deliberative democracy is what kind of influence it can have. In the UK, the Assembly on Brexit was convened after the referendum but before the final form of Brexit was agreed (Renwick et al 2018). Although there were political speakers, there was no commitment to the views expressed. This may mean, as with other more institutionalised public consultation methods used in planning, that people will not participate, even on an invited basis, if they realise their input has not contributed to the outcome. This might be improved if the assembly could determine the issues to be discussed in detail and the form of the event (Elstub et al 2021). While Gray (2024) has asserted that Citizen's assemblies cannot be controlled, research from Ireland demonstrates that they can be influenced in their views if all the presenters agree and take the same position (O'Malley 2024)

Policy bandwagons

Policy bandwagons operate by creating a coalition of interest for specific policy influence on governments and the civil service (Baumgartner and Leech 2001; Halpin 2011). Policy bandwagons may be associated with opportunities created by policy windows (Kingdon and Stano 1984) offered by changes in government. Governments can use policy bandwagons to pursue a policy that might be unpopular for part of the electorate. The decision to hold a referendum on Scottish independence in 2014 and on Brexit in 2016 can both be seen within this context. Pressures for these votes had been building through public discourse – in Scotland since the previous failed referendum in 1978 and on UK membership of the EU since the successful referendum to remain in membership in 1975. In both cases, the pressure had been generated in periods of Labour government and referenda held in periods of Coalition and Conservative administrations.

Halpin (2011) found that civil servants were active in promoting the development of policy bandwagons through the stimulation of the participation of particular groups in consultation processes. These captured attention through invitations to round tables or special closed meetings with the civil service. At the same time, Halpin found that widening the scope of participation in a policy consultation helped civil servants identify those who might be opposed to the proposed policy change and find ways of dealing with their potentially negative responses.

Who makes policy – ministers or civil servants?

In the process of policy development, do ministers or civil servants generate most policies and what is the balance of influence between them (Headey 1975)? As indicated above, the provenance of policies derives from a range of sources, not only from party manifestos. However, within this range, ministers determine the order in which policies are progressed and may be pressured by their party, including donors, government or on advice from their civil servants. They may be waiting for funding to ensure that the policy has a smooth passage through the core executive. They also need to consider the views of other ministers and departments on whether they will provide support. An issue that is not often discussed, but understood implicitly inside government and the civil service, is the degree of competition between departments for resources, parliamentary time, media coverage and support from the core executive (King and Crewe 2014). Some departments can be isolated, such as the Home Office with its longstanding place in Whitehall (Jenkins 1975; Barwell 2021). The abilities of functional departmental ministers to promote their proposed policies cannot be underestimated and the most capable civil servants will not be able to progress policies where the ministers are not well regarded. As Playfair states:

> One can see it in the very peculiar psychological reaction of the ordinary civil servant when there is a matter in dispute between two Ministries. Great passion can be worked up – we get our Ministers involved (they may even have started it) – we feel desperately about it. Then finally, after tremendous manoeuvres and lobbying it goes to the Cabinet and a decision is made. (1965: 262)

The exception to this may be where Permanent Secretaries have decided that a policy needs to progress and, in this case, will work round ministers (Barberis 1996a). Civil servants may have definite views and seek to influence ministers: 'I do not deny that sometimes officials do have strong views and insinuate them in a pretty determined way' (Boyle 1965: 256). Civil servants can also keep ministers in the dark about a wider range of views on a policy from elsewhere.

In a debate about who makes policy, ministers or civil servants, held in 1964, the answer provided by the Minister, Sir Edward Boyle, was that the Minister's policies would depend on them obtaining funding from the Treasury, although officials could do the 'softening up' (Boyle 1965). He emphasised how important it is for a minister to be on top of his brief – as the Treasury 'rather like to feel that they know rather more about the departments than they themselves know' (1965: 252). It is also important for ministers to be aware of the interests of other cabinet members as, through its committees, it acts as a clearing house for policies being taken forward (Hennessey 1986). A similar point was made by Sir David Lidington (IfG 2023a) in relation to proposed legislation. The Institute for Government (IfG) (Urban et al 2024) has argued that there needs to be a change in the leadership and management of policy in government through a merger of the Cabinet Office and Prime Minister's office if any government is to successfully implement its policy programme. The IfG proposes that this should be through greater control of this reformed department in the core executive and its widened role in holding departments accountable for their performance in policy administration.

Some ministers emphasise that the impulse for policy development can come from within the government, the Prime Minister or other cabinet members (Boyle 1965). Ministers are subject to the ministerial code in terms of with whom they can discuss issues and when, and these discussions need to be declared (Daintith and Page 1999). The type of policy can also be dependent on any minister's reputation for being successful in proposing policy into government. The ways in which other members of government and their departments view a proposed policy may make a difference. There are also issues to consider in its framing. As ministers will need to make an argument for a policy with their peers, this will require some understanding of the ways in which they are likely to view any proposals. Ministers also have to consider how any policy will be received in the House of Commons and amendments from the House of Lords. These will vary on the issue and size of the government's majority. However, as King and Crewe (2014) note: 'Britain's political system is a power-hoarding system ... ministers and officials, although ready to consult others, are usually reluctant to engage fully with them and to see them as active participants in the policy-making process' (p 389).

While ministers have responsibility for policy, there have also been concerns expressed about the generalist nature of the civil servants advising them and their ability to frame and develop it (Bailey and Lloyd 2017). The role of specialists will be further down the departmental structure or appointed externally as advisers. Their advice will be filtered and interpreted by Permanent Secretaries before being presented by ministers (Barberis 1996a). Some Permanent Secretaries do not consider issues to be important such as the long period in the policy wilderness experienced by building control regulation reform before the Grenfell Tower fire in 2020

(Apps 2022). This issue of specialist vs generalist has been at the core of the civil service culture since the Northcote Trevelyan reforms (1854) and attempts to change it have been thwarted by the senior civil service, where 'everybody but us' changes (Rhodes 2001). As a consequence, ministers have increasingly sought advice from SpADs. The increase in government failures, Maude (2023) has argued, is a result of the breakdown between the civil service and ministers.

Civil servants are permanent in their appointments and are not changed at the top when there is a change in the political control of the government, as in the United States and some European countries (Daintith and Page 1999) (see Chapter 1). This continuity is regarded as a particular strength in the policy advice role of the UK civil service by those at the top of it (Rhodes 2001). At the same time, members of the SCS will have spent their careers instigating or implementing change (Part 1990) and are skilled in managing, modifying and minimising it (Theakston 1999) within the context of existing traditions (Rhodes 2001). This includes the departmental 'cocoon' (Bevir and Rhodes 2010: 108) which ministers enter when taking office. In Rhodes's view (2001), the principle of the generalist was not a legacy from the Northcote Trevelyan reforms but rather from the 1920s and 1930s, promoted by the head of the home civil service Warren Fisher and his protégée Edward Bridges. Successive attempts by ministers to employ external experts from a range of sectors including local government or the private sector to challenge this tradition have been made. The individuals appointed become part of a revolving door of short-lived appointments (Toynbee 2023; NAO 2024). Members of the SCS consider that those appointed later in their careers will not have had the mentoring or acculturation necessary to operate effectively within the system. Others, including Normington (Foster-Gilbert 2018) argue, without citing any evidence, that external appointees have been the cause of many civil service problems. On matters of internal relations within government and between minsters and the civil service, the courts take the view that, in the WM, these are internal matters held by the crown and not a matter for them.

Governments have used many mechanisms to introduce a wider range of views beyond those proposed by their civil servants. Mrs Thatcher brought in external advisers including Lord Rayner who undertook scrutinies and Prime Ministers Cameron and Johnson appointed SpADs who were regarded as less conventional and anti-civil service in Steve Hilton and Dominic Cummings. Some governments have chosen other routes including the appointment of task forces and policy tsars – both used by the Labour government 1997–2010. The task forces were more flexible and seen as more inclusive than Royal Commissions, focused on cross cutting issues to overcome Whitehall departmental silos (Richards 2008). Policy tsars were appointed to provide alternative advice to ministers or to move on difficult issues (Levitt and

Solesbury 2013; Clifford and Morphet 2023). More recently these have included the Dilnot Commission on Social Care (2011) for Ageing and Leitch report on skills (2006).

When ministers enter government they bring a growing number of SpADs with them and this differs from longstanding views describing civil servant and ministerial relationships. The role of SpADs in connecting ministers into the political context in which they work, with other departments and No 10, can only partly be emulated by civil servants. Since Brexit, the politicisation of central government has been outside the remit of the civil service (Bevir and Rhodes 2010) which has been 'othered' by the governing elite (Shipman 2016). By engendering this alternative advice, can we say that Whitehall has become more politicised in the advice provided to ministers as a consequence? Since 2010, this WM has been changing without any indication of a reset. The increasing role of SpADs, funded in some cases by lobbyists or special interests, can create an environment where civil servants have to work differently to provide advice. There have been periods when ministers or their advisers have denigrated civil servants such as Dominic Cummings who argued that they are too centrist in their thinking – a charge also made by the incoming Thatcher and Truss administrations (Richards 1997). Some civil servants have been clear that they consider the separation of roles between ministers and civil servants in Northcote Trevelyan was a mistake and that civil servants should have a greater role in policy making (Playfair 1965) while Urban (2024) argues that SpADs should have a larger role.

While there may be no neat divisions between civil servants and ministers, the development of policy will be strongly related to the personal relationships between them. As Headey (1975) points out, both civil servants and politicians can be silent in the policy development process and signal their views through passive aggressive approaches of non-engagement. Some Permanent Secretaries indicate that their main role is to persuade ministers to take on policies, while some ministers have little or no role in policy making (Headey 1975). Some departments develop a departmental view which may only be held by the Permanent Secretary (Barker and Wilson 1997). Headey (1975) relays a situation where all briefings to the Home Secretary were put in common notes under the signature of the Permanent Secretary and views in the department were 'coordinated' through this means although one of Headey's interviewees stated that this tended to produce a coordinated silence around the table (Headey 1975: 76). Putnam (1975) argues that civil servants control the policy agenda as they have the evidence on the shortcomings of existing policies and expertise on how to craft alternatives as well as control over the evolution of the agenda. Civil servants want strong ministers who can promote their Department's agenda but they also experience a range of ministerial engagement with policy matters on their departments. Headey (1975) analysed ministers into five types:

1. Policy initiators
2. Policy selectors
3. Executive ministers
4. Ambassador ministers
5. Minimalists

For the civil service there is an expectation that policy options will be evaluated and that this will include an assessment of policy effectiveness within the context of the ideology of the current government (Gray and Jenkins 1983). For the Thatcher government this was related to the costs of delivery whereas during the Blair government the focus was on the effectiveness of delivery for targeted outcomes (Richards 2007). There have been periods when more analytical techniques have been used such as by Heath and the Central Policy Review Staff (Blackstone and Plowden 1988) or more recently through the Treasury's Green Book evaluation process which examines any policy or project using five methods of assessment – strategic, economic, commercial financial and management business cases (HMT 2022). However, policies and their subsequent administration are selected primarily using political objectives, although the array of policy administration within any department may mean that many of the decisions are taken by civil servants acting in their minister's name. However, there remains a culture of secrecy and lack of transparency in access to information and wider policy considerations discussed which inhibits questioning of decision making (Wiliams 1983).

How are policies constructed?

Once it has been agreed that a policy needs to be developed or reviewed there are a number of considerations as to how it should be constructed and designed.

Recycling past approaches with new names

While government departments have no institutional memory, there is a restricted range of policy models that appear to re-emerge, although with different names and minor variations. Sometimes the same policy is reannounced several times to catch public attention or suggest a new issue.

Copying another country – policy transfer and convergence

When the UK has close political or treaty ties with other countries there can be policy copying or transfer between them. It may be possible to demonstrate to ministers that a policy has worked successfully elsewhere. It may be a shortcut to finding a policy rather than thinking this through *ab initio*. The process of policy transfer may include copying a whole initiative or applying a hybrid approach using part of another country's policy approach (James and Lodge 2003). Policy development can include 'lesson drawing' from other countries which may also include what has failed as well as what has been successful (Rose 1993). Policy transfer can include a range of components including construction, presentation and techniques (Dolowitz and Marsh 1996).

Are there also international pressures for policy convergence? Some organisations such as the OECD provide research on policy approaches to different economic, social and environmental issues making it possible to look elsewhere. Ministers have commissioned reviews of other countries as part of their own evaluation processes (Lodge et al 2013). The OECD also compares and scores policy implementation effectiveness between its members and this can be differentially influential in policy sectors such as PISA in educational performance. The introduction of competition in education in England was compared with Sweden and workfare models have transferred between the UK and the United States. During the Blair government, there were exchanges of officials with Australia which had an impact on e-government and the smoking ban for successive age groups proposed by Prime Minister Sunak in 2023 was based on New Zealand.

When the UK was part of the EU, policies across member states were similar and could be described as convergent (Bennett 1991; Page and Wouters 1995), as they were all engaged in delivering the same policy with the same goals and content. However, in the UK there seemed to be a particular interest in giving these policies non-EU names. Since Brexit, there are issues of maintained legal alignment by the UK of EU legislation rolled into UK law (Gibson and Cowie 2024). There were also other policy similarities including the use of missions in the Levelling Up agenda that have also been adopted for the EU policy programme for the same period. In some cases, ministers want policy variation in comparison with other countries to show their distinctiveness. This was a key component of the Brexit argument and is retained as a key tenet of those in favour of Brexit although businesses and institutions have argued for dynamic alignment and maintenance of policy copying in order to support their trading links across European and global markets. Adopting different policies can require businesses to offer different standards in different regulatory regimes which may be costly and make them less competitive.

Why does policy transfer occur rather than preparing a new policy? James and Lodge (2003) state that this question is less frequently discussed with more focus on the policy content and process. There a is a currency in ideas associated with particular ideologies enabling funded influencers in think tanks or operating as SpADs to limit a range of policy options through means such as social media and political coercion. The failure to reform housing tenure legislation by successive Conservative governments up to 2024 is an example of government stated intention being held back by party political mobilisation within parliament.

Policy communities and networks

In some areas, there are longstanding policy communities and networks comprising of individuals who share a common identity or interest who shared views on how policies can be improved. Those involved in policy communities and networks can be coalitions of think tanks, professional and trade bodies and academics who may work together or with other allied groups. Policy communities can be accelerated in their growth and influence at times of policy change such as the introduction of devolution in the UK in 1999 and may maintain their connections and interests subsequently (Keating et al 2009).

Civil servants can use policy communities for advice or to take soundings about the potential response on government proposals. Relationships might be clientelist with policy networks depending on privileged access to government thinking to ensure policy networks have salience and an inside track (Richardson and Jordan 1979). The competitive and sectoral nature of the structure of Government departments means that specialist advice can be useful because it reflects the silos inside departments and restricts wider considerations which might transcend boundaries. Civil servants might also like to have groups 'on side' (Jordan and Cairney 2013: 254) while providing extra validation for silo approaches.

Evidence based on pilots or previous policy roll out

Evidence-based policy making has been used in medicine while the ESRC established a centre for its practice in 2002. There have been periods when it has been a preeminent model in government. The approaches to evidence-based policy making are located in pilot or test bed programmes where policies are trialled and outcomes examined before being applied to the rest of the country. However, trials and pilots take longer than Parliamentary terms and politicians prefer quicker wins. They may seek to obtain cross party support so that policies can be continued after general elections or political changes but these are difficult to achieve. Some governments undertake reviews of policy effectiveness, which was prevalent during the Labour government 1997–2010. However, there is little indication that these studies were used to develop new policies. For an incoming government from a different party, there is a break with past policies and civil servants will not want to suggest previous evaluation studies, as they may be regarded as serving their past and not current ministers. Some ministers have had a stated preference for quantitative studies over qualitative approaches, for prediction over understanding of mechanism, and this was a key element of the *Modernising Government* White Paper (Cabinet Office 1999a).

Publicly adopting an evidence-based approach also brings its problems. Does it suggest that previous policy making has not been based on evidence (Marston and Watts 2003)? There are also issues about who frames the issues and whether evidence is available that reflects the policy questions and concerns (Bovaird and Russell 2007). There is also a hierarchy that places evidence from the community at a lower level than that from experts. Another issue is that there may be too much evidence rather than not enough. Other issues include time periods used and replicability between places. Approaches to evidence-based policy making has been translated into a 'what works' policy agenda (Sanderson 2002) which allows for differences and policy adaptability between places and communities. It is associated with the introduction of behavioural insights or 'nudge' approaches to policy making (Einfeld 2019). There is some evidence that where evidence-based policy making was too wide and difficult to manage, civil servants selectively used the evidence to reinforce their positions to create 'tough' policies (Stevens 2011).

Conclusions

The provenance and development of policy is more complex than is frequently considered, and the policy agenda for government ministers comprises only part of their manifesto commitments. Both long-term obligations and short-term political issues play a part in the use of time in developing policy and some government activity can be seen as a backwater and not addressed for long periods. Some ministers have a strong interest in policy and regard it as the height of their careers to be able to introduce it in their chosen areas, but for others, there can be other objectives on their career ladder with priorities focused on party or political objectives.

4

How Does the Civil Service Administer Policy?

Introduction

Administering policy into effect is considered to be less important than its formulation by the senior civil service (SCS) both in the core executive and functional departments and can be of less interest to some ministers. The extent to which governments place emphasis on the implementation of policy varies, with the Thatcher and Blair governments regarded as most active in this approach (Urban et al 2024). Governments also use different strategies to frame policies at the point of implementation, so the Coalition government (2010–15) wanted to reduce public delivery and did this directly through Osborne's austerity programme that removed funding (Gamble 2015).

There have been discussions and reviews about the effectiveness of the civil service in administering policy during most governments since 1918, related to tensions between the political and administrative interface in the Westminster Model (WM) (Richards and Smith 2016). Even those governments not focused on the detail of policy delivery and outcomes want to demonstrate to the electorate what has been achieved during their period in office as they progress towards the next general election. For civil servants, this is regarded as the administration of policy and those who surround ministers will not have this as their highest priority. They pass policy administration further down the organisation or to external agencies. As part of their 3-year postings, they do not have any long-term career commitments to achieving the outcomes included within these policies. They will expect to leave their post before policy can be evaluated and will not obtain their next post based on the successful administration of policies for which they have been responsible.

The strategies used by the civil service to address policy administration are based on a number of factors including ideological framing to meet the objectives of the political party in power. There will also be temporal considerations for policy administration (Goetz and Meyer-Sahling 2010) including the range of election cycles across the country and the emergence of expedient policy windows (Kingdon and Stano 1984). Unless there is ministerial pressure, the policy design for delivery may not foreground users or how its design may influence success (Kelly et al 2002). Rather, civil servants may consider the pressure placed on funding by the Treasury and any commitments made in Parliament while progressing legislation preceding implementation. Where delivery may have some relationship with other departments, then this will reduce its priority, as the sponsoring department may not be able to claim full success and there will be competitive negotiations including other agreements. Even within departments, there are competitive silos seeking ministerial attention (Urban et al 2024), where policy responsibilities are held separately under Directorate Generals and only meet at Permanent Secretary level. There are other influences on the administration of policy, including whether there should be direct delivery by government, its agencies or local government, or outsourced to the private sector. These decisions may relate to lobbying on the part of private sector businesses who may have been advising on policy development and its implementation earlier in the process. There will also be interest expressed by specialist and general lobby groups, sector associations and professional bodies.

The civil service has found the concept of being held responsible for the delivery as opposed to the administration of policy, to be difficult. All practical matters of management including procurement, finance, personnel and facilities management have low status within the civil service and these are areas that have been put into agencies or the private sector (NAO 2024a). While the WM places responsibility for policy administration decisions with ministers, the Accounting Officer role of Permanent Secretaries gives them absolute control over expenditure (HM Treasury 2023), creating a contradiction in accountability.

Consideration of how policy is designed and successfully delivered has been a consistent tension between ministers and civil servants. It was at the centre of discussions of the Fulton Committee (1968), where it was considered that more skills were required to meet changing demands. Prime Ministers seeking to increase their control over departments and their delivery outcomes have used a range of methods. The introduction of Public Service Agreements (PSAs) by Blair and Brown were associated with their delivery agenda and directed through the Treasury as part of Brown's control of the domestic agenda (James 2004). The focus on setting an agenda and then avoiding distractions in delivery requires control across departments that the Prime Minister's office does not have but can be achieved through financial management. The PSA created priorities for each department and used the experience of Thatcher's Financial Management Initiative (James 2003). PSAs were intended to deal with internal competition and incentivised working together on issues that stretched across more than one department. The PSAs included performance monitoring of these targets, which had internal and external purposes. Externally, there was an implied incentivisation to meet public service delivery which the PSAs would provide (James 2004) and assumed the existence of a public service bargain in the WM which was never explicitly included (Van Dorpe and Horton 2011). Three rounds of PSAs were issued, 1998, 2000 and 2002, and by the time of the last round, further delivery reinforcement was introduced through the creation of the Prime Minister's Strategy Unit (PMSU) and the Prime Minister's Delivery Unit (PMDU) (Barber 2007), although it was argued that they duplicated PSA monitoring systems (James 2004). Much of the focus on the delivery of the PSAs was on ministers and there was little success in transferring responsibility and accountability to the SCS, although there was an expectation of a link between the PSAs and their personal performance assessments. After this, departmental objectives were introduced (Maude 2014), similar to PSAs. The SCS disliked and resented these systems, considering that they changed their roles away from policy to more mechanistic delivery (Richards 2007).

Thatcher used other methods to focus on changes in delivery, including introducing external special advisers such as Lord Rayner, with direct experience of running a large retail business (Marks & Spencer) and Cameron later brought in Stuart Rose, also formerly of the same company (Gamble 2011). Rod Eddington, formerly chief executive of British Airways, was appointed as a policy tsar to review major infrastructure by Chancellor Gordon Brown and Louise Casey was appointed to various roles in relation to social exclusion by Tony Blair (Levitt and Solesbury 2013). These and similar appointments were used to introduce the working methods and focus of their respective sectors to reform and reorganise the way in which government departments worked internally and with each other.

As ministerial frustration levels have grown, there has been an increase in the appointment of special advisers (SpADs) who perform a range of roles including being specialists in their subjects but more frequently adept at political liaison and processes to help ministers gain influence for their policies (Gay 2009; Durrant et al 2020). A further approach has been to appoint Non-Executive Directors (NEDs) on departmental boards (PAC 2021) to make them operate in a more businesslike manner. NEDs were introduced in an attempt to improve the experience available to Departmental decision making, including the consideration of business cases for the options for policy delivery. NEDs also advise on operational matters such as recruitment and management and can recommend the dismissal of the Permanent Secretary (Gill et al 2021). NEDs work more or less effectively, with some senior civil servants and ministers regarding them as a distraction. However, since 2015 there have been increasing concerns that NEDs have a political rather than a commercial background and are being used as a mechanism to politicise or 'colonise' (Ungoed-James 2024) departmental decisions. NEDs are not subject to the Code of Conduct in public life and are not registered across Whitehall, nor are the appointments publicly advertised.

The context for the administration of policy

In understanding the administration of policy by the civil service, it is important to consider the traditional cultural context in which it lies. The way in which the civil service administers policy has been termed constitutional bureaucracy (Chapman 2004), where the form of the constitution has a direct effect on the way in which the civil service can undertake its role of delegated functions of administration (Riggs 1994). In the UK, the WM is a more fluid statement of respective powers than in those countries with written constitutions and, in practice, the guiding principle that appears to frame the structure of policy administration relates to the final responsibility for expenditure (Richards and Smith 2016). Most discussions of constitutions do not include much on the role of the bureaucracy and the limits of their powers (McLean and Tushnet 2013). Where these are public services, then the Permanent Secretary will have responsibility as the Accounting Officer (HM Treasury 2023; Kaye and Powell 2024), requiring less consideration of the framing of delivery as the Permanent Secretary can always intervene. Where implementation is in the private sector, then much of the regulatory environment between 1972–2020 was generated by the EU, and the UK had to ensure compliance in those areas (Morphet 2013). For policy administration outside these two key areas of activity it would either be pushed down the agenda or be subject to lobbying.

The extent to which the World Trade Organization (WTO) Government Procurement Agreement (GPA) has changed the nature of constitutional bureaucracy in the UK was initially considered to be significant, with suggestions that outsourcing and agencification reduced the responsibility and accountability of civil servants, transferring this to the private sector (Grimshaw et al 2002). Over time this view has shifted, at first to an intermediate position, where the management of agencies and outsourcing contracts evolved to be a blend of the pre-1979 position and a mixed bureaucratic settlement (Rhodes et al 2008). More recently, since the Brexit referendum in 2016, there has been an increase in the extent to which the SCS has incorporated the functions of agencies and other parts of the public sector in a process of re-embedding them into departmental control (Ward 2020; Greer et al 2021) which reflects a return to the traditional modes of departmental power. This has also included powers that were given to the Devolved Administrations as part of the devolution settlement in 1999 (Morphet 2021b).

There is also some evidence on the way that civil servants consider their own position and enduring roles, with their traditions refracted over time, to build a precedence of expectations about their functions (Barker and Wilson 1997; Rhodes et al 2008). To achieve this they use two consistent touchstones of tradition to reinforce their roles in the face of change. The first is Northcote Trevelyan (1854) and the second the WM. Proposals for change continue to be measured against these models by civil servants. There are also considerations of whether civil service practices evolve within the context of institutions or the cultures that operate within them (Bevir and Rhodes 2006). Writing immediately before the Fulton Report was published, Parris (1969), an advocate for the status quo, questioned whether the type of changes proposed in the report for the role of the civil service would be consistent with its longstanding independence. Parris described Fulton as superficial in its understanding of the constitutional role and responsibilities of the civil service which led the Committee to make controversial suggestions for reform. However, the reforms of the structure of the civil service implemented by Thatcher for agencification appeared to have gained more contemporaneous favour from the civil service (Fry 1995). The Blair period of government was seen to break the longstanding working arrangements suggested by the WM of civil servants and ministers working together to one that was more command and control. This approach was not welcomed by the civil service who argued this shifted away from the norm, having effects on the quality of decision making within government (Richards and Smith 2016).

In the period between 2010 and the 2024 General Election, the UK had five Prime Ministers, but all governments except one were controlled by one political party. All have been turbulent and disrupted civil service traditions for policy administration into more short-term, chaotic and politicised modes, also reflecting the speeding news cycles. The Institute for Government concluded in its commission of the centre of government (Urban et al 2024) that the core executive is no longer capable of meeting the challenges faced by the UK in the 2020s. The diagnosis of the problems included increased centralisation generated by a weaker centre and filled by a dominant Treasury. Further, the separation of policy making and its administration means that one is not considered when formulating the other. The IfG concluded that the civil service needs change in order to be able to support the country and has compared 2024 with the changes that were initiated through the familiar touchstones – Northcote Trevelyan (1854) and Haldane's Machinery of Government (MoG) (1918). The traditions used by the Treasury to maintain control over departments and expenditure (Beer 1955) are regarded as problematic but specific reforms have not been proposed.

The focus of policy making is primarily internal and short term (Bailey and Lloyd 2017). The extent to which a department has direct relationships with the public is in inverse proportion to its status in Whitehall. The Treasury has the highest status and no direct involvement with the public, followed by the Cabinet Office and those working within the Prime Minister's office. Officials in these departments are unseen and structures are not transparent, but all have significant power over the administration of policy. The SCS were known as administrators or rather as the administrative class until 1971 (Christoph 1975) and there has never been an alternative term that is acceptable. The SCS baulk at being given operational roles as managers, deliverers or implementers (Foster-Gilbert 2018).

The role of the civil service in administering policy is divided between three levels – the SCS within the core executive who transfer responsibilities for the administration of the policy, within the terms they set, to functional departments who form the second level. At this functional level, members of the SCS are concerned with legislation to enact the government's policies and to advise whether this should be primary or secondary. Until 2019, legislation was developed more fully but since then there has been a focus on the introduction of primary legislation as scaffolding, with little detail as to how it will be implemented when Bills are debated in Parliament. Once passed, implementation is through secondary legislation that is unscrutinised as it can be implemented by statutory instruments delegated to ministers and only debated in Parliament through the use of special and cumbersome procedures which are rarely used (Vicary et al 2020). This provides more political flexibility but also means that the administration of these proposed policies is more difficult to appraise.

One consideration for civil servants advising on the administration of policy is the extent of their minister's experience or knowledge of the issue, which may come from time spent in local government or a specific sector. Ministers drawn from the House of Lords can have more specialist knowledge and be included within a departmental team as junior members (Riddell et al 2012); otherwise ministers are generalists and receive no training (Andrews 2024). Some effective ministers have focused on issues over a period of time and have been kept in these roles such as for sport, arts, culture and disability. Some specialist knowledge is provided by SpADs, who bear some of the ministerial administrative load (Yong and Hazell 2014) or by specific appointees such as policy tsars (Levitt and Solesbury 2006). During the Brexit debate Ministers and MPs in favour of the 'leave' campaign stated that they had had enough of 'experts' and decisions should be made on political grounds (Andrews 2017). However, the system favours ministers and civil servants who have no specific expertise. While ministers might be regarded as strong or weak, effective or ineffective in getting their agenda put into legislation and then enacted (Barberis 1996a), the UK political system means that there are always tensions in the requirements for time and space. The Blair government used a grid so that each day would be planned for announcements and media coverage to ensure that departments did not undermine each other. This was also a process of political control, ensuring that announcements were not made by freelancing ministers hoping to catch the public's attention for matters not supported by the Prime Minister (Wilson 2004).

While it is sometimes difficult to understand the balance of the provenance of any policy, who determines its administration? Memoirs of civil servants and ministers relate that civil servants had a departmental view that was strongly put to ministers (Bridges 1950; Barker and Wilson 1997). At the same time, it is clear that this departmental view may only have been the view of the Permanent Secretary (Jenkins 1975). Where ministers encourage wider discussion, those civil servants who offer views different from the department could be met with sanctions in the face of the maintenance of a 'reward structure based on ideological conformity' (Christoph 1975: 43).

The UK civil service may consider the administration of policy within its preparation and design. Civil servants have spent their careers developing policy, a much longer time than the ministers they serve, but have no accountability or seeming interest in its delivery (Bray 1979). Barber (2015), who ran the PMDU, defines this as the 'missing science of delivery' (p xv) in the operation of government, with no similarities in approach to other institutions, public or private. Some ministers and governments are more concerned with outcomes such as the Thatcher governments 1979–90 and the Blair governments 1997–2007. Under these two Prime Ministers, there were policy reviews and changes in approach to find ways in which policy could be delivered to achieve the intended results. However, as the poll tax demonstrated for Thatcher, even after a lengthy period in government, it was possible to introduce a policy that was politically undermining in delivery (McGrath 2002). The increasing frustration of ministers for policy delivery failure has led to a range of actions including reviews (Common 2004), the increase and changing role of SpADs (Durrant et al 2020), the political alignment of think tanks (Arshed 2017) and the rise of All Party Parliamentary Groups (Thomas 2015). There has also been an increasing role in policy delivery through the Prime Minister's Office (Richards and Smith 2006). There have also been short-lived attempts to work across departmental silos to focus on specific groups in society or types of location (Bullock et al 2001).

Administration vs implementation and delivery

Until 1971, the civil service used the term administration to describe the process of the application of policy. There was an administrative class of the civil service which was the most senior in its stratified hierarchy, and administration was the primary responsibility of Permanent Secretaries. In the SCS, there was an assumption that administration was for the public sector while management was for the private sector (Bunbury 1928; Self 1965). The term administration embraced working directly with ministers, advising them on policy options and how these might be put into practice. The change came with the Heath White Paper on the Reorganisation of Central Government (HM Government 1970), which was described as the most significant change in the general structure of the MoG since the Haldane Review (1918) (Rosson 1971) and can, in the longer term, be seen as part of the UK's preparation to join the EU in 1972. It also established the Central Policy Review Staff (CPRS) changing the way in which civil service functions are described (Blackstone and Plowden 1988). Since then, governments have termed turning policy into practice as delivery or implementation, which civil servants have baulked against, regarding it as a transfer of responsibility and accountability to them and not administration.

The creation of the Next Steps Agencies from 1987, followed by Major and Blair's reforms, were intended to focus the civil service on delivery using competency frameworks (Horton 2000), outcome measures, targets and departmental performance agreements which were all tools of internal control by the Treasury (James 2004) but never incorporated into government in practice (Aucoin and Heintzman 2000; Bovaird and Russell 2007). Would the SCS be more content with their roles if the term administration were reintroduced or would this be unacceptable to ministers? Administration can be defined as 'the arrangements and tasks needed to control the operation of a plan or organisation' (Cambridge Dictionary 2024), controlling the means and the ends. It has been associated with supporting a generalist civil service and describes an overarching approach that provides a means of controlling outsiders or incomers, particularly where they have been associated with specialist skills and knowledge which the SCS is seen to lack. When proposals for change in the SCS have been made, to become managers to enhance implementation and delivery, this has met with a consistent response that if Permanent Secretaries spent their time managing they would have no time to support ministers (Self 1965). Being a manager is also seen to be moving away from being an impartial adviser to ministers (Davies 1998). Thus, the UK government has both ministers and civil servants who take a generalist view about the responsibilities they have been given. The term administrator is one which is distanced from the subject of delivery, contains an implied detachment and a lack of accountability for the selection of the policy or the way it should be implemented. Administrators advise on options, they are not seen to have an active role in their selection, although there will always be a departmental view.

The civil service dislike of management has a long history. In considering a traditional approach to administration compared with any merits of scientific management, Bunbury (1928), relying on the Treasury Memorandum of 1868 (HM Treasury 1937–38; Beer 1955), stated administrators have 'an inherited and traditional belief in the merits of control' p 96) which still persists (HM Treasury 2023). In Bunbury's view, control could be protective, coordinative and directive and it is possible to see these three dimensions in the approach taken by the SCS today. Bunbury also discussed many of the issues that have arisen more recently – targets, performance indicators and how to achieve effective efficiency. Bunbury dismisses the appeal to measuring efficiency because it relies on statistics, which are collected on the basis of judgement. He argues that incentives to achieve efficiency in the public sector are less valuable than in the private sector because the public sector is stable and not subject to market conditions with the only incentives in the public sector relating to honours and pride in work.

There is also a dislike of the term implementation and delivery by the SCS, regarding it as a lower status activity and not cerebral like policy making. While this perception and categorisation of policy delivery or implementation is regarded as an activity for functional and operational civil servants, the predominance of this culture has increasingly caused ministerial frustration. Politicians are concerned to see their policies in operation in ways that the electorate will find effective and associate with them. The SCS is less interested in policy design from intention to outcomes (Bailey and Lloyd 2017). For the Blair government, after initial attempts to change the way it worked, the PMSU and PMDU were established, led by the Prime Minister's adviser on delivery, Michael Barber. Appointed in 2001, after the general election, Barber (2007) states that he was appointed to address Blair's frustration with the lack of progress on public service reform and focused on education, health, transport and Home Office in conjunction with the relevant Secretaries of State. Barber describes the process he established as the right to work with the Treasury first and then with the Permanent Secretaries of the four departments, whom he assumed would undermine the work of the PMDU, perceiving it to be another in a long line of short-lived political initiatives. Barber started with the Cabinet Secretary, Sir Richard Wilson, stating he was unsure about who was manipulating whom. However, it is instructive that much of Barber's account on the delivery process is focused not on designing methods of delivery but managing the SCS in order to be able to discuss delivery before departmental discussions took place.

This Blair focus on delivery was termed by Nick MacPherson, a former Permanent Secretary at the Treasury, as 'deliverology' (Barber 2007: 70) and encompassed the work being undertaken by the PMDU encapsulated by Barber in five questions:

- What are you trying to do?
- How are you trying to do it?
- How do you know you are succeeding?

- If you are not succeeding, how will you change things?
- How can we help you?

(p 73)

After considering a range of texts on implementation in government, Barber determined that a main cause for implementation failure was that practical issues were not incentivised in comparison with more general strategic and analytical thought, where failure might be an issue to be argued rather than measured, and blame could be distributed rather than focused. Initially Barber asked each department for some 'quick wins' only to receive complaints from a Permanent Secretary that this would distract focus away from the requirements of implementation, which, as Barber points out, is a fundamental civil service strategy of establishing a false dichotomy to avoid challenge and change. Another Permanent Secretary accused the PMDU as seeking to micromanage their department. As the PMDU started work, it asked each Permanent Secretary to develop a delivery plan for the objectives of their Secretary of State. While civil servants and ministers were content to establish targets for others such as the NHS and local government, they were less sanguine about targets being set for them as part of Public Service Agreements (PSA) linked to funding. Barber lists the series of civil service stock responses to ministers seeking to introduce change or new policies:

- Can we afford it?
- Do you want to take the risk?
- We tried it before and it failed
- Perhaps we should have a pilot study?
- Should we do some more research?
- What about phasing it more slowly?
- Why not try it north of the border first?

(pp 82–3)

When asked for plans, Barber found a lack of skill and experience in preparing these and instead 'Whitehall writes "essays decorated with the occasional number", the hope being that the recipients will be so impressed by the prose that, after reading it, they will leave you alone' (p 84). In order to assess progress, PMDU introduced stocktakes, with a focus on performance attended by the Prime Minister and Secretary of State based on agreed data. After the first year of work by the PMDU, Barber concluded there was a general commitment to delivery but that progress was slow, with a lack of urgency and weak planning. There was no devolution to the front line and cross-departmental working was poor or non-existent. There was little belief that anything other than crisis management or incremental change would work in Whitehall which was also the case 10 years later (Bailey and Lloyd 2017).

Issues to be considered when designing the administration of policy

When civil servants design policy for administration, there are a number of different issues that need to be considered:

Demand management

In any examination of the administration of policy is the consideration of demand management. Within the welfare state model since 1945, there was an initial assumption that, based on the Beveridge principles, demand for services would be free and available at the point of need, although there was also an understanding that provision would never be enough. However, over time, demand for services has grown and access limited by introducing payments, such as for dentistry or medical prescriptions. Demand has also been managed through access to drugs through budget cuts and approval restrictions by the National Institute for Health and Care Excellence (NICE). Less public forms of rationing are applied through prioritisation within reduced public sector budgets for housing, parks, libraries, pest control, children's and social care and public transport. Other rationing is inherent in health services by delays in appointments and treatment plans for patients with chronic and life threatening conditions (Locock 2000). Most public services will have a greater demand than the public purse can fund and principles of demand management need to be incorporated into policy administration (Self 1965). Even where there are regulated services, which require funding not from government but the user or producer, there are considerations of reasonable costs of the administrative process. It is also noticeable that services that are provided on a 'rationed' basis are delivered by others than civil servants, including the NHS, local authorities and agencies, but within powers and budgets set by them.

Competing policies

The administration of policy must recognise silo interests of different government departments that compete with potential conflict (Self 1965). The attempts to develop joined-up government (JUG) in the Blair government (Ling 2002; Pollitt 2003) were an explicit expression of the disbenefits of each department having competing policies undermining cumulative benefits and impacts that integrated policies could achieve. Silo based policies were also regarded as inefficient. Similar approaches to joining up budgets including the creation of the Government Offices for the Regions 1993–2010 (Mawson and Spencer 2014) and Total Place 2008–12 (Hambleton and Howard 2013) have been dissolved and a version of this policy through Trailblazer Devolution Deals single settlements (HMT/DLUHC 2023) was proposed by the Conservative government 2019–2024, to be implemented in 2025 (Morphet and Denham 2023). A civil service argument against JUG was that it blurred accountability for the integrated services being delivered (Wilkins 2002) and created difficulty for the Accounting Officer role held by each Permanent Secretary (HM Treasury 2023). Others criticised it for being a thoughtless and ill-informed approach because it did not consider civil service culture and traditional, endemic, departmental competitiveness to the point of institutional conflict (Kavanagh and Richards 2001).

Regulation

The administration of some policy may require a regulatory regime and, if so, which organisation will apply compliance processes such as inspection, penalties or legal remedies. This includes an assessment of costs and consideration in the design of the policy where these costs will fall – on government, on the user or the provider. Regulatory regimes are also required to be accountable with independent inspectors. Those that relate to services of general interest will also be accountable to the WTO through the GPA. Since 2019, there has been evidence of increasing political interference in regulatory bodies through the appointment of chairs and Koop and Lodge (2020) describe this shift in regulatory approach from responsible to responsive.

Redistribution

Redistribution is a common basis for government policies whether of wealth, economic growth, infrastructure or public services. It was the basis of industrial and employment policy in the 1930s and 1950s, including the creation of the post-1945 New Towns programme which were promoted while firms could not locate or expand in more prosperous urban areas. It also included regional economic planning. Redistribution can be a key feature of fiscal policy providing greater allowances for less well-off or older people and increased tax for those with higher incomes. This is not a policy approach that only operates in the UK but across OECD and EU states, where there has been a focus on policies to redress unequal income redistribution related to gender, ethnicity or location (Immervoll and Richardson 2011). Some aspects of redistributive policies are implemented through formula-based assessments of need to local authorities but these have been reduced since the austerity period (NAO 2021). While in the EU, areas with lower per capita incomes received cohesion funds to support their communities and economies. After Brexit, the UK government introduced the policy of Levelling Up across the UK (DLUHC 2022) and a Shared Prosperity Fund for those areas formerly in receipt of cohesion funding. However, neither were regarded as replacements for what had been in place before and used to support the government's constituencies regardless of need and based on elections (Hanretty 2021; Mabbett 2021). Further, the policy approach to redistribution was not applied across government as an administrative principle. While this lack of concern for redistributive administration might be defended by civil servants as a reflection of government policy, the introduction of pork barrel politics has led to the UK falling to its lowest ever ranking in the Perceptions of Global Corruption Index (Transparency International 2024) and against the principles of public life, appearing as less explainable SCS behaviour.

Short or long term

There is likely to be some consideration in the design of policy as whether it is short or long term. This may be because there is a specific action required. Some policies may be interim or staging posts on the way to greater change such as the administration of policies to achieve climate change.

Determining the mechanism for delivery

Once a policy has moved into an administrative stage for its application, then there is discussion on the selection of a method for its introduction into the public sphere.

King's speech

The most frequently used mechanism for the administration of policy is through legislation which the government announces through the monarch's speech from the throne, usually annually, at the beginning of each Parliamentary term. In order to have a bill included within the speech, each department will be required to make a bid to the Leader of the House of Commons (Lidington 2020). This is a political process where ministers are not supported by civil servants, although they will have been prepared. To be considered for inclusion in the speech, departments have to demonstrate that legislation is in the manifesto, which means that there will be no opposition to it from the House of Lords using the Salisbury Convention. Other legislation might be included if it necessary to meet emerging issues or, when the UK was part of the EU, for policy agreements made there under treaty obligations. Where EU legislation was set out in Regulations there was no legal requirement for Parliament to approve UK legislation for implementation but governments used this mechanism to create a domestic rather than EU provenance for any initiative (Morphet 2013; Gibson and Cowie 2024). Outside this, legislation can be introduced by government if there is an urgent need to do so such as during the COVID-19 pandemic (Vicary et al 2020).

After a general election, the first monarch's speech might include proposals that last longer than a year to include more preparatory time and may include more controversial bills, claiming the benefit of a recent electoral prerogative (Ludlow 2005). The King's speech is not only used to set out how the executive is proposing to use Parliamentary time but also provides policy signals on the relative importance of issues to the government (Jennings et al 2011). While the speech, as read by the monarch, is a list of Bills, the government also publishes an explanatory note which details intentions and content of the bills. This note indicates how the civil service considers government policy can be organised and communicates the relative importance of different agencies in the legislation's administration. From the point of view of the executive, ministers and the civil service, Secondary legislation is regarded as more flexible for policy administration than having debates in committee or on the floor of the House and considered preferable. This increasing use of secondary legislation has been seen as part of the 'hollowing out' of the state. On the other hand, debates on the monarch's speech can be used in other ways by backbench members of Parliament to signal disagreements (Kelso 2017).

Machinery of Government

One of the first considerations in the administration of policy is whether it fits within existing frameworks of government departments or whether a new departments or agency is needed. This will be through MoG processes. Hogwood (1997) argues that the role of the MoG that is not significant but receives most headlines is the reattribution of functions between departments, but White and Dunleavy (2010) argue that it is an important tool and all Prime Ministers since 1950 except John Major have used it. MoG changes offer the opportunity to signal the Prime Minister's priorities and align the Whitehall Departmental structure with them as this determines membership of the Cabinet. However, it can also be viewed as a blunt instrument, as frequently these changes are not planned and occur over a short period of time. They can also be associated with additional costs. One department was created over a weekend and officials then become overloaded trying to make strategic decisions while keeping core functions going. MoG changes also attract little support from the Cabinet Office and Treasury.

Some MoG changes are seen to have worked well where there is sense in the new alignment of functions and where staff can be involved in implementing change. However, as in the private sector where these changes occur through mergers and acquisitions, it can take 2 years for new departments to settle down. There will also be winners and losers in the competitive world of Whitehall and this can affect the ability of departments to progress their business through government. John Major was the only Prime Minister not to use MoG changes and Edward Heath went much further in his 1970 White Paper on the Restructuring of Government, which was said to defy the Haldane (1918) doctrine of having the right structures to achieve the right functions of government. The SCS are most concerned about the lack of preparation for MoG changes but also recognise that they are mostly driven by political priorities than other motives. The use of MoG was seen in the creation of the Office of the Deputy Prime Minister, which was a department specifically created for John Prescott who had a significant role in managing relationships between Tony Blair and Gordon Brown.

Spending reviews

A major consideration in administering policy is whether it is to be implemented through Parliament's decision making, whether it should have a sunset clause or if it is a policy tied to a specific initiative such as those introduced through spending reviews (SR). While SR are regarded as important in terms of reviewing the base line of departmental budgets (Robinson 2014), departments include new initiatives and have introduced change when there were contests for implementation outside the manifesto. In this case, a programme may be short term and fixed to the period of the SR, which can be 2 or 3 years, with 2 years either side for preparation and then completion to be absorbed into departmental budgets. The lack of transparency and internal character of an SR is a way of inserting policies that are specifically supported by HM Treasury or No 10 without wider discussion in Cabinet or Parliament. The process of competitive bidding by departments means that they are not aware of the bids made by others, with the only view across all departmental requests held by Treasury, which will determine the outcome. There are no incentives for departments to work together by submitting joint service or policy programmes for older people or housing, for example, as all formal assessment and informal ascription of success between Permanent Secretaries will be for the amount of funding which each has obtained for their own department. The most important feature of the SR process, which appears counter to the WM, is that they are led by civil servants who determine when ministers should be involved (Robinson 2014; Tryggvadottir 2022).

The process of the SR 2010 and 2015 were described as being 'bottom up', that is constructed through departmental bids, suggesting that there is no strategic dimension to the process. However, these bids are also set within the requirements of departments to demonstrate how they could reduce their budgets by specific defined percentages such as in 2015 where this was for 25 per cent and 40 per cent reductions over a 4-year period. Once agreed, each department prepares to Outline Delivery Plan for their components of the SR.

The SR can be used to achieve the redirection of policy without wider debate. The SR was used for strategic planning in UK after the financial crisis in 2008 and then to introduce austerity in 2010 after a change in government (Eckersley and Ferry 2011; Agasisti et al 2015). In setting the budget for a department, the SR can lead to policy changes through funding reductions for staff or specific initiatives. SRs can be used to reshape the internal workings of government departments in significant ways. SRs are used across 75 per cent of OECD countries in similar ways (Doherty and Sayegh 2022) and are seen as legitimate tools to meet objectives, particularly those that might have occurred in government mid-term. The effects of SRs on policy administration may only be drawn to wider attention through Parliamentary Select Committees rather than ministers having to seek agreement for any changes in priority from Parliament.

Agents of delivery

When civil servants advise ministers about the administration of their proposed policies, they prepare a range of options which may be influenced by political issues, experience with similar policies, examples from other countries or a new approach (Davis et al 1999). As the civil service is competitive, ways that other departments have delivered policies may also be a consideration. Since the GPA, there are considerations about whether policies should be directly delivered by the public sector or indirectly through an agency or an outsourced provider.

Territorial scales of government

There are considerations about the territorial scale policy that should be implemented and whether the devolved administrations will be delivering the same policy in the same way. Since Brexit and subsequent legislation, there has been increased pressure to develop single approaches to policy delivery across the UK without variation (Morphet 2021b). Within the Devolved Administrations and England, there is also an option of administration through local authorities. The selection of the delivery scale is haphazard and not informed by any framework within British public policy legislation or practice. Some local services are delivered by central government while others are local. Some are hybrid such as the housing of asylum seekers which is in part undertaken by central government through contracts with hotels or other providers but can also be the responsibility of local authorities such as for Ukrainian, Afghan and Syrian refugees. When asylum seekers are registered they may be turned out of their government-provided hotels and then become homeless and caught by local authority legal requirements to house homeless people.

In other countries, such as France, there are operational rules which assess the appropriate scale for policy administration with accompanying funding (Rouben 1995). There is also a default to the local in some states and there have been arguments for that approach in the UK. Kaye and Powell (2024) in a think tank report, *Devolve by Default*, argue that there should be an interdepartmental group on devolution that includes local authority leaders for England. While addressing efficiency arguments, they do not examine why there is a reluctance for delivery at sub-state levels as a first consideration, even where the WM and accounting officer roles provide a backstop retention of power to the centre (HM Treasury 2023). Others reflecting on the failure of regional economic policy provide more detail of the ways in which the centre considers sub-national government and its potential role in delivery in a negative way (Turner et al 2023; Balls 2024).

Agencies

Government departments may have some agencies or non-departmental bodies to provide specialist services or expertise. These are part of functional departments but established to operate at arm's length, outside day-to-day ministerial control (Barberis 1996a). They have boards appointed by ministers and their accounting responsibilities remain primarily with the Permanent Secretaries of their sponsoring departments. Since Brexit, the functional departments have been exerting tighter control of these agencies in determining priorities and budgets. This may be because of continuing financial pressures within government and Permanent Secretaries' decisions that cuts can be achieved by squeezing agencies rather than central departments. The second reason may be that after Brexit, financial support for policy agreed within the EU is no longer a consideration and there needs to be tighter control of the policy process to maintain the allocation of funding for the department (Lloyd 2019; Morphet 2021b).

Outsourcing

When the civil service was first involved in implementing the GPA through the outcomes of the Next Steps agencies, there were concerns about the ethical role of the civil service (Du Gay 2000) and whether, in a constitutional bureaucracy, the civil service could give responsibility for services to third parties outside government in return for payment. This was a failure to understand the provisions of public procurement where the responsibilities for services remain with the client (the Government Department). Any failures should be investigated through the contract management process. In larger contract failures there have been discussions about whether the government should be prosecuting the private sector providers and their auditors for failing to alert their government clients of structural weaknesses in contractor companies' finances. A major case was being developed against the contractor Carillon to be taken through the courts but this was unaccountably dropped on the Friday before the case was due to commence in court, without any reason being given.

Some departments have taken a cynical view about contract prices where they are seeking more funding for projects from the Treasury. This is particularly so in the case of the Ministry of Defence, which has accepted prices for contracts and then assumed that further funding will become available once the project is underway (NAO 2022). The country cannot be left with 50 per cent of a battleship.

When a government department or one its agencies agrees to outsource a service, it has to go through a formal process of public procurement. The processes are set through the UK's membership of the WTO GPA. When the UK was part of the EU, then the compliance elements of this agreement were undertaken on WTO's behalf by the EU through the single market and procurement legislation. While no longer part of the EU, the UK continues to comply with its WTO treaty obligations and those of other countries if procurement is outside the UK (Morphet 2021a).

To commence a process of procurement, it is necessary to establish a specification against which any commercial organisation can bid. This specification determines quantity, time period, quality and how the contract will be monitored. Contracts can be measured on frequency, reach or delivery of outcome measures. The WTO specifies that the way in which a contract will be assessed has to be set out in the contract process. This includes whether the contract assessment is based on price only or whether there is a combination of price and quality factors, including social value. The weighting and assessment criteria are required to be set out. A company which has assisted in the preparation of the specification is legally barred from bidding for the contract. In undertaking this process, the administration of the contract within the department or agency is led by a team that has the client role and manages the contractor. The client is required to monitor the contract, approve payments for delivery against evidence of contract completions and keep the contract within price, particularly where there are requests for contract variations.

Within the civil service, contract management and client side roles are low status and are not regarded as a route to achieving top roles. Outsourced services are those that the department does not prioritise and includes routine activities such as payroll, payments and recruitment. Outsourcing can also be used for what the department may consider routine operational functions such as the removal of asylum seekers (Gentleman 2019). The low status of these functions means that service failures or poor performance are not brought to the attention of ministers until there is a severe breakdown in the contract such as the salmonella outbreak on the Bibby barge used for asylum seekers in 2023. While these contracted activities remain a low priority for Permanent Secretaries and their ministers, scrutiny of their operations and civil service management of the contract, is undertaken by the National Audit Office (NAO) and the Public Accounts Committee (PAC) in Parliament. In one example, a review of the provision of accommodation for asylum seekers, the NAO (2024a) found that the Home Office pursued contracts for large camps and the use of barges despite these approaches being rated 'red', that is, at risk of being unable of being delivered, by the Government's Infrastructure and Projects Authority in three reviews during 2022–23. The same conclusions were made by the Home Office's internal reviews of policy delivery. The Home Office also awarded contracts to existing suppliers through modification rather than seeking new competitive bids. Overall, the NAO concluded that the Home Office, in its provision of asylum seeker accommodation, had incurred nugatory spending which provided no value and increased risk.

Some civil servants may have their careers in operational delivery but those in strategic and functional roles seek to spend short or no periods of their careers in this type of policy administration. High levels of turnover means that the client function can be weakened and the contractor will have more power in the relationship because the contract and how to manage it will be more well known to them and have greater salience. Client civil servants are not held accountable for the management of the contract. They may also be drawn in by the contractor to achieve what is known as 'low hanging fruit' (those targets that can be easily fulfilled). The deportation of the Windrush generation is an example of the way a contract was exploited to meet targets not envisaged, with the specification for the removal of 'over staying' in the UK by those with no right to do so having been drawn up in the Home Office (Gentleman 2019).

5

Relationships with Ministers

Introduction

The relationships between ministers and civil servants are critical to successful careers for politicians and the Senior Civil Servants (SCS). Together they are the most powerful elite group in the government (Barberis 1996b; Kavanagh and Richards 2003; Peters 2013) and there are assumptions of co-dependency as they each reach for the most senior posts in their respective spheres (Davis 2018). To achieve the role of Permanent Secretary or Cabinet Secretary, senior civil servants have common career paths that include roles in ministerial teams, serving as a principle private secretary or being a member of a Bill team (Barberis 1996b; Rhodes et al 2007). Civil servants review their departmental ministers annually and poor gradings can lead to the Prime Minister moving ministers (Barberis 1996b). Some ministers have been moved frequently for being too direct in their questions on policy, delivery and performance while later regarded as effective chairs of Parliamentary Select Committees. Others have been found to be bullies and not immediately moved (Monaghan 2022). For ministers regarded as ineffective, who cannot be moved for political reasons, they can be kept away from London on ministerial visits. Some Cabinet Secretaries have worked for Prime Ministers in more junior roles and returned later to serve them when they have achieved higher office (Barberis 1996b). These ties have also been reinforced through similar education and background – including attendance at public schools and Oxbridge (Fulton 1968; Kavanagh and Richards 2003; Fitz and Halpin 2013) and exemplified through the friendship since university of Prime Minister Johnson and his Chief Executive of the NHS, Sir Simon Stevens.

Yet the roles of ministers and civil servants are different, and a number of challenges have emerged in these relationships which are discussed in this chapter. These have been present since Thatcher and particularly highlighted during the Johnson Government 2019–22. They were confirmed in the first actions of Prime Minister Truss to remove the Permanent Secretary of the

Treasury (Wilkes et al 2024). The gap in working relations between those occupying ministerial and administrative roles has been supported through a political narrative of the civil service having its own agenda (Blair 2010). Johnson and his advisers thought a large Parliamentary majority meant exercising a more presidential style of government (Brown 2020), bypassing Parliament, was legitimate. Truss, reliant of the same parliamentary majority, used this to exclude the Office of Budget Responsibility (OBR) on a major economic policy shift after taking office.

One of the key issues in the relationship between ministers and civil servants is trust. When a new government takes over, how far are civil servants still under the ideological influence of the previous government? This was an issue for Blair (2010) in taking office, making him more cautious about the speed of change. However, this lack of trust between ministers and civil servants is longstanding and apparent in a range of countries (Plowden 1994). It may be based on civil servants promoting their own policy preferences or competition between departments. There can also be breakdowns in trust between the strategic and functional departments in Whitehall. The centre can be regarded as too dominant, particularly when the Prime Minister is in a more presidential mode or has a particularly strong adviser. At the same time, how is a Prime Minister to implement their manifesto and exert power if there is no central direction (Urban et al 2024)? There is also a consideration of how far external advisers are used to triangulate civil service advice or to filter it before it reaches politicians.

Prime Ministers have views on the effectiveness of the civil service (Drechsler and Kattel 2020; Pyper 2020; Maddox and Thomas 2021), but these are not primarily focused on successful delivery of government policy but the advice and options provided to ministers. The weakness of the role of Cabinet Secretary in comparison with the Prime Minister's advisers is increasingly discussed (Urban et al 2024) and can be illustrated in a number of ways from breaking COVID-19 lockdown in No 10 (Gray 2022) or ensuring that there were appropriate procedures for procurement of PPE through the use of a 'known individual's' fast lane for suppliers (NAO 2020). Ministers have always been critical of the civil service with Crossman being the first to break the omerta of the relationships between minister and Permanent Secretary in his political diaries (Bogdanor 1977; Crossman and Howard 1991).

The period since 2010 has seen a reducing level of trust between ministers and civil servants (Diamond 2021; Lowe and Pemberton 2020), higher levels of senior staff turnover (Sasse and Norton 2019) and less direct experience of those leading specific policy areas (Stokes 2016). The effect has been a recalibration in relationships between ministers and civil servants in which ministers have sought to increase their power over the SCS through mechanisms of managerialism and accountability (James 2004).

Such reforms are not without contradiction. On one level, ministers have berated Whitehall for lack of skills, blaming civil servants for blocking change. However, ministers see reform occurring through officials taking more responsibility – the desire for 'delegated mission command' (PASC 2015). Collectively, these changes reveal a change in the Westminster Model (WM) between ministers and civil servants, instead emphasising in starker terms, a more explicit, binary, principal-agent setting (Lane 2020). This has been further exacerbated by the increased use of SpADs by ministers and the financial support for policy promotion from think tanks, who seek to mobilise political support through the media and frame the context within which civil servants can provide their ministerial advice. This is discussed further below.

The view of civil servants by ministers

The working relationships between ministers and their civil servants is at the heart of the WM and the success of a minister can depend on their relationship with their Permanent Secretary (Barberis 1996b). Where relationships are poor, Permanent Secretaries can be moved or retire (Stokes 2016). However, since the 1970s, the growth in the role of SpADs has meant that there are now three parties in this marriage and how far the civil service has adapted or changed in ways that recognise this now well-established working triumvirate at the top of government. The WM now relies on this three-part operational model with ministers reliant on their SpADs to create political space and opportunities for their policies and initiatives with the Prime Minister and then are reliant on their civil servants to provide the substantive policy briefs that can be used to support their proposals. The opportunity to create policy space has changed since Brexit and this is discussed further in Chapter 7. The relationships between ministers and civil servants can be viewed through political memoirs, although it is important to remember that these are unreliable and 'self-serving' (Rhodes et al 2007: 1) while classified documents may not be released for years.

In addition to political memoirs which evoke these ministerial/civil service relationships in everyday practice, Stokes's (2016) research, based on interviews with former ministers across the political spectrum, found relationships between ministers and civil servants focused on two key issues – control and competence. In the background to his interviews, Stokes periodises the control of civil servants over ministers being more common before Thatcher, switching to ministerial control over civil servants during her time in office. Stokes finds that ministerial concern at the competence of civil servants has been present since the Fulton Report (1968) and grown since Thatcher. While Fulton's proposals for increased civil service skills were rejected and ridiculed at the time (Parris 1969), the issue has come increasingly to the fore while civil servants have not been willing to change their cultural aversion to 'mechanistic' skills (Barberis 1996b).

The extent to which the civil service changed as part of the Next Step reforms was considerable (Lowe and Pemberton 2020) and was said to be the result of Thatcher's focus. While Thatcher saw this as a mechanism for increased ministerial powers to deliver her political agenda, others argued that it detached ministers from the day-to-day running of the department (Peters 2013). The controversial dispute between Michael Howard as Home Secretary and the head of the prison service, Derek Lewis, running an agency, was the epitome of this challenge for power – was it in the hands of officials or ministers? The resulting victory for ministers also confirmed the powers of Permanent Secretaries over their agency heads, even when they were more experienced and better paid. Yet the increased detachment of the civil service and ministers from day-to-day knowledge, responsibility and accountability for a range government agencies or organisations where government is the main shareholder, has had significant impacts on the electorate in cases such as the Post Office, Windrush, infected blood, PPE contracting, crumbling school buildings and poor water quality. What are seen by politicians as their priorities have been overtaken by these public service operational failures.

The introduction of the MINIS system by Michael Heseltine when he was Secretary of State for the Environment (1979–83) was designed to provide a 'management information system for ministers'. Heseltine founded Haymarket Publishing and was familiar with the systematic collection of information on activity within the organisation that MINIS provided. However, his enthusiasm was not shared by colleagues nor by senior officials in other departments, which either adopted a version of MINIS or ignored it completely (Barberis 1996b). The Financial Management Initiative (FMI) that followed was launched in 1982 and was another business practice to assign budgets to individuals who acted as cost centres. The application of the FMI was mixed and encountered cultural objections about whether civil servants should be responsible for budgets in this way rather than ministers.

How far do these tensions in working relationships with ministers have an impact on the recruitment and retention of civil servants and effectiveness in the implementation of government policy? On recruitment and retention, there has been an increasing turnover of civil servants while morale has begun to decline (NAO 2023, 2024b). The IfG has demonstrated that recruitment costs were £74m in 2022–23 while the movement and loss of civil servants between March 2021 and March 2022 at 13.6 per cent was the highest in a 10-year period (IfG 2023b; NAO 2023). In 2024, the number of recruits interested in the SCS through the fast stream was low and promotion expectations, in comparison with other graduate jobs, was one of the issues cited as a disincentive. At the same time, the NAO (2024b) demonstrated that promotion primarily comes from within the civil service rather than through open competition and that this closed employment culture is having an effect on the quality of civil service leadership. There may be other factors which have depressed the level of recruitment interest to the fast stream. There have been complaints about the treatment of civil servants by ministers including those against Dominic Raab and Priti Patel. The case against Patel was particularly important in the relations between ministers and civil servants because it led to the resignation of the Permanent Secretary and the Prime Minister's ethics adviser Alex Allen when the Prime Minister failed to take his advice, stating that there had been no breach of the ministerial code (Monaghan 2022). The Committee on Standards in Public Life (CSPL) stated that these tensions are having a significant impact on the effectiveness of government, noting that comments by ministers have become increasingly disparaging in tone (Woolridge 2023).

Ministers have increasingly been finding ways of meeting this gap, as they perceive it. This has been through appointing external advisers, policy tsars (Levitt and Solesbury 2013) and increasing numbers of SpADs who have a political loyalty to the minister. The increased role of SpADs has served to inhibit the control of the policy menu by Permanent Secretaries (Barberis 1996b; Rhodes et al 2007). Before the introduction of SpADs, contests between ministers and their civil servants could be characterised as being on a continuum. However, the insertion of SpADs into these relationships has made ministers less reliant on their civil servants and made civil servants more reliant on SpADs to help them make informal overtures to other departments, provide support for the department to gain political traction and space in the Parliamentary timetable or as a funding priority (Wilkes 2014; Durrant et al 2020).

All ministers interviewed in Stokes's (2016) research were concerned about the extent to which civil servants attempted to control the agenda as presented to them. As noted in Chapter 2, there is frequently a 'departmental view' of policy proposals and how they should be prioritised which may run counter to a political agenda. The role of control and who holds it lies at the heart of the relationship between the minister and the civil servant. There are a range of means available to civil servants attempting to maintain control of their ministers, including minimising time available for decision making, managing ministers so that Treasury rather than departmental targets can be met and intransigence. As the range of studies and memoirs confirm, attempts to gain control of ministers by their civil servants is understood by them and the main issue is how they deal with it. The negative influences on the relationship between ministers and civil servants from ministers' point of view were expressed as those civil servants who:

- lack competence
- undermine policy and seek control

- are averse to change
- lack external experience
- do not lead, take responsibility, or communicate clearly

(Stokes 2016: 75)

Stokes (2016) also invited former ministers to identify the positive attributes of civil servants working with them. These were expressed as:

- showing commitment and demonstrate expertise
- displaying fearlessness, honesty and independence
- committed to delivering policy once ministers have made a final decision, regardless of their views about the merits of that policy
- understanding their Minister's philosophy

(Stokes 2016: 69)

Many ministers are critical of civil servants with whom they have worked (Stokes 2016) including David Blunkett who stated that often the only way to remove an incompetent civil servant was to promote them (Blunkett 2006: 314, quoted in Stokes 2016: 29). The relationships between civil servants and their ministers can be weak where there is little opportunity for them to progress their agendas. When cabinet is stronger, ministers and civil servants can work together more positively (Thomas 2022). Weak ministers find it easier to blame their civil servants for their lack of progress. However, the public attacks on civil servants by members of the government and their advisers have been accelerating in the period since 1979.

Thatcher wanted to 'deprivilege ' the civil service by reducing the size of state as set out in her manifesto (Hood 1995; Kavanagh and Richards 2003: 181) and her advisers from the new right argued that the civil service would prevent change and seek to reinforce the status quo. The Conservative Party was consistently advised that the civil service would hinder change to the post-war consensus for the welfare state. This view is maintained in Conservative thinking with the civil service being described as the 'blob' by Michael Gove when Secretary of State for Education (Robinson 2014) and a term that has been used since (Seddon 2023). The 'blob' is described as an unaccountable liberal elite which has seized control of the agenda and culture on how public services should be run; being a minister who wants change means having to fight this within the civil service. There has been a growing sense in the Conservative Party that there should be a post-bureaucratic era for the civil service, less bound by the targets introduced by the Labour Government for civil servants through the use of public service agreements (Barratt 2014) and more focused on being agents of delivery of a political agenda (Hanretty 2021). Cameron's adviser Steve Hilton was part of this reform dialogue and took it to a further level, stating that 4,000 officials could run government (Pyper 2013). There have been direct briefings to the media by those around ministers about specific officials (Stokes 2016). These criticisms of the civil service were accelerated during the May government by her advisers Nick Timothy and Fiona Hill (Stafford 2022) and then through the Johnson government, primarily in relation to public criticism of the civil service being opposed to Brexit. These criticisms were expanded through Johnson's adviser Dominic Cummings, who argued that there should be wider recruitment of 'weirdos and misfits' for the Prime Minister's office (Syal 2020) who could 'think outside the box'. This criticism was expanded by Jacob Rees Mogg when he was the minister for the civil service in the Truss government.

While the WM makes ministers responsible for decisions, Stokes (2016) found that blaming civil servants was also a frequent option. However, civil servants are not generally named and even when there is a public dislike of bureaucrats and their perceived competence, failures remain in the political domain. Everyday relations between civil servants and their ministers vary. In addition to regular business meetings, contact can relate to issues in the media. When requesting an update or discussion on a particular policy, ministers cannot demand to see any specific civil servants apart from the Permanent Secretary, although some adopted this practice (Stokes 2016). Some ministers became known for their disagreements with their Permanent Secretaries including Richard Crossman and Evelyn Sharp (Barberis 1996b).

The view of ministers by civil servants

Much of the literature about civil servants is concerned with them being an elite (Barberis 1996b; Kavanagh and Richards 2003; Rhodes et al 2007) and in the past there was a considerable overlap in elite membership between civil servants and ministers. Although the Northcote Trevelyan reforms (1854) were designed to open the system by removing patronage in appointments by politicians, these continued (Guttsmann 1969: 231-34). The potential role of patronage by ministers of civil servants for promotion re-emerged during the Thatcher era and is now at the centre of a debate about whether the civil service has been increasingly politicised, and this is discussed later in the chapter. While serving civil servants are forbidden by law to be MPs, former civil servants can stand for Parliament, and those who have included Harold Wilson and Keir Starmer.

Civil servants also gain a sense of power through long hours and low pay in a form of 'bureaucratic enchantment'. As former cabinet ministers state, the control of civil servants over every aspect of life begins from the moment of appointment as a minister, both as a bureaucratic (Crossman and Howard 1991) and a companionable embrace (Castle 1973). In particular, the civil servants take over diary, contacts and existing commitments. As Castle commented, the Permanent Secretary is fully prepared for this in ways that ministers are not, at least on their first appointment. Following this, the ministers' life is controlled through the diary and excludes political and other opportunities to interact with real life.

Civil servants come to a very quick view about their ministers once appointed including whether they are likely to work hard and how they will respond to their brief (Stokes 2016: 54). They can classify ministers according to their competence and style – policy entrepreneurs, management technicians and zealots (Rose 1987) and manage them accordingly. For a civil servant, particularly a Permanent Secretary in charge of a functional department, it is important to have a minister who can exert some authority in Cabinet (Headey 1972) and be heard by the Prime Minister and their advisers. Relationships between ministers and Permanent Secretaries are symbiotic and vary according to the characters of the individuals (Barberis 1996b). The ways in which civil servants work with their ministers providing advice varies and has changed over time. In 1972, Headey wrote that the key role of civil servants was policy formulation and then for 'ministerial rubber stamping' (p 41). Civil servants might obstruct or use delaying tactics and a 'still more sinister interpretation would be that not just individual civil servants but the Civil Service as a whole is in favour of certain policies and tries to force these on all governments' (p 41). In some cases, Permanent Secretaries can become a single channel of advice to ministers, having corralled the views of their department and external experts before putting them into a single view (Headey 1972; Barberis 1996b; Stokes 2016).

Civil servants can also use a range of means to undermine the decisions of their ministers that they do not support. These will include press leaks (Barker and Wilson 1997), private briefings or discussions with other departments, such as the Treasury, to reduce available funding. They can also have long relationships with specific specialist lobby groups to change the climate of the discussions (Headey 1972). The regular meetings between all Permanent Secretaries each Wednesday morning can be a way of sharing information about a minister's position and gaining support from other Permanent Secretaries (Barberis 1996b; Rhodes 2007). The *Yes Minister* and *Yes Prime Minister* series (Lynn and Jay 1988, 1989) demonstrate the range of ways in which civil servants could manage their ministers into taking a line that they preferred (Riddell 2019).

Permanent Secretaries may disagree with the decisions made by their ministers despite their advice. In these cases, the objections may be on grounds that are so severe that a Permanent Secretary may request a ministerial direction – that is a written instruction to act in a particular way which indicates the extent of the civil servant's disquiet on an issue. The request for a ministerial direction may be based on legal advice, because a decision appears to be too political or unethical (Barker and Wilson 1997; Freeguard et al 2017). If less than this, the Permanent Secretary can resign, retire or request to be moved to another department (Stokes 2016).

The extent to which the civil service seeks to control ministers has been affected by increased role SpADs. At the time of *Yes Minister* (1988), SpADs could be excluded through a range of means including proximity and access to ministers being restricted. However, this is no longer the case and ministers and their advisers belong to WhatsApp groups that are not accessible to the civil servants (Durrant et al 2022). As ministers have become more politicised in their decision making, civil servants have had to deal with increasingly complex and sophisticated contracting arrangements (Stokes 2016). The dividing line between politicians and contractors has become more blurred and civil servants do not seem to have had the strength of case to demonstrate what might follow if particular courses of action are taken. While COVID-19 reduced the legal procurement process requirements for government as it was an emergency, this did not explain the introduction of a fast lane for contractors who were political contacts and their prioritisation over existing suppliers (NAO 2020). In the provision of accommodation for refugees, competitive contracting has been undermined through the use of contract variations to existing contracts for speed, despite any assessment of quality. Government data systems in health have been contracted to a major Conservative party donor (Mason 2023). These contracts are considerable in value and it is unclear why civil servants have not been more forceful in explaining the risks. This may be because the civil servants have taken less interest and take the view that a contract will offload their responsibilities, although this is not the case. The pressure for speedy action within a wider context of civil servant criticism over their ability to respond may also be a consideration. The institutional framework for ethical practice in government was reduced through the resignation of two ethics advisers to Prime Minister Johnson. Members of the SCS might wish for a reset of former operational norms with a change in government but it is unclear whether those who have entered the civil service since 2010 will have much experience of these. Further, the wedge that SpADs and think tank funded advisers have inserted between civil servants and politicians has increased since 1997 and it has become an operational practice to be considered in any government reform. Calls for reform in the relationships between ministers and their civil servants provide a range of prescriptions but not why these behaviours have changed (Urban et al 2024) and run the risk of being ignored (Dunleavy 2024).

In his research on the relationship between ministers and civil servants based on interviews of former ministers, Stokes (2016) identified a range of factors which civil servants identified that ministers should display in their relationships with them and concluded that the positive traits included:

- showing leadership, direction and set clear expectations
- understanding the importance of the embryonic relationship
- having energy and charisma, even though they may overstep their bounds
- treating their Civil Servants with respect
- are able and are perceived to be so by their Civil Servants
- challenging their Civil Servants
- carrying their Civil Servants even when making wholly political decisions

(p 49)

There were also negative traits of ministers identified in their relationships with their civil servants:

- mediating their relationships with Civil Servants through Special Advisors
- lacking experience outside of politics
- not working cohesively with departmental Ministerial colleagues
- openly criticising their Civil Servants
- frequently changing their mind about policy or not thinking strategically

(Stokes 2016: 59)

The role of any Permanent Secretary is to be accountable to Parliament for its work and expenditure under their control, which will include agencies and sub-parts of government. While Permanent Secretaries are responsible to their Secretaries of State for the delivery of government policy in their area of responsibility, their financial accountability is to Parliament rather than ministers. Ministers, including Prime Ministers, do not appoint Permanent Secretaries nor do they dispose of them in general. This makes a Permanent Secretary more of a free agent that is generally recognised.

Following their periods as Permanent Secretary, a few may expect to continue to become the Cabinet Secretary but others have moved to other roles – including to head government regulators such as Melanie Dawes and Sharon White, who also went on to join the private sector. Others have moved to run charities such as Dame Helen Ghosh formerly of Defra who moved to be Chief Executive of the National Trust before becoming Master of Balliol College Oxford. These roles are also important consolation prizes for those which might have expected to become Permanent Secretaries or who have headed government agencies. These continuing links with regulators and third-party bodies are important and provide spheres of influence potentially in both directions, although more effective in the direction from government to other bodies than the other way round.

Ministers need to be able to rely on their Permanent Secretaries for a clear analysis of policy proposals. One consideration is how far down inside the functional departments briefings should be provided directly to ministers rather than through Permanent Secretaries. This may be a matter of preference (Playfair 1965) or the technical elements of the briefing. More frequently, the interchanges may take place between civil servants in the department and SpADs. When ministers appear before Parliament or Select Committees, they will have been prepared by their civil servants and have extensive briefings including lines to take and answers to potential questions that might be raised. Informal relationships between Permanent Secretaries and ministers are important. Civil Servants can be on hand when ministers are tired and there are issues that need some attention, but not at the top of the agenda. (Heseltine 1987). The relationships between ministers and civil servants are frequently expressed as a partnership which suggest they are equals. There is also a view that civil servants do what they want but dress it up as the will of the minister (Peyton, quoted in Nairne 1980: 80). Dennis Healey's view was that politicians who say this are too weak or incompetent (Nairne 1980: 81).

Has the civil service become more politicised?

There have been claims that the civil service has become more politicised although it is difficult to find evidence of this (Worlidge 2023). Unlike other countries, such as the United States, Germany and the Netherlands, in the UK civil servants do not change with the government (Page and Wright 1999; Peters 2013). Civil servants are expected to have 'neutral competence' (Aberbach and Rockman 1994). The argument that the civil service has become 'politicised' in the UK has been alive since the introduction of neo-liberal models of government in the 1970s (Peters 2013) and particularly apparent since Thatcher (Hennessy 1989: 628–87; Page 2010). The new right's agenda was to neutralise or 'deprivilege' the civil service from acting as the main source of advice to ministers which it saw as reinforcing the status quo rather than being willing to introduce competition into the welfare state model (Hood 1995; Peters 2013). The Next Steps agencies introduced change into the relationships between ministers and their operational understanding of their departments, providing potentially less control over everyday services. However, ministers remain responsible for their operation and successes in addition to their failures. This has increasingly led ministers to re-introduce political priorities in the operation of their whole departments not just the policy focused part at the top. This has been exacerbated as the role of cabinet government has diminished and the Prime Minister has moved to a more presidential style (Bevir and Rhodes 2006; Peters 2013). Further, it can be argued that ministerial interest in direct control over their departments has increased since Brexit, where formerly policy, legislation and funding were guaranteed within the policy areas that the UK pooled within the EU.

Has UK public policy has become more politicised since 2010, moving from a public service bargain through periods of austerity, Brexit, the use of specific funds in marginal constituencies (Hanretty 2021), political appointments and award of contracts to political allies (NAO 2020) and Partygate (Gray 2022)? Has the civil service become more politicised in response to these changes in the focus of their ministers or is there an expectation they should provide stronger advice on increasingly politicised uses of public policy and funds? Ministers have long been involved in making appointments, as well as encouraging their senior officials to find jobs elsewhere or retire, although this falls short of ministers being able to appoint political friends. In 2003, the Labour government suggested that it wanted to change the appointment of senior officials to give ministers greater involvement (Cabinet Office 2003: 6), but withdrew its proposal shortly afterwards. The appointment of those politically aligned to top posts has not occurred in any systematic way (Page 2010) although short term appointments from outside the civil service have been made throughout the last century including Edwin Plowden, Derek Rayner and Louise Casey. These outsiders may not have been appointed for their political allegiance but for their experience and focus being aligned with the government's objectives.

Other external appointees have been political advisers and not civil servants and there has been a longstanding tradition of these appointments including Steve Hilton and Dominic Cummings. Some SpADs, such as Geoff Mulgan, went on to become civil servants, but this was short lived and did not mark a strong, general or lasting trend (Page 2010). The visibility of politicisation has been more apparent in the appointment of those politically aligned to boards of inquiry, government owned businesses such as the Post Office or to the major cultural institutions and as NEDs to Government Departments, being described as colonisation (Ungoed-James 2024). In March 2022 there were 4,476 public appointments by ministers. The evidence of the politicisation of public appointments made by ministers is more transparent than those made within the civil service. These issues are of greater public concern than in the period before the 1970s, when there was an assumption that public appointees would be members of the establishment and be at least partly aligned with the government's position expressed as 'The traditional Westminster–Whitehall system sustained by informal restraints and conventions – what has been called "club government"' (Marquand 1981: 565).

Other forms of politicisation can operate within the civil service. This can be in the way that policy recommendations are tailored to fit specific ministerial ideology rather than taking a wider public service position. This may be termed unconscious bias and an effort by civil servants to translate options for public policy into forms that are politically acceptable to ministers. However, this political focus may assume that options are edited for political acceptance rather than being drawn up within the code of neutrality (Hood and Lodge 2006). Some civil servants may seek to closely align with the government's agenda and be more proactive in working with SpADs and think tanks. The issue here is whether civil servants aligned more closely with the ideology of the government have greater influence in the preparation of policy options or gain promotion compared with others (Peters 2013) which extends the benefits of politicisation to individual civil servants.

This potential politicisation of officials in the civil service lacks transparency. In local government, officers are required to make public in a register their meetings and any offers of hospitality from the private sector together with any family or friendship ties with potential contractors. This information is in the public domain. While covered by the same Nolan Code of Public Life, civil servants do not have to record meetings or attendance at social events. Meetings with think tanks may be regarded as standard business and happen regardless of the party in government. Ministerial meetings with think tanks and interest bodies are required to be recorded and are in the public domain.

Unwelcome intermediaries

In addition to the relationships between ministers and civil servants, there are others engaged in providing advice on policy and administration. These are generally considered to be irritants by the civil service and, like other unwelcome changes, removed after short periods of time, never being absorbed into the mainstream (NAO 2024). The role of SpADs has become a more permanent feature and has not been resolved by the removal of their influence by the civil service but rather being an expanded and functional feature of everyday life at the top of departments. Does this suggest that the fundamental triumvirate within the WM – of ministers, civil servants and Parliament has now been broken or needs to be reformulated to consider their role and presence (Russell and Serban 2021; Urban et al 2024)? These political insertions by ministers to provide advice and change are considered in turn.

Wider external recruitment

Recruitment of outsiders by ministers, to provide experience or skills, has been a longstanding practice and consistently accompanied by antipathy by the SCS (Plowden 1989; Barberis 1996b; NAO 2024). This is a widely reported issue and described as an 'inhospitable environment for outsider or "irregulars" joining in this capacity' (Christoph 1975: 32). The lack of trust and interest in the recruitment of external experts at a senior level can be seen as part of the internalised community or village culture within Whitehall (Heclo and Wildavksy 1981) or organisational culture focused on cosmopolitans or locals (Gouldner 1958). Within the village there are shared interests, practices and actions that can promote conformity within a closed system (Putnam 1973), reinforced through a promotion system that is mainly only open to internal candidates (NAO 2024). While civil servants might be in competition with each other, their external position is of being at one. When there is an external threat from an individual or an idea, the civil service can, through its regular permanent secretaries' meetings (Barberis 1996b; Rhodes 2007), develop a strategy of resistance aligned to their own departments. The reinforcement of the village culture is through locations in and around Whitehall and a fear of losing influence if relocated away from Whitehall. These fears can be justified when considering the creation of the decentralised government offices and civil servants within them are regarded as policy takers rather than policy makers (Mawson and Spencer 2014).

The introduction of those in their mid-career into the civil service is regarded as undermining to those in post (Page 2010) and while initially envisaged as a route into the top of the civil service by Northcote Trevelyan (1854), was dismissed as a working practice by Haldane (1918) and later by Fisher and Bridges. Those who undertake these tasks for ministers have a difficult time in practice (Plowden 1989). They are regarded as dangerous external appointments to an internally focused organisation (Weller and Haddon 2016). Civil servants also expect external appointees to fail to understand and recognise the relationships between ministers and their civil servants (Foster-Gilbert 2018) and its essential political nature even where civil servants are expected to be neutral (Plowden 1989). As an outsider appointed to the Treasury as an economist, Hall was ridiculed as a 'mad technician' and 'too clever by half' (Jones 1994: 191) but as a specialist, he worked in the same team for much longer than members of the SCS and with a wider range of ministers providing a continuity in policy advice that was otherwise rare.

Special advisers (SpADs)

While the civil service has an important role in advice, there is a continuing question about SpADs and their appointment by ministers. As Boyle (1965: 258) states, 'the government machine does not have a monopoly of wisdom or good ideas'. The development of the role of SpADs emerged in the 1970s and their recruitment, age and experience has changed over time. Thatcher's advisers were older than more recent appointments (Yong and Hazell 2014). Many SpADs transfer into government as MPs. At the start of his career, Prime Minister Cameron was a SpAD to the Chancellor of the Exchequer Norman Lamont during a turbulent financial period in Major's government. The role of SpADs may widen as the period in government progresses. Some help to manage internal government relationships while others are policy specialists. Secretaries of State may see their SpADs more frequently than their junior ministers, who they may not have selected directly but rather appointed by the Prime Minister to create balance within the Parliamentary party. Ministers can also feel isolated in their private offices and find SpADs provide a sympathetic ear aligned to their objectives (Yong and Hazell 2014).

The growth in the appointment of SpADs, whose role is overtly political, has created a change in the relationship between ministers and civils servants (Hennessey 1996). SpADs have different skills and objectives in comparison with civil servants. Foster and Plowden (1996) argued for a return of the old way of policy making without SpADs, but this seems unlikely and their role is now established. This leaves a tension in the role of civil servants, with ministers regarding them as administrators more than policy advisers. In March 2022, there were 126 SpADs listed by Parliament although this says nothing of the specific roles that they fulfil. SpADs can be the eyes and the ears of the minister, which civil servants might expect to do on departmental business across Whitehall but cannot be political fixers (Page 2012). The appointment of SpADs has primarily been a matter for each minister, although since the period of Johnson and Dominic Cummings, there has been a tendency for advisers in the Prime Minister's office to seek to approve all SpAD appointments, leading to the resignation of a Chancellor, Savid Javid (Walker 2023). The Prime Minister's SpADs can be policy leads but also enforcers across the government. SpADs are party loyalists and see their role as a pathway to their own political careers – as MPs, running think tanks or lobby groups. Their access to ministerial offices and the Parliamentary estate gives them networking advantages that can last for many years. They also provide ministerial access long after they have left their SpAD role and retain their links with civil servants as they also rise through the ranks.

The number of SpADs brought into support ministers can vary. There was an increase between the Major and Blair governments when the number increased from 38 to 72 and their appointment became more routinised with specific terms and conditions (Page 2012). The extent to which SpADs have been brought into the offices of ministers and Prime Ministers was extended further by the Truss government, whose chief of staff, Mark Fullbrook, had been involved in lobbying scandals (Stafford 2022) and the policy communications team was recruited from right wing think tanks.

There have been other significant external political appointments in the Chief of Staff and head of communications roles in 10 Downing Street including Jonathan Powell and Alistair Campbell under Blair, Steve Hilton in the Coalition, Fiona Hill, Nick Timothy then Gavin Barwell (2021) under May and Dominic Cummings in the Johnson period. Sunak has had Isaac Levido, a protege of Lynton Crosby, a longstanding polling adviser. Sir Keir Starmer has appointed Morgan McSweeney his former political adviser as Chief of Staff.

Stafford (2022) has set out the four functions of Downing street staff – press, politics, policy and private office and it is in the private office where the civil service has attempted to retain its role. When Blair wanted to change this, arguments about the role of the private office, the monarchy and the honours system were used to retain its status as having a Parliamentary Private Secretary (PPS) who was a civil servant and not a SpAD. Incoming Prime Ministers such as Brown and Cameron stated that they wished to reduce the number of SpADs but ended up appointing more because they considered progress in achieving their objectives was too slow. These appointments may also reflect the relationships between the Prime Minister and their ministers. There have also been suggestions that a Prime Minister's office might be established (Urban et al 2024). While there have been arguments in favour (PASC 2002), there are those who consider it would be too bureaucratic, create congestion between advisers and potentially distance the civil service from their discussions (Diamond 2022).

How do SpADs work with civil servants and have they replaced them as the most senior policy advisers? Experience varies depending on the issue and the minister. Most SpADs appear to operate across the whole department, rather than focusing on specific issues (Page 2012). Civil servants obtain the views and position of the minister from their SpADs and there are occasions when they work together across Whitehall when in agreement. Good relationships within the private office between SpADs and civil servants are seen to be important as otherwise there would be a tendency to exclude either side and create conflict and competition. Yong and Hazell (2014) found agreement that No 10 worked best when there was a mixture of civil servants and SpADs working together. Page (2012) found the primary contacts of SpADs were with civil servants at levels lower than the Permanent Secretary, particularly those civil servants who were concerned with policy detail and administration. While seeing Permanent Secretaries daily, any direct contact would suggest that things had gone wrong and SpADs attempted to avoid this. However, Page (2012) found that SpADs had considerable contact with their peers in other departments when acting in a 'fixer' role. The extent to which civil servants are more careful about taking political roles following the increase in SpADs has also been noticeable (Yong and Hazell 2014). Where ministers rely on their

SpADs, this can insulate them from the civil service (Stokes 2016) which can be problematic.

Events

The relationship between ministers and their civil servants can be shaped by events where the power dynamic between them is thrust into the public's attention. This has been apparent in the past in the way in which specific issues have been dealt with including more traditional whistleblowing, issues such as Partygate and the role of the 'ministerial fast lane' for procurement in COVID-19 (NAO 2020).

Whistleblowing

Whistleblowing or public interest disclosure (Hunt 2013) may occur when individual civil servants decide that they wish to make public events or practices of their department, including decisions or communications by ministers. They may undertake this as principled dissent (Graham 1986) taking the view that they have a responsibility for the contract between the state and the citizen (Hunt 2013) or because it crosses their own personal boundaries. For professionals, such as those in medicine, witnessing poor practices without commenting on them may break their professional codes or standards and render the practitioner liable for censure as well as the individual who has perpetrated the initial acts. One of the first whistleblowers was Leslie Chapman (1978) who broke with civil service convention to write about waste and collusive fraud in government (Vinten 2003). Whistleblowing is a perilous activity for a career and despite statements about protection, it frequently ends in dismissal and opprobrium. In the 1980s, whistleblower Clive Ponting broke the Official Secrets Act during the Falklands War and was prosecuted. Ponting was acquitted, after which, the law was strengthened (Vinten 2003). More recently, whistleblowers in the NHS have been suspended from their posts despite the Public Interest Disclosure Act 1998 and institutional safeguards for whistleblowing employees.

There are personal pressures against whistleblowing for civil servants, not least the experience of other whistleblowers that can be a disincentive. What is more likely is that civil servants apply for a posting to another role. Those whistleblowing can be portrayed as having a grudge against their employers and using this in an attempt to discredit them. The Permanent Secretary of the Home Office faced criticism of this kind when complaining about the bullying behaviour of the Home Secretary towards him in 2021. Further, there is always peer pressure to remain silent, as part of a tacit acceptance of practices in that workplace. Employees may also take the view that they will lose their jobs if managerial practices are disclosed. Hunt (2013) argues that whistleblowing is strongly associated with the principles of freedom of information which should, in his view, be considered with freedom of expression which is not permitted in the civil service within the Armstrong doctrine (1985).

There have been calls for change, although there are critics of attempts to codify the role of the civil service through legal means as inappropriate where the UK does not have a written constitution (Chapman 2005). These matters are also included in reports of the Committee on Standards in Public Life (Chapman 2005), but do not apply to civil servants working for ministers as they are required to abide by the Armstrong doctrine and the Civil Service Code to represent their ministers and not their own views. The 2010 Constitutional Reform and Governance Act guarantees civil service neutrality. However, the Rwanda Act (2024) contained proposals to amend the Civil Service Code so that civil servants would be required to act in accordance with ministerial directions, which has evoked legal action from civil service trades unions, on the basis that their members are being asked to break the Human Rights Act. Other forms of whistleblowing include leaks to the media and it is unclear whether these are by civil servants, SpADs or politicians. Worlidge (2023) argues that these are unacceptable as a means of defence against ministerial attacks on civil servants.

Partygate

Relationships between ministers and civil servants can be framed by specific events that become notorious in the public's mind, such as Partygate which occurred during the COVID-19 lockdown. This related to breaking COVID-19 regulations and guidance that banned social mixing. Prime Minister Johnson denied that gatherings not authorised under the COVID-19 regulations had taken place. The nature and timing of these gatherings, including one on the evening before Prince Philip's funeral, when the Queen sat alone, appalled the public including many whose relatives had died during the pandemic. This was also a major element in the first part of the COVID-19 Inquiry (2023). Partygate was one of the rule violations of politicians and some public servants who resigned included the Secretary of State for Health, Matt Hancock and the Chief Medical Officer of Health for Scotland (Gorton et al 2022). Johnson evoked a range of formulations of words which attempted to demonstrate that the COVID-19 rules and guidance had not been violated in answer to questions in Parliament but this was found to be the case both by the Metropolitan Police and, on the basis of a limited inquiry, by Sue Gray (2022). Subsequently fixed penalty notices were given to a range of Downing Street staff, mostly comprising more junior civil servants and SpADs, leaving concerns about the civil service and its behaviour (Thomas 2022). While there were calls to strengthen the guidance for civil servants after the Partygate events, this was left to an ongoing civil service review undertaken by Maude, in 2020–23. Johnson set the tone for the activities in No 10 during the pandemic, including pressure on over 200 individuals to participate in these social events. However, the Gray report criticised the way in which civil servants did not account for their own behaviour and lack of leadership from the Cabinet Secretary and Head of the Home Civil Service Simon Case.

6

Devolution and the Role of Civil Service in the Union

Introduction

The introduction of the 1999 Devolution Settlement by the Blair government was a major point of punctuated equilibrium on the UK state, including for the civil service (Thelen 2009). While more attention is paid to the effects of the Northcote Trevelyan reforms (1854), Haldane's Machinery of Government (MoG) dictums including the Westminster Model (WM) (1918), Heath's Reorganisation of Government White Paper (1970) and Thatcher's agencification (from 1987 onwards), the devolution settlement was under-recognised because, as administrative devolution (MacKinnon 2015) or, more correctly, delegation, it was not considered important by the civil service who saw it as a continuation of the British centrist approach of permissive autonomy (Warner et al 2021; Sandford 2023). Like the creation of the Irish State in 1922, when the UK lost more of its territory than Germany after 1918, those parts of the UK distant from Whitehall were regarded as less important and a residual colonial administration culture was in practice (Hechter 2017). Yet the Heath, Thatcher and Blair reconstructions of government all had their provenance in unintended consequences of external of agreements made by the UK state. In 1971 and 1999 these were as a direct consequence of the UK's membership of the EU and in 1987 of the UK's membership of the WTO's Government Procurement Agreement (GPA) (see Chapter 2). As these reforms of the way in which the state conducted its business were external in their origins and bound by treaties, they had to be implemented and their requirements persisted through changes in government.

When the modern civil service was formed after 1854, it was modelled, in part, on the Indian civil service created by the East India Company (Elliott et al 2022). At the time, the UK was a colonial power and its views were shaped by these practices. Hechter (2017) argues that the English state and the subsequent creation of the Union was a product of colonial ideology, with the centre in the south east and the rest of the country being regarded as a peripheral and subordinate domain. There was no initial coming together in an equal way – Wales was conquered, Scotland was in a weak position financially and Northern Ireland remained after many years of policy discussion and subsequent compromise in an ongoing state of internal colonialism (Hechter 2017). Movements for devolution or to protect cultural identities such as in Cornwall reflect a return to this Anglo-centric power distribution within the state and Brexit can be interpreted as an external version of this through the dominance of British exceptionalism (Whitham 2023). To this can be added the growth of local democratic administration. As Hechter states (2017), the practices of colonies required the definition and acknowledgement of two cultures – that of dominant, elitist ideology and practices and the rest. The focus of colonial relations was London and this is echoed by those who came to Britain in the Windrush generation – the centre of the empire was Piccadilly Circus underground station (Selvon 1956). The Colonial Office was abolished in 1966, shortly before the UK joined the EU, creating a double sense of loss of Britain's power to determine its own destiny. At the same time, UK colonial practices of public administration have continued their influence through the institutional structure of the UK state following a range of reforms (Elliott et al 2022).

While the loss of colonies and their rebirth as Commonwealth states occurred over a relatively short period in the 1960s and 1970s, it might be observed that the practices and culture of London and the periphery were transferred to bring the internal administrative relations within the state into focus. Movements for cultural and political independence emerged in the EU and beyond, demonstrating that smaller states could be both viable and influential with their peers. The response of the UK civil service to these changes and then devolution has been to continue the same practices through the use of delegated powers within an unchanged constitution (Woodhouse 2004). The promise of devolution, with a differentiated and reformed civil service (Rhodes et al 2003), supported by EU treaty principles of subsidiarity (Arribas and Bourdin 2012) have not survived Brexit. The delegated powers included in the 1999 Devolution settlement are gradually being returned to the centre, while civil servants have been requested by Government to reinforce Union roles and powers (Savoie 1999; Cabinet Office and DLUHC 2023; Morgan and Jones 2023).

The WM did not change as a result of either the end of colonisation or the introduction of devolution and has been returning to its centralised control model (HMT 2023a). Does this matter? The ability of the civil service to return to overt control rather than operate this behind the mantra of devolution might be considered a success and rescued before it went too far. The threats of independence in Scotland have been seen off, although support for independence remains higher than before the referendum in 2014, support for independence in Wales has grown from a small base (Martin 2022) and the potential for pressure for a united Ireland poll, as set out in the Good Friday agreement grows (Renwick et al 2023). Further, economic orthodoxy has moved away from a model dependent on international, external trade to one which is balanced between internal and external exchanges (Krugman 1991). The focus on centralised power without a consideration of the effects of its practices on the continuation of the Union and the state's long term economic standing are a weakness of the civil service and may be defined as a failure in due course.

Within the Union, the centre may find new ways of creating a narrative for more devolution, but unless there are fundamental changes in either the WM and the practices of the Treasury using direct approval mechanisms for local authority projects in deals across the UK (Morphet 2022), the economic consequences will continue. Proposals in the Labour Party Manifesto (2024) for mission-based organisation of government, the introduction of a UK Council chaired by the Prime Minister comprised of First Ministers and Mayors of Combined Authorities in England and proposals for the reform of the House of Lords to comprise of national and regional may bring more reform (Balls 2024).

Operating within the WM that is centralising, hoards power and focuses on ministerial responsibilities (Lijphart 1999; Flinders 2011), devolutionary changes were not taken to be necessarily long lasting or binding. As the history of the civil service demonstrates, changes in the relationships within the WM are considered as impermanent, with their return to the previous state of power distribution to be achieved over time (Dahlström et al 2011). While central government departments do not wish to reverse the Next Steps reforms of 1987, by taking back agencies or outsourced services within their core departmental structures, they have increasingly sought to regain control of their activities in other ways. These include budget tightening and intervention in prioritisation which has returned more control than was anticipated when these arrangements were first established. Similarly, recentralisation of the powers of the devolved administrations (DAs) since 2014 and more particularly since Brexit in 2016 (Andrews 2017; Brown Swan et al 2024) has been increasing. When the Devolution Settlement was introduced in 1999, there were no attempts to change the UK constitution and, as with other responses to pressures for reform in the civil service, there was always an assumption that these could be recentralised in due course.

Before devolution in 1999, the main relationship between Whitehall and other parts of the UK was through the territorial offices of state based in London. Devolution delegated responsibilities from the centre to the new administrations (Flinders 2011) and the selection of the term 'devolved administrations' over the use of the term 'government' is significant. The

DAs are decision making bodies with responsibility for matters which are specifically delegated to them. Further, the decisions that were delegated were primarily those which the UK had pooled within the EU and thus this delegation was for their administration within the EU framework. This meant that the UK government did not have to exert any direct control over this delegation of the administration of functions as it had already been involved in setting them in EU negotiations (Morphet 2013). Some functions in the DA settlement such as housing and planning were not part of the EU portfolio of pooled responsibilities but had already been within the delegated practices of local administration in Scotland and Wales.

The relationships between the centre of UK government, Scotland, Wales and Northern Ireland, together with local authorities, was subject to increasing EU treaty obligations for subsidiarity in decision making from 1992 onwards. After 1999, the initial relationship between the DAs and the centre was one of devolve and forget. However, the increase in EU subsidiarity obligations in an amended Article 5 of the foundational treaty, after 2009 (Arribas and Bourdin 2012), appeared to stimulate a Whitehall re-evaluation about whether devolution had gone too far. This was exacerbated by austerity after 2010 and Brexit after 2016, when central departments were initially reduced in size and then could no longer rely on EU decisions to ensure that the Treasury allocated funds to them as before.

The Dunlop Review (2021) of the operation of the Union, focusing on the centre and the DAs, was instigated by outgoing Prime Minister May in 2018 with the resulting relationships between the centre and the DAs dependent on stronger civil service machinery of government (Sandford 2023). The change was noticeable through the response of the DAs during the COVID-19 pandemic. In this period, for the first time, it became clear to the UK national media that the DAs had different powers that could be exercised independently of the centre in London (Cushion et al 2022). Johnson, when Prime Minister, spoke of a need for 'muscular unionism' (Sandford 2023) and steps were taken in a subsequent White Paper on Levelling Up (LUWP) (DLUHC 2022) to set missions and targets for all local authorities in the UK, regardless of the existing devolution arrangements. These requirements were translated into the Levelling Up and Regeneration Act 2023 (LURA). Deal funding, which had been one of the tools of the post-2010 changes in devolution practice, was extended and by 2021 at the publication of the LUWP, all local authorities outside England had a direct funding deal with HM Treasury in London. In these deals, civil servants acted with delegated responsibilities for their departmental accounting officers to centrally approve local authority programmes, projects and specific allocations of funding (Morphet 2022). In England, some councils had these deals and the primary focus in the LUWP was to establish similar, civil servant led deals for the whole of the nation.

What is the case for devolution of decision making?

The adoption of a devolved or delegated system of government using a principal agent model (Dehousse 2013) has a number of perceived benefits over a unitary state. It provides an answer to criticism of an overcentralised bureaucracy and democratic deficit which is made at all government scales. It also allows for cultural differences across the country to be addressed through the institutions of the state without having a common approach. It allows for local administration of justice and service accountability while allowing the state to benefit from distancing itself from blame and more detailed accountability. By devolving decision making on service funding, it may be more efficient for the centre and reduce the scale of political bargaining over individual policies. It also helps to support a local political system that can reinforce the centre when required. It also allows for separation and distance between systems within a state which helps accommodate difference (Majone 2001) without seeking separation. For civil servants, this approach gives power without responsibility. While there is some accountability for the distribution of funding and its application, any failures or political fallout can be held to be the responsibility of local politicians and their officers with central intervention only when required. The maintenance of financial control is through the accounting officer system, although each of the DAs has a single accounting officer rather than one for each functional department as in England. This can provide a significant advantage for the DAs in operating policies across traditional functional departmental boundaries, although, in practice, this has not occurred.

The debate on devolution and decentralisation within the state has been made in the context of the success of national economies (Krugman 1991; Ahrend et al 2014) and this has shifted economic orthodoxy on the role and type of trade within the economy. As a response, the EU extended its founding treaty principle of subsidiarity in 1992, 1999 and 2009 to reflect this (Barca 2009). In practice, this has resolved into the recognition of functional economic areas with strong local democratic leadership. Here the argument relates to the benefits to nation states of internal trade between functional territorial entities that mirrors the traditional orthodoxies of international trade (Alesina and Spolaore 2005), and which, at the same time, supports the use of more sustainable practices for movement of materials, goods and services. However, the success of this approach depends on strong subnational democratic leaders and the extent to which this is devolution rather than decentralisation or delegation (Ahrends et al 2014). There have been critics of the creation of functional economic areas that use soft governance models (Brenner 2019) which are operational across OECD member states. Or turning this on its head, what is the rationale for increased centralisation (Self 1965)? The danger is that too many central staff will be used in the exercise of control rather than that of initiative (Self 1965). As Harris (1925) stated, civil servants are compelled towards centralisation both through their accountability to Parliament and Treasury control: central decisions mean uniformity.

For devolution in the UK, the case was made that it would bring quangos in the DAs into a democratic framework by making them accountable to ministers (Flinders 2011). This was argued as a main function of devolution implementation by Blair (Norton 2007). Over time this was expected to lead to a simplification and centralisation mechanism for quangos that had been established to bypass civil service and government control. While the arguments varied between Scotland and Wales as to the drivers of these reforms, they were central to the argument for devolution for the civil service as they were about regaining control not losing it. Thus devolution in the UK has remained within the 'shadow of hierarchy' (Flinders 2011: 25). Delegation of administrative power is also considered to be a more acceptable bureaucratic practice where there is political alignment between tiers of government (Volden 2002). At the time of the implementation of devolution in the UK, there was political alignment between central government and the newly elected DAs for Wales and Scotland. While inter-governmental arrangements were established at the time of devolution, the common political party in power meant there was less apparent need for the institutions established to hold together the devolved settlement and these were not strong or based in the constitution. These institutional arrangements were therefore slow to establish and have been weak or non-existent in operation (Jeffery 2009). The Labour Party Manifesto for the 2024 General Election included new institutional relationships between the DAs and Mayors of English Combined Authorities.

Relationships between Whitehall, Scotland and Wales before 1999

Before the implementation of the devolution settlement in 1999, there was divergence between Scotland and England on legal and educational systems and land law which all had their origins in the Act of Union 1707. Wales had less autonomy as a principality which had been part of Great Britain since 1592, although there had been an increasing tendency to separate the legislative components for Wales in Acts of Parliament for England and Wales before 1999. Following a referendum which sought to separate Scotland from the UK in 1978, the Barnett Formula was established to allocate specific funds triggered by decisions for expenditure in England, known as Barnett consequentials. Before the Barnett Formula, the Goschen formula existed for Scotland from 1888 and there were bilateral discussions with Northern Ireland after the creation of the Irish Republic with Wales being treated as part of England. In the period up to 1999, the role of the Treasury was to use finance to ensure that UK policies were implemented in Scotland and Wales (Thain and Wright 1995). The Barnett Formula was based on a population base ratio between England, Scotland and Wales at 85, 10 and 5 and territories received an increment based on spending decisions for comparable English functional programmes. Northern Ireland was added as 2.75, based on a population share of the United Kingdom rather than that of Great Britain. Associated with the Barnett Formula was the ability of the territorial Secretary of State in central government to vary expenditure propositions within their budgets rather than following England. By 1992–93, the block allocations for each territorial Secretary of State covered more than 90 per cent of expenditure under their responsibility but excluded some specific matters such as social security (Bristow 2001).

Policy differentiation after the Devolution Settlement 1999–2010

Before devolution, the territorial departments were part of the wider policy web within Whitehall and were included in circulation lists as part of the Government Department networks (Keating 2002). This enabled territorial departments to maintain awareness of the extent of potential divergence in Scotland and Wales although the role of quangos and other bodies allowed for some distancing from Westminster pressures in decision making.

The apparatus of devolution was established to ensure that there would not be a wide variation between the DAs and the centre. There was an administrative committee and concordats on policies which limited variation and gave Whitehall the last word on any disagreement. Many of the policy areas that were included within the Devolution settlement were already within the remit of the territorial departments in Whitehall (MacKinnon 2015) and beyond this, Keating (2002) argues that there was little opportunity for variation. This was within the wider frame of the UK policy, while ignoring the EU policy context. Keating argues that there was less flexibility in Wales than Scotland, as legislation was set in the same format as England and civil servants were more dependent on London networks. After the establishment of the DAs, there was some surprise when Wales started to diverge on matters of policy, including planning and there was a sense among Welsh civil servants that this needed to be managed back into the former model (Cole 2012) The Welsh Assembly Government changed the civil servants so that a wider range of policies could be developed.

While the arguments in favour of implementing the devolution settlement in 1999 offered the opportunity to generate better differential policies for places, their economies and people than could be provided in a unified state (MacKinnon 2015). While the establishment of the DAs was expressed through a narrative of separation, as there was no constitutional settlement, powers exercised by the DAs are set within the UK Parliamentary framework and can be removed at any time. Devolution of control has been less than promoted at the time with the focus on the powers to vary delivery rather than overarching policy (Greer 2007). While there are arguments for divergence in the administration of policy there are also public pressures to have similar minimum standards across the state to avoid a 'postcode lottery'. As MacKinnon (2015) states, many of the devolved powers for delivery were those already set within the territorial offices of the state and therefore did not require any fundamental arguments in Whitehall about loss of control. While promised, some longer-term powers for revenue raising, to reflect differences in DA priorities, were small and marginal when implemented, even when related to the effects of the potential for differential income tax rates. Where variations in policy within the DAs occurred, there was no need for the UK government to set parameters as they were already contained within EU treaties and legislation. While the Scottish government attempted to engage directly in the negotiation of policy relating with the EU, this was not permitted by the UK government (Keating 2002) with the most involvement achieved by Scottish ministers and civil servants being that of attending meetings as part of the UK delegation.

The implementation of devolution led to changes in the mechanisms for policy making in the DAs. In Scotland, this included reform of civil service organisation, moving from departmental to a single service or strategic state model (Elliott 2020). Much of the early discussion about the implementation of devolution was focused on whether it would lead to policy convergence or divergence, where the weight of pre-existing agreements could limit the extent of innovation in administration (Keating 2002). Further, convergence might occur between the DAs rather than between the DAs and England (Clifford and Morphet 2015). There was also a process of policy divergence resulting from pent-up demand for change within the system and the development of a new policy style (Greer and Jarman 2007). At the same time, there were policy making traditions and cultures which continued despite changes in the party in control. The civil service provided some of this continuity.

In Scotland after devolution, Greer and Jarman (2007) indicate that the main policy concept introduced was one of partnership, 'based on universalistic, directly provided, undifferentiated public services that use networks rather than competition and are governed based on a high degree of trust in the professionalism of providers' (p 13). This was an opportunity to continue and reinforce policy culture (Elliott 2020). Civil servants working in the Scottish Office would have been part of this process for decision making in policy areas where there were both *de facto* and *de jure* policy differences, for example in health, education, justice and land. After devolution there were still expectations of vertical relationships with civil servants in Whitehall. However, these relationships reduced to the point where it is stated apocryphally that civil servants in the Cabinet Office affixed 'post it' notes to their computer screens which said, 'remember Scotland' and the DAs are colloquially referred to as local authorities.

In Scotland, the implementation of a partnership philosophy included local government. Through the 2003 Scotland Act, community councils were established and an obligation on public services to work together was enshrined in legislation. The local authority boundary and function reforms in Scotland in 1992 into 33 local authorities meant that it was possible to have representatives of all local authorities together in the same room. This led to a more developed set of working relationships between civil service officials and local government officers. As in Northern Ireland, many had known each other for some time and they had a platform of trust before 1999. The focus on partnership working in Wales has also been a feature post-Devolution (Greer and Jarman 2007), particularly across local government and health, primarily using carrots rather than sticks. While there is contempt for local government in Whitehall, this is not expressed in Scotland and Wales (Greer and Jarman 2007).

Post-devolution policy styles and cultures were located in the principles of the welfare state rather than the neo-liberal market orientation in England, where there has been a significant step away from the precedents and norms of the post-1945 settlement. In comparison, Wales, Scotland and Northern Ireland have maintained and continued to develop welfarist policy ideology across central and local government.

Recentralising the state and muscular unionism after 2010

While the change in the fortunes and relationships between the UK central government and the DAs from 2010 was characterised as a change in mood related to a change in government, from Labour to the Coalition, there were other issues which led Whitehall to reconsider the relationship between the centre and what they saw as the periphery. The first was increasing pressure for an independence referendum in Scotland, to which the Coalition gave agreement in 2011 to be held within the period of the Parliament in 2014. A second concern in Whitehall was the negotiation of the EU Lisbon Treaty, following on from the Amsterdam Treaty and EU Government White Paper (2000). This changed Article 5 in the Treaty for the European Union (TfEU) to increase the role and application of subsidiarity to sub-state democratic institutions within the EU (Arribas and Bourdin 2012). The Scots could claim more power, even short of independence and this applied to all other parts of the UK. Gordon Brown was the last of the EU member state leaders to sign this treaty in 2009 and his reluctance to do so was never discussed or understood. Thus, while the UK had been able to implement devolution in 1999, including the Good Friday Agreement in Northern Ireland, based on the level of subsidiary included in the Maastricht Treaty 1992, it did not have to make any constitutional reforms and accommodated this level of subsidiarity within the WM to meet its EU Treaty commitments. The changes introduced by the Lisbon Treaty required more formal and lasting subsidiarity over a wide range of state activities including powers and funding. In effect, this changed aspects of the UK Constitution and the WM while the UK was part of the EU.

These pressures for independence and the obligation to devolve central government powers and funding led the UK civil service to take a more active interest in devolution than initially after 1999. It was recognised by the civil service that the formulation of policies in relation to English local government, would require less directive and assertive framing. Another apparatus that could not be sustained was control of local authorities through performance targets and a new approach was needed if the relationship between the centre and substate administrations was to retain the same balance. The answer that was selected and used across the whole of the Union was for 'deals' which were couched in voluntaristic, competitive terms, initially expressed as 'contracts' between the centre and substate administration, reflecting the Partnership Agreements that the UK state had submitted to the EU for delivering substate cohesion programmes (Bachtler and Mendez 2020). The contract format was eventually dropped in favour of a clientelist competitive model for funds (Morphet 2022) and for the creation of new, bespoke structures for functional economic areas – combined authorities (CAs). These CAs were established using legislation originally implemented by the Brown Government in the Local Democracy Economic Development Act 2009 and subsequently amended in the Cities and Local Government Devolution Act 2016. They created administrative groupings of local authorities through secondary legislation, with each having a bespoke range of competences. However, CAs have no powers and reflect no change in the constitutional structure or WM. Increasingly, the offices of the CAs are managed by seconded or former civil servants rather than local authority officers (Anderson 2024). The introduction of Trailblazer Devolution Deals with integrated financial settlements for two CAs in 2023 (Sandford 2023b), confirmed the limited range of funding and competences to be included, but the extent of devolution of decision making was questionable (Morphet and Denham 2023). The mechanisms for determination of projects within the CAs were to be retained within the power of civil servants, exercising accounting officer control (HM Treasury 2024a HM Treasury 2023) in a similar model to that used elsewhere in deal structures across the UK (Morphet 2022).

The growth in support for Scottish independence during the referendum campaign in 2014 was attributed to the introduction of devolution in 1999 and it was increasingly suggested by those in favour of retaining the Union, there should be more assertive Britishness by politicians (Martin 2024). The Cabinet Office Devolution Unit was strengthened with a new programme for civil servants, 'Devolution and You' launched in 2015, designed to 'improve devolution capacity across the One Civil Service' (Cabinet Office 2015: 12). Guidance was issued to civil servants (Cabinet Office et al 2015) and devolution coordinators were appointed in each of the functional departments as well as the Core Executive.

Following the Brexit referendum in 2016, an opportunity to review the 1999 devolution settlement presented itself in Whitehall. As the basis of the 1999 settlement was the delegation of the administration of agreed EU policies, if the UK was no longer part of the EU then it would be possible to return these powers to the centre. The development of the post-Brexit referendum legislation did this through the establishment of the UK single market in the Subsidies Control Act 2020 (Brown Swan et al 2024). When the DAs attempted to challenge the reduction in their powers, through the use of the courts and the Sewel Convention (Keating 2021), the Constitution, WM and Parliamentary sovereignty prevailed. At the same time, the operational relationships between the DAs and the centre were reviewed to reassert relationships that had dwindled after 1999. These included May's Dunlop Review on UK Government Union Capability (2018–21) with recommendations including a new Cabinet sub-committee, the appointment of a Minister responsible for the constitutional integrity of the Union in Cabinet and the appointment of a new single Permanent Secretary for the three territorial departments. It also proposed a new intergovernmental council, to replace the Joint Ministerial Council established in 1999, which was also set out in more detail in the Intergovernmental Relations Review (Cabinet Office and DLUHC 2022). Most of these proposed reforms have not been implemented and may have been more performative than operational in intent. However, the lead official for this review, Sue Gray, subsequently took on the role of managing the office of the Labour Leader and these proposals for an intergovernmental council reappeared in the Labour Manifesto for the General Election in 2024 (Labour Party 2024) and was subsequently established.

The differentiation between the leadership of the DAs in the COVID-19 pandemic was further evidence of the evolution of public relationships within the DAs over the preceding 20 years. There was an assumption that their powers, reduced by Brexit and the operation of the UK single market after 2020, would undermine the pull of Edinburgh and Cardiff and their differentiation from the UK wide policies. However, the continuance of the culture of welfarism and care of the citizen in the state was starkly represented in the COVID-19 pandemic. Was the Prime Minister speaking for England or the UK in his regular press conferences? As the pandemic continued, the national media in London learned about the effects of DAs on public health and local government (Cushion et al 2022). Unable to gain control of the actions of the First Ministers in Scotland and Wales, the Prime Minister refused to speak with them or maintain liaison arrangements. The Prime Minister then began to attack the directly elected mayors in London and the CAs in Greater Manchester and the West Midlands, the latter representing the Government's political party. The focus on privatising the pandemic rather than adhering to the long established emergency planning procedures with local government meant that local leaders, including these mayors, had to manage their own approach through their local directors of public health (Kippin and Morphet 2023; Urban et al 2024). The centralised approach to the pandemic from No 10 Downing Street served to galvanise the substate apparatus, leaving the civil service to appear to be undermined by adopting a centralised approach.

Johnson's response through speeches on 'muscular unionism' (Andrews 2021) was followed by attempts by Prime Ministers Truss and Sunak to reassert the British case and political tradition of the WM and its power hoarding. The Government has reiterated the role of the Union in policy papers and speeches (Sandford 2023). Despite the Conservative party being positive about devolution in 1999, Johnson described devolution as a 'disaster', in the context of the WM being the basis of the UK's administrative apparatus (Warner et al 2021). In this approach, Westminster and Whitehall control has been asserted with the role of the DAs being regarded as 'pageantry' (Martin 2022).

Civil servants in the DAs

After the creation of the DAs in 1999, civil servants in Scotland and Wales remained part of the UK civil service but served ministers of their administrations. Did the allegiances of these civil servants change as their role in the WM was demoted from serving a Cabinet Minister to a First Minister, from the cerebral to the mechanical? Was this a stark difference in practices in comparison with their previous working lives (Parry 2012) or did these relationships replicate a degree of latitude that civil servants based in Scotland, Wales and Northern Ireland had before devolution? Cole (2012) argues that the way in which each nation entered the Union had a major effect on the operation of the government and civil service. In Scotland, the Act of Union in 1707 incorporated a compromise between two systems of law and education which were never unified, whereas in Wales, the Act of Union in 1536 did not allow this variation. In Northern Ireland, the division of the state in 1922, created a separate civil service in Northern Ireland

and these distinctive characteristics have remained. However, despite the centralised character of the UK state, before devolution, there was practical devolution of funding for example to the level of 70 per cent in Wales. At the same time, there was a view that civil servants in Wales were secretive and not locally accountable. The political objectives for devolution sought to make these transactions more open and transparent, so it might have been expected that these civil servants would not have welcomed changes in their reporting arrangements. After devolution the introduction of a Welsh Assembly Government Cabinet meant an increase in the work of civil servants to service the portfolio of each post holder (Cole 2012).

Overall, has devolution affected or influenced the role of the civil service, particularly in Scotland and Wales? Keating and Cairney (2006) have argued that devolution made little or no difference to the civil service in Scotland, despite there being a pre-devolution view that civil servants in the Scottish and Welsh Offices, based in London, had too strong an influence on decision making (Cole 2012.) At the point of implementation of devolution, it was decided that a single civil service should be retained for Great Britain, so that officials could move between national and DAs with Northern Ireland retaining its separate institution. Before devolution, senior civil servants working in Scotland had expected to spend their careers there, with a short time spent in Whitehall, preferably in the Treasury or Cabinet Office, to find out how things work and obtain contacts (Keating and Cairney 2006). However, the recruitment and background of members of the SCS has differed from Whitehall since devolution with more officials in Scotland being born/and or educated there and a high percentage having attended Scottish universities rather than Oxbridge as for senior officials in Whitehall (Keating and Cairney 2006). When devolution was introduced, officials in the Scottish Office based in Scotland were moved into the Executive of the DA. The maintenance of the unified civil service that was said to reflect the concerns about a lack of mobility for the SCS between the DAs and the UK government, was not based on practices (Keating and Cairney 2006) and may rather have been a mechanism to ensure that Whitehall could still place officials in the DAs.

How far has there been policy convergence and learning across the civil servants in the DAs since they were formed? One issue to consider is the introduction of the three DAs was based on asymmetry with the Scotland having more powers than Wales and fewer powers granted to Northern Ireland (Keating et al 2012). Over time, devolved powers have increased in all administrations but they remain asymmetric and not converged to a single model. Since devolution, the DAs have also been excluded from policy discussions by Whitehall and the networking that inevitably occurs in attendance at meetings has reduced (Cairney 2011). The DAs in Scotland and Wales have been developing their own policy capacity since devolution and maintaining contact with each other on issues rather than with London (Clifford and Morphet 2015). In Northern Ireland, the creation of the Assembly was accompanied by other institutional changes with Ireland and the cross border nexus of officials in Armagh has provided a space for discussion and development of joint services in education and health (Heenan 2021). In Northern Ireland there was also a Review of Public Administration which included the transfer of powers from the civil service to local authorities (Knox and Carmichael 2024). This was not welcomed by the Northern Ireland civil service who instituted independent reviews in order to hold on to powers (Morphet 2018), although these were not effective in retaining control.

The opportunity for policy divergence was restricted by the framing of the UK's membership of the EU (Keating 2002; Morphet 2013). In the early period, the 'photocopy' approach to policy replication from London was apparent (Keating et al 2012: 292). The opportunity for difference was through the administration and implementation of these policies and the relative importance given to them within each of the DAs. In all DAs, the civil servants in the executives were not in favour of more internal devolution as part of the changes to Article 5 in the EU treaty after 2009 and considered that they had gone far enough. In Scotland, the Convention between the executive and local authorities, together with the community planning functions at the local level, offered more opportunities for internal devolution.

However, despite the differences in their powers, there has been close working across the DAs together with Ireland on a range of issues through the institutional framing of the British Irish Council (BIC) which was established as part of the initial devolution settlement. The BIC has a public role in the DAs and Ireland while being almost invisible in the UK broadcast news and English media. The BIC chair rotates between the members with the DAs being represented by the First Minister with Ireland, Jersey, Guernsey and the Isle of Man represented by their head of state. There is no separate representative for England at this level and it has been represented as part of the UK by the Deputy Prime Minister and demoted to representation by the First Minister for the Union in the Conservative Government 2022–24. Some significant political moments have occurred at BIC meetings such as the Queen's handshake with Martin McGuinness and the launch of the Dunlop review by Prime Minister May in 2018 but its role has not been acknowledged nationally in the UK. This lack of interest and support on the part of the UK government has not deterred other members of BIC from using the apparatus to discuss and share experience on matters of common interest. Working groups have been established on a range of issues such as planning, drugs and early years (Morphet and Clifford 2018). These groups are proposed by one of the DAs and then reports are prepared for consideration when that member is in the chair. While not explicitly being acknowledged, a number of the topics discussed were of common interest while the UK was a member of the EU, and there was often discussion about how different EU directives and regulations were being implemented in these groups. Where there was a wish to promote a view into Brussels about a specific policy issue, the DAs did not only use the mechanisms available to them through Whitehall but also worked with officials in Dublin to create a second route of influence and lobbying.

Has there been coercive policy transfer between Whitehall and the DAs? While working within the EU, there was no need for Whitehall to exert power. The failure of the independence referendum in Scotland in 2014 was accompanied by a centralising and more coercive approach to local funding which started to insert a wedge between local authorities and their devolved government. With a promise of funding direct from the Treasury in London, for matters that were otherwise devolved, local authorities began to recognise that they now had two sources of funding and priorities (Morphet 2022). Whereas the DA's influence was over policy and direction, together with some directed funding, resources available from London were controlled on an individual project basis while also seeking to commit the DAs to long-term funding to the same projects. This had the effect of reducing DA freedom to use funds in order to support their own priorities. Since Brexit, EU cohesion funding, from which the DAs benefitted in a significant way given their higher levels of deprivation, has been replaced with a more tokenistic levelling up policy and Shared Prosperity funding which was not based on a transparent formula. The local authority deals have been rolled into this, together with a UK-wide approach to managing and monitoring local government in a single system across the UK, through the requirement to pursue a set of Government determined missions set out in LURA 2023. Together, the deals and the monitoring systems can be viewed as a coercive approach to deliver Whitehall-led priorities. This coercion significantly reduces the potential of local authorities to respond to local needs or to implement policies prioritised by the First Ministers. In England this process of measuring and monitoring of local authorities was being led by a newly formed Office for Local Government (OfLog) but the methods for implementation within the DAs were not revealed at the same time. Further, the measurement of the outcome of these missions across local authorities in the whole of the UK appear difficult as the objectives are broad and can only be implemented with central government support.

Devolution in England

There is also a need to consider the governance of and within England. Since devolution in 1999, Cabinet Minsters for functions which are devolved have held a dual mandate for the United Kingdom and for England. This has maintained an Anglo-centric focus on UK-wide policy making and a confusion in the minds of ministers about the extent of their control and responsibilities. This issue was demonstrated in practical terms through the management of COVID-19 when the responsibilities of the DAs allowed them to use different mandates and operational codes in comparison with England.

The development of the reach of the civil service into sub-national institutions of administration has grown significantly since Brexit. The introduction of the deals mentioned above has created programme management committees chaired by Whitehall civil servants for all local authorities in the DAs and for those with deals within England (Morphet 2022). Within the CAs in England, staff supporting the directly elected mayors are now typically secondees or appointees from the civil service rather than from local government (Anderson 2024). There appears to be evidence of these civil servants crowding out local agendas which Mayors of Combined Authorities have with their constituent local authority leaders and being pressured into making decisions without the consultation that the CA governance framework expects. In the leading CAs, Greater Manchester and the West Midlands, mayors have been offered Trailblazer Devolution Deals which will require them to work on policy development and implementation directly with ministers in channels established by civil servants at both the CA and national ends (Morphet and Denham 2023). A settlement for England will be set out in an English Devolution Bill.

The future role of the civil service in drawing together the Union

Since 2014, there has been a significant and growing effort to reduce the powers that were devolved in 1999. This was initially focused on the actions of the DAs but the Dunlop Commission (2018–21) focused on the way that UK state was organised at the centre, with a reassertion of control. Reviews of the civil service also indicate that it is a significant agent of state re-unification (Cabinet Office, Civil Service and DLUHC 2023) and a statement on this role as part of a modern civil service (HM Government 2023).

Conclusions

As Parry (2003: 4) points out, if we consider the significant growth in managerial responsibility for pay and recruitment given to Whitehall departments, then:

> from central civil service management in Whitehall, the DAs are like government departments. In terms of delegation of management

responsibility, they have little more than any Whitehall department or agency ... [T]hose delegations extend to recruitment, pay and grading at all grades below those in the Senior Civil Service, and to the definition of posts in the SCS under common job evaluation methodology.

As Parry further points out, the impact of devolution on the UK civil service, and in particular the prospect of a separate Scottish civil service, is a possible 'sleeper issue'. Major constitutional conflicts involving the devolved civil services of the Welsh and Scottish administrations are not yet apparent (Parry 2008: 413).

7

Policy Formation after Brexit

Introduction

The development of policy to advise Ministers is regarded by the civil service as its main responsibility, with an assumption that this is derived primarily from the application of the Westminster Model (WM) (Richards and Smith 2016; Cooper 2020). Specific government policy that is drawn from party election manifestos provides the starting point for these discussions prior to general elections through access talks (Norris et al 2024). During the course of a government's period in office, requirements for new policies to be formulated relate to events such as the global financial crisis in 2008 (Pautz 2017) and the COVID-19 pandemic. As discussed in Chapter 3, there is rarely, if ever, any consideration of the role and shaping influence on policy of the UK's international obligations as set out in treaties such as those with the EU, WTO and UN. At the point of Brexit, the *Financial Times* estimated that the UK had engaged in 750 treaties and 168 countries were involved (quoted in Larik 2020: 447). These treaty obligations transcend Parliamentary terms and were the main determinant of domestic policy when the UK was part of the EU. The absence of discussion of these significant shapers of policy can be noted in UK public discourse (Morphet 2013) and is described as a wide gulf of incomprehension, illustrated in the EU/UK Balance of Competences Review undertaken prior to the Brexit referendum (Emerson et al 2014). This was also exemplified by the lack of expectation of changes in the Machinery of Government (MoG) after Brexit (Dudley and Gamble 2023).

The implementation of Brexit in 2020 leaves a policy and priorities vacuum in the UK where these were set as part of its EU membership (Gamble 2021). These include a wide range of domestic policies for the environment, employment, trading, consumer and business standards, financial services, immigration, economic support for lagging regions, transport and the quality of the UK's internal institutions to achieve these policies. After Brexit, the UK retained some of its policy obligations with the EU through the Northern Ireland Protocol (McCrudden 2022) and the Trade and Cooperation Agreement 2020 (Peers 2022). In an attempt to fill this vacuum, the UK has rolled over almost all EU law that was operational at the point of exit, 11 pm on 31 December 2020, and appears to be keeping these up to date on a specific website as Retained EU Law (REUL) (Gibson and Cowie 2024). Successive governments have also confirmed that this EU legislation retains primacy over UK legislation in any legal determination. However, this position does not represent dynamic alignment with the EU as it does not include new policy and legislation that has been agreed by the EU since the point of Brexit. At the same time, some of the legislation was dependent on EU treaty obligations to override individual rights such as that for land and property in the Town and Country Planning Act 1947, which allowed land owners to challenge any compulsory purchase orders (CPOs) or refusal to use their land through the legal system. These appeal rights for planning applications and CPOs were removed by EU TEN-T and TEN-E regulations and have not been restored. The legislation remains in place, while the Treaty backing for legislation has been removed (Clifford and Morphet 2023).

While the maintenance of the platform of EU legislation that was operational in 2020 reduces the abrupt rupture to the UK's economy and disruption of extant programmes such as those for transport projects which continued until 2025, there remain major issues about the derivation of new UK policy in those areas which were previously pooled. Further, even less acknowledged, these policies represented the EU's attempt at a coherent approach to regulation and investment across its member states and indicated to each member state, including the UK, where it was lagging behind other members and thus needed to apply specific policy priority. There were examples of this in the post-2008 EU Macroprudential policy programme and in the Cohesion Fund. Further, not only did this process identify which policy areas should be given priority to make good these areas of poorer performance but, like the OECD, the EU advised on the points where institutional strengthening was required as part of these improvements. Once agreed, these programmes, projects and institutional changes were implemented by functional departments who did not then need to make a separate case to the core executive for political time or funding for implementation.

Since leaving the EU, this coherent approach to policy making and the identification of support programmes to address the gaps has appeared to be dormant although the number of civil servants in the Cabinet Office has rapidly increased (Urban et al 2024). It is clear that ministers in some functional departments did not welcome having to enter into EU negotiations in order to determine their approach to domestic policy, although this varied over time. Some recognised that an EU agreement could guarantee resources to their departments without a negotiation with the Treasury. In other cases, civil servants were able to advise on framing and presenting methods for EU policies which aligned with ministers' political ideology. The policies of some departments since Brexit, like Defra, focused on reducing EU standards and much of the legislation not retained was environmental. However, the incoming Labour Government has introduced the Product Regulation and Metrology Bill 2024, which, when passed, might restore some of these regulatory requirements and keep them up to date. In other areas, where major gaps have opened, such as trade with other countries, the UK has adopted a policy of making agreements in a sporadic way. The approach to international affairs has been criticised by former members of the Foreign Office as being non-strategic and colonial in its focus (Fletcher et al 2024).

While there was considerable expectation that procurement legislation would be loosened once the UK left the EU, this failed to recognise that the UK remained a member of the WTO and, as such policies and their implementation for the Government Procurement Agreement and trade continue (Dawar 2018). In this case, the EU's role was to provide assurance of member state compliance to the WTO (Semple 2012). Given the global response to Prime Minister Truss's economic package in September 2022, the role of the IMF is also central to future policy making (Marsh 2023). The UK also has Treaty obligations with the UN on climate change while energy security and commitments to NATO may also become more significant. Other international organisations and individuals such as the OECD, the World Economic Forum and United States' Presidents also have an influence on UK policy making, although with no treaty obligations.

Despite commitments to roll back EU legislation after Brexit, the global trading environment has changed since the UK entered the EU in 1972 and the opportunities for self-determined regulations and trading agreements are far less. In order to maintain international trade, the UK has to operate similar standards which, in the case of the EU, may depend on their dynamic alignment (Armstrong 2018), although this may be addressed by the product Regulation and Metrology Bill 2024. The failure of the UK to agree cooperation on financial services, for example, has led to the relocation of UK jobs to other financial centres in Europe and New York. On domestic policy, there is widening gap between an auto-pilot mode of policy development based on pre-Brexit discussions and relationships and the establishment of mechanisms to create new policy. Given the length of time taken in the preparation of EU legislation, the UK will have participated in some of what was developed before the 2016 referendum for the 2021–27 Cohesion Programme, for example (Bachtler and Mendes 2020). What is less known is whether civil servants can remain informally connected with EU officials and institutions or whether this can occur through proxies such as the OECD (Wright et al 2020). However, being outside the EU offers a different policy context for the UK. In terms of trade, in order to replace the benefits of the membership of the EU single market, the UK has made some trade deals with individual countries such as New Zealand and Australia and other trading blocs such as the Trans Pacific Partnership, although negotiations with Canada stalled over agriculture in 2024. Some of the trading agreements will include policies that will lead to divergence from EU standards.

However, after 50 years of civil servants working in policy development and framing within the EU, where is the new provenance of the UK's policy stimulus and how will the gap created by Brexit be filled? How strong is the UK's international soft power when treaties are being negotiated now that it has left the EU? In terms of UK domestic policy, how aligned does this need to be for the economy, as UK companies want to retain their ability to trade within the EU? The issues in the implementation of the EU border on the island of Ireland have demonstrated how complex this is in practice but there are also longer and more strategic economic issues to consider. Businesses do not want to see their markets being shrunk. As this chapter examines the sources and influences on UK domestic policy making after 2020, it is important to recognise the continuing role of the EU as the UK's largest trading partner and the legislation which is still in place in the UK after Brexit. An attempt to improve trading relationships with the EU was an issue included in the Labour Party's approach to economic growth in the 2024 General Election campaign (Fleming and Parker 2024) and has subsequently been acted upon through new regular relationships between the EU and UK.

It is also noticeable that since the Brexit referendum in 2016, when the UK started to withdraw from making new EU commitments, there has been a growing instability in government (Fletcher et al 2024) and in the relationships between minsters and civil servants. The power dynamic within Whitehall is changing and has yet to settle into a new set of working relationships. The Treasury has stepped into the policy vacuum increasing its control over domestic policy through tighter control of programme and expenditure at national and local levels (Morphet 2022). Functional departments have not established policies that are distinctive from the EU nor given this high priority as they have been able to retain most EU legislation. Within the Whitehall system, functional departments do not have sufficient power to progress new or replacement policies without strong support from the core executive, while deviations from the retained EU legal platform in the UK are closely monitored by a range of interest groups and institutions. Where EU membership provided a policy coherence across much of the UK's domestic agenda and within Whitehall departments, new arrangements are being tested. These have included having a strong Prime Minister in Boris Johnson, who set an agenda without discussion in Cabinet and expected the Whitehall departments to fill in the gaps created through his policy announcements (Brown 2020; Hayton 2022). There was no coherence between policies and no sense of following through these announcements with wider support across government or through the Treasury. Another experiment in how the government should be run was through the short premiership of Liz Truss when the civil service was pushed to the edge, in an echo of the Thatcher view that the civil service prevented change in its centralised position (Cliffe 2022). The Sunak premiership has been one that was dominated by external influences, through donors and think tanks leaving an incoherent set of policy announcements. In these post-Brexit experiments in government styles, as viewed through the lens of the role of the Prime Minister, the role of the civil service has been weak and perceived as not being able to check the operational changes in the constitutional model as set out in the WM (Sergeant et al 2023).

The role of the EU in shaping UK domestic policy 1972–2020

The role and extent to which the UK's membership of the EU and the UK's membership of the WTO have influenced its domestic policy programme has been seldom discussed in British public policy reviews (Morphet 2013; 2021a). This is in part because the links have not been openly acknowledged by civil servants or ministers and attempts to discuss them have been actively discouraged. These policy negotiations were also transactional in character and differ from domestic policy making. Further, the long tail of time that it required for these policy negotiations – sometimes between 10 and 15 years – means that there are now temporal and political challenges to be considered (Kingdon and Stano 1984) as these policy certainties have been removed. During the internationalised and opaque process of negotiation between the UK and other institutions, these long time spans lead to a lack of public awareness of the discussions underway (Goetz and Meyer-Sahling 2013). When policies are finally agreed, their implementation has been fashioned by civil servants to sit within a domestic narrative and disassociated from their wider contexts (Morphet 2013).

While a member of the EU, the UK would have been aware of developments where it had retained policy competencies or had EU targets to implement such as in e-government, where it took its advice from Australia rather than the EU member states. However, it is also the case that a vast tract of policy would have been sourced within EU discussions and considered by the civil service as it affected the UK domestic policy narrative rather than being a policy idea generated internally. These EU policies provided confidence to the civil service in relation to their implementation and meant less Whitehall competition for policy space and Treasury funding.

This confidence also allowed the civil service to generate domestic policies in the knowledge that they had to be accepted and implemented. The main challenge was to find a policy formulation and framing that would align with contemporaneous political ideology and ministerial preferences. Outside the EU, the UK needs to make choices about policy development and selection without this certainty. The UK may choose to retain its alignment with the EU but be outside the policy discussions or work more actively with the OECD to influence its work and, through this, its relationship with the EU (Wright et al 2020).

International sources of UK government policy post-Brexit

Treaties and obligations

Although seldom discussed, much of the development and delivery of government policy by civil servants is to implement the UK's international treaty obligations (see Chapter 3). Although some of these are fixed at the time that they were signed, others are more dynamic with evolving principles and application methods. In some cases, such as financial regulation, the UK was both bound by its membership of the EU and also through its other bilateral agreements (Poulsen 2017). For the UK's agreements as part of the WTO on issues such as public procurement and trade and environment, the EU acted as a means of assuring member state compliance through the adoption of their own parallel regime in the European single market which went further than the WTO requirements. Other matters in these WTO treaties including state aid and procurement remain (McGowan 2023).

One of the key issues for the UK Government post-Brexit is to determine how far they should redefine their relationships within these international treaties. There could be greater dependence on them or should there be a maintained alignment with the EU as it remains a key trading market for the UK? There may be damage to the UK economy if the divergence is too great, with companies having to use parallel sets of regulations in order to do business outside the UK. In some areas such as investment and taxation, there may be incentives to determine a more attractive financial environment for investors and businesses, often called making London Singapore-on-Thames (Nesvetailova et al 2017). However, as the short-lived Truss government demonstrated, any attempts to step away too far from a conventional financial and economic policy can result in a run on the markets and retreat.

When the UK exited the EU, there were a range of views about what the implications would be of continued WTO membership arrangements and commitments. There were some arguments that this meant that the UK would have to renegotiate some its existing arrangements and agreements, particularly those which were operational across the whole of the EU rather than earlier agreements which the UK entered into individually even within its early days of membership of the EU (Bartels 2016).

In addition to the powers and obligations on the UK from existing treaties, Brexit has also opened up a space for the negotiation of new international treaties for the UK. This is an emerging legal context and requires that the civil service has or acquires new skills. The creation of new treaties can be driven by the political ideology of the government such as that with Rwanda for receiving UK asylum seekers and migrants, or can be for trade such as the treaties agreed with New Zealand and Australia. Without its membership of the EU, the UK has to develop and negotiate its treaties independently, and as Poulsen (2017) points out, most treaties are for 10 years after which they can be unilaterally terminated. Most of the UK Investments treaties are older than 10 years and there is a growing practice of treaty parties exercising their withdrawal options or threatening to do so unless better terms are offered, for example India. There are also new arrangements within the EU which may build on the existing bilateral cooperation agreement between the UK and France for defence and through the new European governments group established by President Macron.

Influencers and policy diffusion

In addition to the formal obligations for policy and delivery set through treaties, the UK is a member of many other international organisations which provide advice, research, comparisons and benchmarks. They provide opportunities for policy transfer between states as civil servants are able to compare and contrast experience of effectiveness and messaging for policy delivery through discussions framed by these international organisations. The extent to which other states that might act as a reference point for the UK may also be an influencing factor in their creation as a norm (Towns 2012) and one that civil servants can use with ministers in their advice on policy administration. These norms might also have an element of force or coercion to comply as part of wider influencing of decision making.

While not an organisation with binding treaty implications for the UK, the OECD has a role in assessing and comparing different policies and programmes of their members and their effectiveness in practice. The OECD also provides templates and guidance such as those used for investment regulations between countries (Poulsen 2017). The UK is a founder member of the OECD and the organisation provides research and comparative performance data between its member states on a wide range of issues that have an economic impact including taxation, transport, housing, education, skills and sub-national governance. Much of the OECD's work is derived from comparisons on the effectiveness in policy selection and adoption. It comes to conclusions about effective management and delivery in government but has no powers to see any of these practices put into effect. However, as White (2020) has shown, the OECD, like other international organisations, can have a considerable influence on domestic policy making, although this can vary between states. Further, cross-memberships with other supra-national organisations such as the IMF or World Bank can create a stronger influencer role for OECD. Working in alignment, if not explicitly together, these organisations can create a policy climate that can establish norms or a range of actions within boundaries that are established through the OECD's work. These use soft power and there is a tendency for states to move together in matters of public policy such as health. White (2020) describes them as epistemic actors who create the knowledge space within which domestic policy decisions are taken and post-Brexit, these actors may take on a more important role for the UK. However, this should be seen in the context of UK exceptionalism which is most apparent in economic and financial policy. There is a view from parts of the UK core executive that as founders of these international institutions, the UK should not be rule takers but rule makers where they are concerned. This may create difficulties in the development of policy in the post-Brexit period.

Other sources of policy advice and influence are derived from policy transfer, policy communities and policy diffusion (Marsh and Sharman 2009). These processes may be regarded as less attractive to governments who have criticised the use of experts and they may prefer to depend on their own policy advisers. In the definition provided by Dolowitz and Marsh (2000: 5), policy transfer is a process by which: 'knowledge about policies, administrative arrangements, institutions and ideas in one political setting (past or present) is used in development of policies, administrative arrangements, institutions and ideas in another political setting'. This suggests a deliberate method of seeking to use wider policy experience in developing domestic policies. However, agenda setting (Kingdon and Stano 1984) might also serve to set the menu of options to be considered and which states most closely align institutionally or politically to the domestic landscape. Whose priorities are being used to frame the issues where policies are required (Cairney and Kippin 2023)? The broader agenda for considering policies which are seen to be acceptable or successful in achieving the objectives or enabling a successful implementation from wider political objectives or international obligations and public acceptance also have to be considered.

Much of the formal policy exchange will be hosted by organisations such as the OECD but think tanks who commission research which is line with their own objectives are growing in influence. Policy convergence may also be used as a 'pick and mix' approach where policies are chosen for a specific reason – including political alignment or public acceptance – where there may be no other similarity in the policy regimes of the states. There can also be convergence at different scales of policy such as for taxation, immigration and health care policies, and there may need to be policy convergence for countries to work together to achieve their different objectives. There may also be a perceived need to emulate others for fear of being left behind, and here the role of organisations such as the World Economic Forum can be influential (Jakobi 2012). At its annual meeting in Davos, world leaders can explore ideas for change outside their immediate domestic context. There is also an issue as to whether this use of policy diffusion or convergence is outwardly acknowledged. In some cases, political leaders used the example of Thatcher to change the size of their state (Lee and Strang 2006). In other countries, including the UK, such open emulation might be less acceptable and international comparisons have been used on a selective basis such as on health outcomes, educational attainment or taxation.

What was the role of the civil service in developing policy and administration when the UK was in the EU?

While there has been much discussion as to whether the UK was prepared for the pooling of a range of policy areas when the UK joined the EU, 'The British public was still too near to the glory of empire to accept the role for Britain of just another country in Europe' (letter form Lord Home to Edwin Plowden 1985 quoted in Plowden 1989: 172). And making the case for Britian to be at the top table required the UK to demonstrate to the US that it was not part of Europe, stated Ernest Bevin (Plowden 1989: 172).

There is a range of contemporaneous evidence that demonstrates that the issue was considered in the major debates before UK entry on 1 January 1973 and before the second referendum on remaining in the EU in 1975 (Oliver 2015). There was also comment about the ways in which membership would affect the role of the civil service in making policy as it changed parliament's role in the legislative process, which Herman and Alt (1975) describe as making it more an international than national process. However, what was unknown from the outset was how a blame culture might be used to downplay policies which the UK did not like or how new protocols for cabinet decision making might be developed.

Subsequently, the civil service engaged in policy development and delivery at a range of scales in government – from the role of UK's permanent and seconded representatives in Brussels (UKREP) (Kassim 2001), including COREPER (Bostock 2002). These agreements were passed to the core executive, particularly the Cabinet Office who managed the transition from Brussels to London, pre-packaging policies before passing them to functional departments for their administration (Thomas 2008). In some policy areas, such as agriculture and the environment, the role of the EU in UK policy delivery was well known. In others, including aspects of transport, less so. Initially, there was a civil service fast stream route for stagiaires in the EC

(Shore and Thedval 2023) with additional language and coaching to pass the EC's entrance exams. However, after periods in Brussels, civil servants found that their experience and knowledge was not recognised in domestic policy making when they returned and the initiative was ended.

The challenges after Brexit

The anti-expert rhetoric of successive governments since the Brexit referendum, accompanied by criticism of the civil service, undermined any public debate on the ways in which policy is developed in the future. However, there has been an overt recognition that the UK economy requires some stability in its policy and regulatory framework. A proposal to abolish EU law in a sunset clause within the EU Retained Law (Revocation and Reform) Act 2023 was removed and replaced by retention of most legislation apart from some specific exceptions (Diamond and Richardson 2023).

Commentators have now started to identify the need for a strategic approach for policy making (UK in a Changing Europe 2024) with no clear responsibilities for addressing potential gaps in legislation that emerge over time. The only response appears to have been a large increase in Cabinet Office staff although with no transparency on their activities (Urban et al 2024). There is also a need to maintain relationships with the EU on policies and the responsibilities for these are split between the Cabinet Office and the Foreign, Commonwealth and Development Office. The UK is in danger of entering a policy void.

Political

One of the greatest challenges in developing policy after Brexit is the mantra of 'taking back control' (Dudley and Gamble 2023). Brexit was a political process and the resulting context is one where the civil service needs to review each of these issues and present ministers with options. This is a large administrative burden (Poulsen 2017) and one where specialist skills may not be available to the civil service. Those political leaders intent on implementing Brexit did not trust experts or use their experience to prepare for change, and this continued subsequently. There was no programme for departmental or issue reviews and there is a danger of the government and the civil service 'muddling through' (Diamond 2023a) in a responsive rather than programmed and proactive mode.

There were suggestions that Brexit would overwhelm the civil service in both the negotiation, assessing the full load of implications across the operation of the UK state, and also in the preparation of replacement policies where capacity had been directed to negotiation in addition to policy development (Fahy et al 2017). There were different phases after the referendum. The first was during the period of negotiations which were led in a politically charged environment during which there were three Prime Ministers – Cameron, May and Johnson. The MoG was used to create a new department, the Department for Exiting the European Union (DExEU) which was intended to be short lived. The churn among civil servants in this department was high. Democratic and constitutional changes were also to the fore in Brexit (Lloyd 2019).

The COVID-19 pandemic meant that there was not much time or capacity to consider preparations for post-Brexit policy, despite the rhetoric of the UK regaining control. While political positions varied between dynamic alignment and pressure for a complete exit from all EU agreed polices, there remained the issue of how the UK would function in a post-Brexit world that differed from that which existed in 1972. The globalisation of trade and standards together with formal economic alliances are different. This period also experienced a growth in service industries and international regulation, with companies using transfer methods for locations with tax benefits. As financial services were excluded from the post-Brexit Trade and Cooperation Agreement (TCA) with the EU, the UK has experienced considerable economic consequences. In the face of this early post-Brexit experience and the run on the UK markets in the Truss period, the Conservative government appeared to soften its view of complete separation, although this still left opposition from the business sector, normally Conservative party allies (Diamond and Richardson 2023). This also had effects on wider international relations as the EU's global network of offices was used by many member states as part of their own networks and the UK no longer had access to these.

Trust

A further issue that has a longer term impact as a consequence of Brexit has been a breakdown in trust between the Conservative Party in government and the civil service (Dudley and Gamble 2023). As David Davies attested in 2018, there were no Permanent Secretaries who voted for Brexit and this was symptomatic of the open hostility of the government for the civil service that had not been experienced before. The necessity of increasing civil service capacity to deal with the detail of Brexit came after a period of austerity since 2010 (Lloyd 2019). This has been seen as part of the breakdown of the WM where the civil service maintained an independent position (Eleftheriadis 2017). The response has not been a major change in the machinery of government or civil service structures to manage de-Europeanisation of the British legal structures but rather an incremental approach. This is through addressing issues as they emerge (Diamond 2023a) rather than taking a systemic approach through the competencies held by each government department, mirroring the process of their introduction (Bulmer 2013). Others present evidence to demonstrate that the UK is maintaining links with EU policy discussions and adopting approaches that are remaining in alignment such as in police and judicial cooperation matters (Wolff and Piquet 2022). Further, there appears to be no examination of gaps in skill sets nor any attempt to use those experts who understood in more detail the effects of Brexit in the areas and expressed the issues both before and after the referendum (Diamond and Richardson 2023).

The extent to which the UK civil service was prepared for Brexit with contingency plans was regarded as low (Evans 2018). The government made it clear during the referendum campaign that it was not going to plan for Brexit apart from the Treasury to manage any financial instability. This was in stark contrast with the scale of preparation undertaken for the 1975 referendum on maintaining EU membership under the Wilson Government (Evans 2018), although this might have been seen as a continuation of the preparations during the long period of negotiation for UK membership previously. Then the contingency planning group established was restricted in size by the Treasury and economic contingency planning was left to them. Even after such a short period of membership, it was identified in 1975 that withdrawal would be a highly complex issue, which was compounded in 2016 after nearly 50 years of membership, in a process of path dependency (Diamond and Richardson 2023). The civil service did not have the capacity to understand the extent to which UK withdrawal from the EU would affect policy because the lack of transparency about EU policy making within the country was similar inside the civil service. Here the management of negotiations for EU policies was handled by the core executive, only involving the functional departments when they had agreed an approach. This was then often presented to functional departments as domestic policy rather than as implementation of what had been agreed within the EU. This meant that both before and after Brexit, many functional departments had no idea that they had been implementing EU regulations and directions. In areas such as transport, the EU regulations that the UK was implementing covered all transport policy from strategic routes to local transport schemes. The same was true for employment and economic regeneration and, in health, the application of no smoking policy was little understood as an EU policy. For those departments where the vast majority of their functional activities were pooled by the UK within the EU, this was unexpected. It also demonstrated how far the functional departments and the Secretary of State were not in charge of policy and were given their priorities within a Whitehall system where the Cabinet Office and Treasury remained dominant. Yet while the Brexit vote was one for a major change in the UK, the WM has continued with no change or preparations for the future (Diamond 2023a; UK in a Changing Europe 2024).

What are the policy implementation challenges post-Brexit?

While the evidence is that in the short term, there will be alignment between EU and UK policies for economic and capacity reasons, there are also some challenges posed for the civil service for the transposition of policy into delivery. When the UK was a member of the EU, the strategic departments had a long preview and engagement in their development of forthcoming policy. During negotiations it was possible to consider not only what was best for the UK in general but how the emerging policies would fit within the political ideology of the then and any future government and how it should be framed in this context. The implementation period for EU Directives, for example, was always given as 7 years to allow for political change in implementation. The ability of the core executive to frame policy and package it as part of other government episodes such as Spending Reviews, manifestos or machinery of government changes helped to mask its provenance.

The removal of this longer-term policy trajectory will present issues for the core executive and their ability to secure policy delivery and implementation when it is not backed by treaty obligations. This will provide particular problems for the centre of government and the functional departments when dealing with the Treasury, who will have greater control over decisions for expenditure without these obligations. Further, there will be few if any long term projects, particularly for infrastructure. The UK Treasury has a different approach to accounting for capital investment than any other OECD country and has a mindset based in revenue expenditure, that is, government spending being funded from that year's income. The TEN-T transport networks were set in EU Regulations, on which there was no discretion about implementation, although there was flexibility on modal improvements and specific routing. This was expenditure that the Treasury had to agree while the UK was in the EU which is no longer the case. The UK is set in an economic ideology of short termism where each project is at the whim of the Treasury.

In the longer term, there may be a move to develop policies in the orbital Europeanisation model. Otherwise, the UK will have to develop its own policy community that may be subject to the ebb and flow of political ideologies of government and Parliament. The policies that derive from treaties such as the WTO and UN will exist but these do not cover all aspects of government's work. There are ways in which civil servants can engage with practitioner and expert communities, although governments have different views about these. There will be pressures from think tanks and donors that may be more difficult to resist without the baseline commitments and policy trajectories from the EU. There may be the opportunity to take policies from the work of the OECD and the IMF but these face Treasury disinterest. There are other international policy drivers expressed through the World Economic Forum or working with other countries and learning from their experience. This will depend on some synchronicity of political alignment such as between the Trump government and the Johnson administration.

When the UK was in the EU, it also had the opportunity to influence policy development through anticipatory implementation and become first time movers. This would subsequently be less costly when final implementation was agreed with fewer transition costs and would allow the UK government and consultants to sell their services to other EU member states to support implementation of the same legislation.

A further challenge is the extent to which the EU integrates its policies across a range of its core objectives. This can be seen in competition policy (McGowan 2023). While the European Commission has been criticised for being silo based, within each of its Directorates General, it has taken steps to start to reduce that policy separation through a focus on the spatial application of policies and how they interact in practice through delivery. The UK will no longer have this focus on policy integration to frame its own policy development if it decides to move away from EU policy and this may have some critical impacts.

Conclusions

In terms of UK policy making post-Brexit, Dudley and Gamble (2023) argue that the UK is on a course that will see it align with EU policies even if it has no part in their formation and does not agree them through any institutional process, although reengagement may occur in the future (Wolff and Piquet 2022). There is a vacuum at the heart of government policy making after Brexit. There is also a sense of auto-pilot with those EU policies discussed for the 2020 Cohesion programme emerging as similar missions in the LUWP and LURA 2023. Dudley and Gamble (2023) describe this as policy drift with no overt response to fill this gap from the Conservative government. For the civil service, this might be a return to their operational practices before 1972, but even here the role of EU economic and social policy was influencing UK political policy directions.

Does the UK find itself in a situation of 'orbital Europeanisation' (McGowan 2023) or 'satellite cooperation' (Wolff and Piquet 2022), because the influence of the EU, as the world's third largest trading grouping, is simply too big to ignore or avoid? It is no longer possible to adopt a separatist approach and the UK may be forced to adopt the trading rules of one of these other groups if not the EU. Any reforms may be costly and may not be in alignment with existing practices. It is potentially a more efficient approach to align to the EU as the UK already has a system that is in conformity with it.

There is emerging evidence that a continuation of past cooperation practices exist and post-Brexit domestic policies are being rebranded as new replacements for previous EU policy, such as 'levelling up' as a replacement for the EU Cohesion programme including structural funds (McGowan 2023). In this specific case, which has at its heart state aid rules, which are also tied into international trading agreements through the WTO (Ehlermann and Goyette 2006), there was an agreement between the EU and UK on these matters as part of the Withdrawal Agreement (2019), subsequent Trade and Cooperation Agreement (2020) and the Subsidy Control Act 2022. Yet, in the pro-Brexit campaigns, EU state aid rules were seen to be one of the measures that were restrictive and fettered UK decision making, particularly in the delivery of its industrial strategy. However, this is an example of where the UK is obliged to have state aid rules as part of its policies through its treaty obligations to the WTO, and because of a continuing need to ensure business can trade with the EU, it becomes simpler to maintain the EU approach in this orbiting approach and remains the default position of the UK government (McGowan 2023).

8

Civil Service: Weaknesses and Failures

Introduction

While the civil service is proud to retain its reputation, there have been an increasing number of failures in central government policy and its administration which are in the public domain and cannot entirely be attributed to ministers. In this chapter the weaknesses and failures of the civil service in relation to its primary responsibility in advising minsters is discussed. As we have noted earlier, the practices of the Westminster Model (WM) have focused on the preparation of policy rather than its administration which is still regarded as a mechanical function (Haldane 1918). While civil service reforms by successive Prime Ministers have focused on attempts to rebalance these responsibilities, the policy role remains dominant. However, ministers have not been content with this lack of response to their pressures for more focus on policy administration and have instead increased the special advisers (SpADs) available to each minister (Yong and Hazell 2014). While the WM is a triumvirate between ministers, civil servants and Parliament, this no longer represents the operational practices of Whitehall, with two parties providing advice in ministerial offices.

This chapter considers the conditions within which the administration of policy is made including civil service culture, lack of institutional memory, short-termism and relationships with ministers. The second part of the chapter considers more explicit factors which have led to failures in government which might have been avoided if the civil service had been more focused on the administration of policy rather than its development. There is also a consideration of who is holding the government and the civil service to account – particularly Parliamentary Select Committees and the National Audit Office (NAO), though recommendations of neither are binding. Examples of these failures can be found in a range of studies (Runciman 2004; Hood 2011; King and Crewe 2014) but despite continuing efforts to change the culture of the civil service to reduce the risk of these failures reoccurring, a continuing pattern exists and there is no focus on righting the wrongs that have been visited on individuals and organisations. In Chapter 4, there is a discussion about the choices available to the civil service in the administration of policy. This chapter considers in more detail how these choices may lead to mistakes and failures.

The context for decision making

In the WM, the civil service has responsibility for providing advice, ministers decide on its implementation. This gap has been widening since the Brexit referendum in 2016 as Parliamentary Bills have increasingly become scaffolds on which decisions about their implementation are left to secondary legislation through Statutory Instruments (SIs) (Cave and Gibson 2024). While there is a process for SIs to be considered in Parliament, it is rare for this to be the case. This also means that there is less public awareness about changes in legislation and little public discourse, leaving the administration of policy vulnerable in practice. This lack of focus has concerned successive Prime Ministers, increasingly from the post-1945 period onward (King and Crewe 2014). Prime Ministers have made attempts to refocus the civil service towards delivery, including through the Fulton Committee (1968), CPRS (James 1986), Next Steps Agencies (Haddon 2012), Citizen's Charter (Pollitt 1994), joined-up government (Pollitt 2003), civil service reviews (Maude 2014, 2023), proposals to have ministerial advisory groups (Maude 2014), and external appointments to the civil service (Barberis 1996b). Of all ministerial interventions to gain support for policy advice, it is through the appointment of SpADs (King and Crewe 2014) where change has been most persistent and administration more politicised.

The role of policy and its administration as part of the work of government is scrutinised by Select Committees in Parliament and by the NAO, which is independent, also reporting to Parliament. However, while recommendations made by Select Committees or the NAO require a public response from government, ministers are not mandated to implement them and few are translated into policy or action. King and Crewe (2014) argue that despite being thorough and non-partisan, these two methods of assessment are considered in silos rather than within government as a whole, meaning that the 'why' question of what has been undertaken is not addressed.

In functional departments, greater regulation has been introduced within a public interest narrative (Hood et al 2000; James 2003), through quasi-independent bodies including performance management of local authorities, the role of Ofsted in regulating schools and the Care Quality Commission (Smithson et al 2018). This distances government's role of providing resources and setting operational frameworks which may contribute to poor performance and allows for 'blame-dumping' on other parts of the public sector (Hood 2011). Departments also have a role in appointing and framing regulatory activity.

Government policy has to consider reports from coroners, tribunals and inquiries but there is evidence that by lengthening the time between the receipt of reports to dealing with the recommendations, a gap is generated between public concern about issues and their remedies (Hood 2011). This means that they can be only partly implemented. There appears to be a reluctance to admit that the government has had responsibility for failure, leading to an unwillingness to learn from it. The short-termism of both ministerial and civil service appointments means that institutional learning is not valued and lost in the 'now-ism' of any specific ministerial and departmental activity. Relying on what has gone before is not a way to gain promotion. There appears to be little interest in not repeating previous failures or rectifying them, while these failures may be inbuilt into the institutional design of government (Gains and John 2010; Bevan 2023).

Overall, there appears to be no method that has been devised that has had any effect on civil service culture which was expressed clearly by Bunbury (1928) and has been reinforced since. Each new Prime Minister makes statements about change and implements some means of achieving it but there is little evidence that any of these approaches are long lasting (Bovaird and Russell 2007). It suggests that more fundamental change is required potentially through who defines powers and responsibilities in more detail and/or a reform of the constitution, changing the allocation of responsibilities within the WM (Denham and Morphet 2024).

When there is a failure in government then how is it understood and is there any process by which future similar risks can be avoided? The civil servant who developed and advised on the policy is almost certainly two or three jobs on from the time spent working on the failing policy and it is unlikely that they participated in determining its administration, which would have been passed to less senior officials to manage or to contractors through an outsourced process (Morphet 2021a). If the delivery failure is by contractors, a review of contract specifications and monitoring by the client – that is the civil servant who is responsible for the contract – is required. The specification may enable the contractors to maximise their income through focusing on those parts of the contract which are easier to fulfil, frequently referred to as 'low hanging fruit' which, in effect, skews the operation of the contract. The Windrush scandal is an example of this (Gentleman 2019), where the West Indian community had their papers destroyed by the Home Office, then later this lack of evidence of leave to remain in the UK allowed the contractors to reach deportation targets by focusing on this group precisely because they did not have this proof.

To improve change in government, project management methodology was introduced by the Gershon Review (Erridge 2000). This is used to implement a physical outcome such as a building or organisational change. Project management is used across a range of sectors and has common features. A project board is established, which might include stakeholders from other functional departments impacted by the project and an official is appointed as a Senior Responsible Owner (SRO) for the project. At specific points in the project, there are 'gateway' reviews undertaken by those independent of it. These coincide with the Treasury's Green Book (HMT 2022) on project implementation. Not all public policy administration will use this methodology for implementation and there is little assessment of project management in practice. Given the civil service's view that any technique or tool is subject to being bent to the will of the outcome, then critical project boards and SROs can be 'refreshed', gateway reviews managed and project outcome objectives changed as projects progress.

If failure in government does occur, then how is blame allocated and what are the strategies for avoidance? Hood (2011) argues that, like much civil service practice, this is learned on the job rather than through training in risk management. Blame avoidance can be considered in three categories – 'presentational', which attempts to spin the blame, 'agency' that transfers the blame to another organisation and 'policy' which argues that no one is really responsible for what went wrong (Hood 2011: 18). King and Crewe (2014) considered how 'blunders' in government are reviewed and investigated. They found that the reviews focused on the questions of 'what' goes wrong rather than the 'why' questions (p xiii) to prevent mistakes being made again.

One of the key components of Senior Civil Service (SCS) 'control' of policy is civil service short termism, inward focus and being self-referential (King and Crewe 2014). There is little institutional memory in departments which could embody the culture and principles of their bureaucracies, learning from past failures when formulating new policies. Institutional memory can be based on narratives and sagas that become more specific in their lessons incrementally (Painter 2013; Corbett et al 2020), with only some related to experience and 'lessons to be remembered' being foregrounded over time. Cultural memory is socially constructed and not an objective form of institutional learning (Corbett et al 2020). It uses a purposeful process of agenda management through emphasis of past narratives which may reflect on heroic individuals (Bailey and Lloyd 2017; Stark 2019). These narratives become embedded and reinforced, becoming a synecdoche, a mention of which evokes a specific position within the cultural mythology, and are institutionalised (Linde 2015) as static points of reference (Corbett et al 2020).

Progression within an organisation with this culture requires acceptance and repetition of the values these narratives represent. When new policies are required, then past models can be useful as they offer efficiency and speed in being used again, albeit with different names. However, the selection of policies may not be related to their purpose but to an understanding of how their introduction affected the reputation of the department, together with any negative consequences for those administering the policies. Policy selection can be based on this library of memory, which is focused on government inputs rather than policy outputs or outcomes. The longest memories of policy purpose and effectiveness of its delivery can reside outside the SCS with experts and policy networks (Corbett et al 2020) but their contribution can be suppressed, undermined or derided.

While the SCS has a strong culture, the memory for functional departments is less. The churn of 18-month to 3-year postings and character of fast stream members, described as competent and self-reliant with no tendency to 'reach back in time' (member of the SCS being interviewed and quoted in Stark 2019: 150) create no value on situated memory or in annual reviews or promotion boards. Institutional memory is a function of bureaucracies (Pollitt 2009) with punctuations in civil service practice such as Next Steps Agencies weakening ties to the experience of administration (Hood and Lodge 2006; Marsh 2011). Where civil servants have been required to work in more integrated and collaborative ways across government, these new working relationships had no precedent and subsequently disappeared (Corbett et al 2020).

While institutional memory in the SCS might be expected to be a valued principle, it is in conflict with an inward looking dynamic. There is little or no evidence that the SCS is concerned with the effectiveness of policies as they relate to citizens or institutions (Bailey and Lloyd 2017), although lip service may be paid to this (Dunleavy 1991). Instead, focus is on the conceptualisation of their role within government (Bevir and Rhodes 2010) and its continuity (Stark 2019). Further, Pollitt (2009) has suggested that, in the post-Thatcher period, there has been a new 'contempt for the past' (p 207), reinforced by the experience of the Brexit Referendum (2016) and the description of the civil service as the 'blob' characterised by an adherence to past values and practices (Robinson 2014).

What is the role of civil service in the failure to successfully administer government policy?

In considering how government projects and services fail, points of weakness can be identified through the process of the development of policy by civil servants and its relationship with subsequent administration. Why do things go wrong?

Policy design

In the WM there are differences in objectives and responsibilities of civil servants and their ministers including measurement of success in promoted policies. For civil servants, the main focus is in demonstrating to ministers that they are in charge of their brief and do not need additional experts to bring before Ministers to provide advice (Bailey and Lloyd 2017). Civil servants focus on advice on policy options that ministers can consider including their presentation and the ease with which they may be able to attract time in government, agreement in Cabinet and funding from the Treasury. Civil servants in functional departments are competitive and are not incentivised to bring forward policies that include other departments (King and Crewe 2014). Success for civil servants might include piloting a bill through Parliament, experience of which is associated with promotion. Once these tasks have been completed, civil servants expect promotion to their next posting, leaving administration of their policy to lower grade colleagues. Ministers may be, but not necessarily, concerned with policy or legislation implementation as part of their policy narrative. Who will be included in this policy, how will they receive its benefits and will its successful implementation be attributed to the minister, the government or the political party at the time of the next election?

Attempts to introduce training in the relationship between policy making and administration have occurred since Fulton (1968) and included the establishment and demise of the Civil Service College (2010), together with a period of the National School of Government. In the College, there was no feedback to SCS participants of their progress and development as a result of their attendance, with 'training' being regarded as only appropriate for mechanical and specific tasks (Goslin 1979). Instead, civil servants have increasingly employed management consultants who understand how policies can be administered but may never meet the ministers responsible for policies they are employed to deliver.

The Major reforms challenged the civil service, but focus was switched to local government. Blair introduced civil service reform targeting policy design and delivery with customers and stakeholders (Bovaird and Russell 2007). Domestic policy changes were led by Chancellor Gordon Brown using funding to achieve the government's political ends. This included pressure on functional departments to work together. Focus on civil service performance making these policies work was significant and not welcomed (Heywood 2021). The introduction of public service performance agreements and the PM's Delivery Unit were seen as attempts to demote civil servants into mechanistic delivery while policy was retained by ministers with advice from SpADs. Policies were evaluated for their outcome effectiveness so that lessons could be learned for the future.

The push towards a Coalition government by Cabinet Secretary Gus O'Donnell was interpreted as an attempt to move away from the Labour government's focus on delivery to a narrower agenda (Urban et al 2024). Within the Coalition, every issue had to be considered by both parties and slowed policy development. It also returned the role of civil servants to policy away from performance agreements. After 2015, at the end of the Coalition government, the Conservative government had no policy programme and its administration was quickly consumed by Brexit, followed by the COVID-19 pandemic, Partygate and the Truss 2022 financial crisis.

The focus to incorporate delivery into policy design did not disappear as a political objective. Policy Labs were introduced in 2014 through the Cabinet Office, to transform 'policymaking by demonstrating new tools and techniques, generating new knowledge and skills, and facilitating a long-term shift in policymaking practice' (Bailey and Lloyd 2017: 2). This approach represented an attempt at cultural change away from civil service norms of generalists to a more professional approach to evidence, options, evaluation and co-design with recipients. These were regarded as 'tools and techniques' of policy making and it is here that they come into conflict with the culture of the civil service (Chapman and O'Toole 1995). As research by Bailey and Lloyd (2017) demonstrates, the currency of senior officials is to be ahead of ministers and provide Prime Ministers with convincing assurances that problems can be solved (pp 6–7). This culture overrides professional policy design approaches and reinforces 'artful innovations' (p 7) by senior officials who are individualistic and consistent with SCS culture. The norm is that only 'clever' people can achieve the most senior positions in the hierarchy. The culture is managing upwards rather than a consideration of policy recipients. In their study, Bailey and Lloyd interviewees admitted they never considered recipients of policy in design. Their focus was its management through government to the point of delivery (p 7). Policy design tools were regarded as useful but not perceived as important compared with traditional methods and should not replace them.

Managing ministers

Some policy failures relate to civil service advice to ministers, although this may relate to the minister's personality. Before the growth of SpADs, civil servants were principle advisers (King and Crewe 2014) through briefings comprising of essays and textual counterpoints (Bailey and Lloyd 2017). Their role was to alert ministers of pitfalls or likely poor reception (Shergold 2015). While there is competition between functional departments, this can also be between ministers for the Prime Minister's attention. Ministers may be appointed to deliver specific mandates (King and Crewe 2014) or lose interest once announced or legislation has been passed (Barberis

1996b). Civil servants around ministers reflect what is important to them and a Ministerial lack of interest in policy administration lowers its status. Further, ministers, like Permanent Secretaries, cannot have knowledge of all departmental responsibilities, relying on civil servants when crises arise. Incorrect civil service briefings used to inform Parliament have led to ministerial resignations from both main parties (Beverley Hughes in 2004 and Amber Rudd in 2018). Further, the increasingly short time ministers have within a job means that they seldom become fully acquainted with their responsibilities. This is significantly different from practices in other countries, particularly Germany (King and Crewe 2014). While there are arguments that shorter ministerial postings enable ministers to take a pan-government view, ministers may become more reliant on the advice of their civil servants. Aware of short term appointments, ministers may promote headline-grabbing policies in order to make an impact with the Prime Minister, leading to promotion, rather than considering their departmental responsibilities (Riddell 2019).

When ministers or Prime Ministers seize on policies, such as Thatcher and the poll tax, it becomes difficult for ministers and civil servants to argue against or, perhaps more importantly, to undertake stress tests before implementation (Smith 1991). King and Crewe (2014) found civil servants were increasingly reluctant to speak truth to power to their ministers 'because they believe that power does not want to listen' (p 335). They conclude that blunders in government result from a 'formidable combination of ministerial activism and official reticence' (p 335). Civil servants may confuse power with capability. Ministerial activism has been supported through short term appointments, more SpADs and think tanks, which can have considerable influence on the direction of government policies (Pautz 2014). More recently SpADs and think tanks have repeated Thatcher's criticisms of the civil service, who, she said, would always try to argue for the status quo or be too slow in response to changes ministers are seeking (Butcher 1991).

The introduction of agencies and distancing between functional departments and delivery showed no reduction in ministers' views about their responsibilities (Gains 2003) and in some cases, there has been more significant increase in involvement (Koop and Lodge 2020). This can cause the SCS to apply pressure to change reports and minutes. The Independent Inspector of Borders stated that meetings with the Home Secretary were cancelled and civil servants pressurised him to change his reports, making them less critical of government (House of Commons Home Affairs Committee 2024). It is difficult to know in whose interests these civil servants were working but resulting delays in publication left borders insecure and migrants living in poor conditions.

Perhaps the most public case of civil servants failing to advise ministers was in Partygate. Here, SCS participated in drinks sessions with ministers and SpADs, with no observance of government rules or advice (Thomas 2022). The Cabinet Secretary was seen to be weak and demonstrated how the UK constitution has little muscle when individuals push it to its boundaries (Sergeant et al 2023; Urban et al 2024). It is unclear whether civil servants felt obliged to participate as part of their job with failure to comply meaning being moved elsewhere. There were fixed penalty notice fines applied by the police primarily to lower grades occupied by women than men in higher grades. The Cabinet Secretary did not receive a fixed penalty notice (Sanders and Richards 2022).

A further weakness in the relationship between civil servants and ministers during COVID-19 was failure to use emergency planning procedures in place for over 150 years (Morphet 2021a; Urban et al 2024). In the case of public emergencies, agreed procedures operate command areas with local authorities, health services and emergency services working together, usually under a police lead. At the beginning of the pandemic, this procedure was not implemented and uncertainty followed among those expecting to be involved. Instead, the Prime Minister implemented a private sector contract strategy (NAO 2020) which bypassed existing suppliers and contractors with performative procurement for ventilators and Nightingale hospitals. Rather than relying on traditional suppliers for PPE, a fast lane for suppliers known to ministers and, in many cases, with no track record for this provision, was opened by the civil service. Eventually, despite not being provided with adequate resources, Directors of Public Health organised local responses and supported failed private sector track and trace schemes (Ross et al 2021). When the COVID-19 pandemic started, there were assumptions that politically and institutionally inexperienced civil servants and SpADs were unaware of the emergency planning procedures that were in place. At a greater distance, this looks like a failure of the civil service to deal with ministerial activism and appropriately advise the Prime Minister of existing procedures including those for public procurement, and the uncertain legitimacy of 'fast track' arrangements for ministerial recommendations (Sian and Smyth 2022). While the pandemic meant that public procurement rules could be waived, there were still ministerial obligations for the use of public money. As accounting officers, Permanent Secretaries in the procuring departments could have requested Ministerial directions on these privatised and unorthodox processes. The COVID-19 inquiry will assess resulting failures, including excess deaths. However, costs were considerable and expenditure was passed into the private sector rather than the public sector, to whom the population turned for assistance.

Lack of Parliamentary oversight

In the WM, civil servants have no accountability to Parliament, other than Permanent Secretaries for expenditure. They are servants of the Crown which is the government. In this role, civil servants have no relationships with Parliamentarians or requirements to provide them with information or support. The information provided to Parliament by civil servants has to be approved by a Minister. If an MP wishes to raise matters undertaken by a functional department, this has to be through written communications from the MP to a minister or a question in the House of Commons. Failure of ministers to provide truthful answers to the Commons or Select Committees is a disciplinary matter and can result in suspension or other censure. The Armstrong Doctrine (1985) required civil servants to represent the views of their ministers and was established after the enhanced Select Committee system was introduced in 1979 and the Ponting affair (1985). This doctrine is now included in the Osmotherly rules used by civil servants, although this guidance is not adopted by Parliament (Grube 2017). This rule also applies to civil servants who run agencies and cannot respond to criticism (Woodhouse 2013).

The Armstrong Doctrine has proved frustrating to Select Committees who are required to hold ministers to account. Following the Maude review of the civil service (HM Government 2012), that had the ambition of sharpening civil service accountability, the government stated its intention to adjust the relationships between civil servants and Parliament including reviewing the Osmotherly rules. The focus of these reforms was to allow SROs of major infrastructure projects to appear in front of Select Committees to answer questions on performance, changing the then convention that civil servants should be required to defend decisions of their predecessors (Barlow and Paun 2013). There is also no convention that civil servants should keep Select Committees informed of current issues even where there is a relevant inquiry underway. These changes have not occurred. Civil servants are required to provide information to the National Audit Office and the House of Commons Library, which prepares briefings for MPs on current matters.

The main relationship between civil servants and Parliament is through the role of Permanent Secretaries as accounting officers to the Public Accounts Committee (PAC). This is based on a convention agreed between the Treasury and the PAC in 1932 (Harris 2013). The Treasury responsibility for all government expenditure was established in a Treasury Memorandum of 1868 (Beer 1955) and accounting officers by a Treasury minute in 1872 (Harris 2013). The wording applied by the Treasury in describing this role is almost unchanged (HM Treasury 2023). The Treasury can also apply the Fiscal Rules at any time, including during a conversation with a minister (IFS 2024).

The Accounting Officer role attracts little attention although a nexus of the distribution and exercise of power within the state. Some Permanent Secretaries pay scant attention to the PAC despite having to appear in front of it, in what can be a 'bear pit' atmosphere (Harris 2013). Accounting officer roles run counter to devolution (Harris 2013), but subsequent changes were made in Treasury guidance post 1999. These were reversed to the centralised control model after Brexit (HM Treasury 2023). The accountability relationship between the Permanent Secretary and Parliament is an important one and is at odds with the WM, Armstong Doctrine (1985) and Osmotherly rules. If the Permanent Secretary is personally responsible for the actions of their department this appears to be in conflict with the WM and Northcote Trevelyan (1854) principles that it is the minister who is accountable to Parliament. Although Permanent Secretaries, as accounting officers, can request ministerial directions, where they would be the final decision maker, in other cases the Permanent Secretary has equal power to decide, although exercised with accountability only to the PAC. Who is in charge?

Relationships with contractors

The relationships between contractors and government have changed since the introduction of outsourcing. Before the GPA for services in 1994, suppliers were non-existent and were created through market testing and specifications. Over time, these emergent contractors have become dependent on government for their business and, in 2011, the Cabinet Office identified a category of 'strategic suppliers' who hold contracts of more than £100m with government. This process did not identify the contractual risks, instead focusing on faster processes where successful suppliers benefit from subsequent framework agreements, to 50 per cent of the total value of contracts awarded (Meggitt-Smith 2022). Even where contractors have failed, including Fujitsu, they have continued to be successful in framework contracts. Boris Johnson's decision to rely on private contractors for emergency support during the pandemic rather than use emergency planning procedures was unexpected, leaving the local public sector to deal with issues without public funding or support. Existing contractors, as well as new ones, were allowed to operate beyond the scope of their contracts and expertise, as would not normally be permitted before public contracts are awarded. Further, Meggitt-Smith (2022) argues that the incorporation of contractors into the design of delivery without any competition changed the nature of the contracting relationship to one of 'partnership' rather than client/contractor. These arrangements have been sought by service providers since markets were created, where opaque relationships between specification and funding exist (Morphet 2021a).

Low status of contract management leading to perverse incentives

The growth of public service delivery through contracts has been a major influence in the British state. There has been an increase in service failure and over-reliance on some companies. Carillion collapsed in 2018, although issues about its financial viability were known before. The extent to which the regulatory and contract frameworks were able to control the relationship and protect public interest were inadequate. This left the government responsible for £150m costs to keep services running and allow projects to be completed (Hajikazemi et al 2020). Further, the House of Commons Work and Pensions and BEIS Select Committees report (2018) on this contract failure states that it could occur again and that no lessons had been learned.

In considering Carillion and other contract failures such as National Rail contracts (Nash and Smith 2020), accountability is central. This is both individual and systemic (Bell et al 2021) including assessment of contract specifications – that is what level of service government is purchasing – but also standards of delivery stated in the contract. Procurement in the civil service is a middle ranking role, seldom discussed and not provided with adequate policy detail for implementation (Page 2007). These middle ranking officials can be left to interpret the policy intention and may be prey to the influence of the potential contractors in the way in which requirements are included in contract specifications. The advice of these civil servants will not be sought in the design of policy, nor is there any obvious location for the lessons learned from previous contract failures. Ministers will be asked to agree any major contract on their expectation that civil servants have undertaken full reviews of associated risks (Page 2007).

Failure to act on the use of powers held by government-owned bodies

In the 2008 financial crisis, the government provided support for the Royal Bank of Scotland (RBS) and eventually owned 84 per cent of the bank. While the Treasury wished to save RBS, it also wanted to have a return on its investment (Frame 2022). However, in seeking this return, the Treasury had other public sector objectives including maintaining confidence and providing lending to small businesses and households. At the time, the Treasury Select Committee identified these as contradictory objectives, requesting the Treasury to clarify them (Frame 2022). Unlike other bank failures in 2008, such as Northern Rock, the government did not nationalise RBS but kept it under the regulation of corporate law, making the bank's management accountable to its shareholders. The Treasury established UK Financial Investments (UKFI) as a company to hold its shares in RBS, creating distance from the civil service in its management. As the major shareholder, the government, through UKFI, could determine RBS's policies for lending to small businesses. The Government's approach was challenged by Judicial Review when an environmental group argued that it was not abiding by its own rules for investment set out in the Treasury's Green Book. It was accused of failing to direct the lending practices of RBS which were penalising small businesses through targeted action and sequestering their assets when entering liquidation. The UKFI Board took a commercial, hands off approach to managing RBS, acting as a 'firebreak' between the officials and RBS practices. The Treasury had a single member on the Board. The RBS approach did not fulfil the objective of providing public lending but rather in 2009–10 generated more revenue from loans than loans made. The public ownership of the Post Office has also been held at arm's length with a former civil servant as its chair and its lawyers arguing that as a public body it should not disclose evidence to those it was wrongly prosecuting (Post Office Horizon IT Inquiry 2024).

International and domestic rules don't apply to us

One source of failure within the civil service can be related to the doctrine of economic and fiscal exceptionalism which has been in operation since 1945 and exercised as 'Treasury orthodoxy'. In 2022, Prime Minister Truss made a short lived attempt to ignore this orthodoxy in a bid for the UK to buck the markets in a 'go it alone strategy' (Marsh 2023). This resulted in an economic crisis which was exacerbated by the context of Brexit. In other financial and economic matters, the UK does not follow international accounting practice and has always used revenue to pay current costs and to fund capital investment. It also uses revenue to fund its pension liabilities rather than establishing a pension fund, a requirement of all other organisations. In using revenue to pay for capital investment, such as for infrastructure, rather than making a provision for the costs in the accounts, there is always a risk that long term projects will be abandoned before their completion as occurred in HS2.

While the UK was part of the EU, some aspects of economic policy and taxation were subject to Treaty agreements including macroprudential policy and VAT. After the financial crisis in 2008, the EC policy priorities for each member state targeted specific economic weaknesses and those of the EU as a whole (Prodi 2010). Members of the EC visited London every 6 months to discuss progress and subsequently published their reports. The three UK priorities were housing, planning and youth training. The housing issue related to rental supply flexibility to the detriment of labour flexibility in the economy. Government policies were implemented to meet these objectives. While in the EU, the UK was also required to implement major infrastructure projects for Trans-European Networks for transport – TEN-T and energy, TEN-E. These network corridors crossed the EU's territory and provided mechanisms for supply chains to operate across the single market (Clifford and Morphet 2023). They also play a significant role in energy security. The projects were partly supported by the EU and other funding was made available through the European Investment Bank (EIB) and UK funds. These loans also included funds for housing regeneration and local transport schemes. At the point of the Brexit referendum, the UK had the largest loan book in the EIB of all member states. After Brexit, the UK reverted to short termism and major projects and programmes including for transport interconnection within the TEN-T network including Northern Rail were dropped or reduced in their budgets. As government revenue reduced after 2016 and the 2022 crisis, so did infrastructure projects. The UK had the lowest investment levels in the G7 in the period 2019–22, and the lowest level of investment of any member in the period since 1994 (Dibb and Jung 2024).

Is the culture of Treasury more powerful than the Chancellors? There has been a view that this has been the case since the end of the First World War (Plowden 1989). Attempts to change control of the Treasury, by transferring its economic responsibilities into the Department of Economic Affairs by Harold Wilson, when Prime Minister, were short lived (Blick 2014). After Brexit, the Treasury increased its control over the state, including local government, despite economic orthodoxy having shifted to favouring devolved control of funding and policies to functional economic areas (Ahrend et al 2014). Commentators and researchers are united in their view that the Treasury's internal culture of control causes harm to the UK but there appears to be none who will address this issue and revoke the 1868 Treasury memorandum. The failed attempt by Prime Minister Truss to change Treasury orthodoxy is likely to safeguard the longevity of its culture and practices.

Failure to keep regulation up to date

One of the outcomes of the SCS not paying attention to regulation has been building failures evidenced by the Southwark and Grenfell fires (Apps 2022). The pressure to update building control regulations and to ensure adequate inspection services, once partly privatised, were largely forgotten with the team responsible for building control being moved away from the main departmental building (Hodkinson 2018; Ewen 2023). In the past, industrial and public accidents have been independently investigated and recommendations made for changes in standard procedures including inspection. However, since the introduction of outsourcing in the UK, the initially increased regulatory frameworks have been weakened. The civil service has not taken forward all recommendations of independent inspectors such as the Railway Investigation Unit or the Health and Safety Executive.

Short termism and the power of 'now'

While there is little institutional memory for the administration of policy within the functional departments, this is accompanied by endemic short termism within civil service culture. This is characterised by the promotion and progression norms of members of the SCS (King and Crewe 2014), on the assumption that it is better to have experience within a range of functions and not to become an expert on any – the mantra of the generalist (Bridges 1950; Fulton 1968). Members of the SCS do not receive promotion or improve their prospects by demonstrating good administrative outcomes. While internal training on large projects is provided, all members of the SCS know that they will not be in post when their advice is implemented and this will be by those on more junior grades or in other agencies or institutions. For a member of the SCS joining through the 'fast stream', there is benefit in being in the room where decisions are made, developing networks within your cohort and those in more senior roles who might be useful later in your career. The power of the present or 'now' is dominant and there is a desire to ensure that initiatives attracting time from those advising the Prime Minister and funding from the Treasury are prioritised.

Does this short termism matter for the state? There is evidence it has implications for the UK, recognised by the G7 as a failure to invest. As the NAO (2013) states, the provision of economic infrastructure is a core function of the government. As infrastructure projects take time to plan, assess and deliver, they will stretch beyond one term of parliament and need cross party support for delivery. This can be through a variety of means including directly, through the private sector or hybrid funding. The National Infrastructure Commission (NIC), established in 2015, must prepare one assessment of need during each Parliament and the government is required to respond. However, the NIC is a part of the Treasury and has no independent powers such as the Office of Budget Responsibility or the NAO. The government also produces a risk register which includes items that require longer term investment, including energy security, but this was not found to be up to date when the COVID-19 pandemic occurred in 2020.

The short termism over infrastructure investment has its roots in Treasury exceptionalism over the operation of international accounting rules and practices. This can be illustrated through the management of the HS2 project, the provision of PPE in the pandemic, the lack of management of water provision across England, mass public transport systems and energy security (NAO 2013). Short termism can be financially inefficient and policy uncertainty may mean less support from the investment market. Longer term uncertainty can reduce confidence in other forms of investment for businesses and communities. Treasury short termism also encourages poor practices in the functional departments such as the MoD, where estimates for major defence projects are provided at lower levels on the assumption that the government will not want to be left with unfinished planes or ships. Despite criticism from Select Committees, the NAO and politicians in charge of functional departments, Treasury civil servants are obdurate in their practices. Budgets for smaller and more local infrastructure investment were delegated to local authorities after 1945. On agencification, Highways England and the Environment Agency were provided with powers including for flood schemes. However, both funding and independent decision making have been reduced and increasingly centralised by the Treasury, a practice that was supported by the response to the 2008 financial crisis (NAO 2016) and reinforced by Brexit.

There is also no accounting practice applied in the functional departments which identifies the capital assets within their remit or what is needed to maintain them, as required in the private sector nor what new investment is required to meet gaps or further economic needs (NAO 2016). In 2007, the UK adopted the OECD international agreement on the International Financial Reporting Standard (IFRS) to be implemented by 2017. This brought public and private sector accounting standards together and required the UK government to provide whole government accounts (WGA). By 2024, the IFRS has not been implemented in large parts of the public sector including local government, and WGA lag in their preparation and publication. In 2023, DLUHC was forbidden from spending any of its agreed budgets for capital projects without the Treasury's explicit control, without any reason being given. At the same time, those in functional departments responsible for procurement and delivery of these projects are not part of the elite structure of the core executive and have difficulty being heard.

The Treasury recognises the endemic issues caused by its short term approach to capital investment on infrastructure as highlighted in the 2014 Autumn Statement (NAO 2015) although there is no evidence that its practices subsequently changed. The Treasury also has a fixed view on the role of the UK economy with policies and projects with redistributive effects not adopted because they are regarded as a threat to London's contribution to driving the economy (Coyle and Sensier 2019).

Underpowered policy – competition between departments

The way in which the MoG is used to distribute functions between departments is longstanding and focuses on changes at the margin between one or two departments rather than a review of the whole. The creation of individual departments to deal with specific issues such as DExEU for Brexit have a short life and are then disbanded. Other MoG changes reflect the power relationships between government departments and mechanisms used by civil servants to generate reforms they prefer (Gains and John 2010). Over time, the administrative preferences of the SCS, particularly in the core executive, can be reinforced and strengthened in relation to other parts of the WM. The absorption of DfID, with a small but important policy function, into the FCO was an example of where a longstanding department wanted to control a minnow with more public recognition but less power. This has not been successful (Fletcher et al 2024; NAO 2024c). The creation of the Department of Economic Affairs by Harold Wilson with a wider policy brief than HMT was short lived and used as an example to deter those considering strengthening economic policy functions of other departments. The last major review of government functions was undertaken by Edward Heath in 1970 as a prelude to the UK joining the EU. By expanding and strengthening the departments that were expected to have most interaction with the EU, Heath was making preparation. No such similar review or reorganisation was undertaken when the UK left the EU.

Competition between departments provides more power to the Core Executive, who can threaten to move responsibilities between departments if they do not adhere to their direction, go rogue or develop their own policy priorities. There is also competition within departments which have similar responsibilities. Departmental structures are not permanent and there are no legal requirements to report internal changes to Parliament. It is argued that the fluidity of internal structures allows the civil service to respond to changing government demands.

This competitive culture within and between departments leads to a lack of integration across government. This is understood as inefficient for both organisations and the recipient groups (Perri 6 2004). However, there are also considerations of the owners of separate policies and services and the perceived institutional benefits of administrative coordination and integration but not on delivery. Will integration ensure that resources saved will not be lost to other departments? Will promotion prospects be enhanced by achieving integration around people or places when framing norms reward competition? This lack of integration has been tackled through a range of Prime Ministerial initiatives such as JUG or Total Place and children's number for tracking abuse which have all been abandoned. The other feature of internal competition is that functions are split and this plurality creates difficulty in ascribing accountability for taking decisions (Gerodimos 2004).

Corruption

While corruption or the potential for it was one of the reasons for the Northcott Trevelyan review of the civil service (1854) (Heywood and Dobson 2019), it has assumed that it has not emerged since. While corruption is defined as the abuse of public office for private gain, this gain is taken to be financial rather than personal. Corruption in the civil service is not discussed even where it may be on a major scale such as the creation of false accounts to perpetrate benefit fraud or create of passports for bogus people. Corruption within public agencies is discussed more in relation to the police or local government. Within the civil service, studies of corruption have focused on human relations practices, of selection, promotion and pay (Meyer-Sahling et al 2018).

The potential for increased corruption in the civil service has been associated with public service outsourcing and use of consultants to advise government. Although the UK has been regarded as one of the most transparent and open in its contracting process this is not without its risks (David-Barrett and Fazekas 2020). Contractors may be required to have specific experience or their companies have a particular financial standing, yet there are instances in government where contractors continue to be appointed despite failures of existing contracts including Carillion and auditors including Ernst and Young. Extending existing contracts without new competition may not be related to personal gain by civil servants, but rather generated through failure to spend time on the process, low status or a general familiarity with individuals, gained through sponsored attendance at sporting fixtures or cultural events with existing or potential suppliers. When these relationships become formalised in procurement, they are required to be logged as a conflict of interest, but at what point in the pre-contract relationship does this become a necessary declaration? This is better understood when there is a family or financial connection between the contractor and the procurement (NAO 2015). It is an issue for politicians and civil servants, with potential networked relationships remaining in place since school, university or fast stream cohorts.

Other forms of corruption relate to the selection of consultants through competitive or reduced tender processes. Consultants may employ former civil servants to reinforce the comfort of longstanding relationships. Networks may also provide civil servants with access to future jobs through 'revolving doors' (Heywood and Dobson 2019) or a secondment to the private sector, which is important for promotion prospects (IfG 2024). These regular workplace practices may not be considered corrupt when they are endemic and culturally embedded, although they may be outlawed in other organisations.

While the UK has had high rankings in the Transparency International Corruption Perception Index and World Bank Governance indicators, its position slipped to its lowest position ever in 2023 (Transparency International 2024). This reputation ranking reflects contract awards and public servants and adviser appointments (Doig 2003). This decline is related primarily to the politicisation of decision making, whether for places prior to elections (Hanretty 2021) or the access to government contracts by friends and party supporters, with minimal scrutiny (NAO 2020), through crony capitalism (Wood et al 2023). Prime Minister Johnson's behaviour led to the resignation of his two ethics advisers (Durrant et al 2021). There have been earlier warnings and concerns about the ways in which decisions benefiting individuals and their associates through the Nolan Inquiry and subsequent

Standards in Public Life (1995). While prosecutions for corruption are within the laws for bribery or fraud, in the civil service it is misuse of public office and framed within a twin approach of the application of ethics (Heywood and Dobson 2019) and rules in the Civil Service Code.

Can politicisation be regarded as corruption, where SCS members may be subject to advice and pressure from advisers, SpADs and donors represented in think tanks? The processes of politicisation of the civil service has been increasing across a number of countries both in the behaviour of politicians and officials (Halligan 2021). The civil service has a code of neutrality, and while this politicisation may not be described as partisanship, there is also a desire to fulfil the administrative requirements of presenting policies and advice that ministers will find acceptable to their ideology. As the political context becomes more defined, this becomes more challenging. Failure to follow a minister's views in the advice provided may result in bullying, being moved to another job or ignored. Increased interference of politicians in senior SCS appointments characterised the breakdown of the post-war consensus of the role of the state (Theakston 1986), there is less consideration of the relationships before this which might be described as the 'good chaps' (Blick and Hennessey 2019) or 'chums' (Kuper 2022) theory of government. Here members of the SCS, MPs and leading figures in public life were educated at the same schools and universities. This network had their own version of 'one of us' and the broadening of the administrative classes after Fulton, was in recognition of the wider number of graduates and stimulated by mechanisms to maintain control, over selection and recruitment. Overall, Heywood and Dobson (2019) argue that the civil service may appear to be clean in respect of corruption but it is compromised.

Conclusions

Does having a lack of institutional memory for policy administration matter? There can be a range of costs associated with poor policy and administration including inadequate targeting of intended beneficiaries. Similarly, there can be poor targeting of those which need to be controlled or regulated by policies (Wettenhall 2011). The failure to remember past experience may lead to wastefulness (Morphet 2021a; Urban et al 2024). However, an over reliance on the past can stultify innovation and make policy static. It may also generate 'muddling through' (Hennessey 1996) or iterative policy when more punctuated approaches may be required to reset expectations or policy models. There can also be costs in not learning across functional departments or from inquiries. While this failure to learn lessons from previous administration of policy, there are two other concerns that are highlighted here for SCS practice. The first is a lack of interest on the effectiveness of any policy in administration and these issues, not included in assessments of performance or promotion, are not valued. The second is that, in a 'sitting by Nelly' tradition of SCS learning, there is a dominance of the interests of the SCS over any other part of the WM. The legacy of memory is selective and reinforces SCS power structures in government. Adherence to these cultural norms is essential to promotion and any attempt by Minsters or Parliament to change practices are held to be warnings internally and criticised externally (Hood 1990; Pollitt 2009).

9

How Does the Civil Service Survive Change? The Persistence of Power

Introduction

The role of the civil service in the constitution, as set out in the Westminster Model (WM), is persistently reinforced despite constant pressure for change. This chapter examines how this is achieved and what effects it has. Some argue that the WM operates too loosely to have any meaning (Bevir 2008; Rhodes et al 2008; Russell and Serban 2021), its flexibility, ambiguity and slipperiness are attributes which the civil service favours and to which it returns after periods of disruption, through different political interventions (Richards and Smith 2016). However, can the WM survive, not least as it has failed to incorporate the growth of special advisers (SpADs), who are ignored in this narrative?

The rhetoric about the quality of the civil service and the way it differs from other countries (Greer and Jarman 2000) is located in its specialism of generalism. There have been successive efforts to change it by those in power (Lowe 2010; Lowe and Pemberton 2020; Maude 2023), through a range of methods including formal inquiries, critical speeches and the insertion of advisers. However, since its foundational reform (Northcote Trevelyan 1854), it role has been reinforced by Haldane on the Machinery of Government (MoG) (1918), Fisher's reform of the Treasury (Greenaway 1983) and Bridges' view on the power of the generalist (1954). These have created a living tradition of practice (Bevir and Rhodes 2010). None of the proposed and adopted reforms have made lasting changes to civil service practices and powers. Sometimes, regaining lost powers can take time but the continuity and permanence of the civil service compared with shorter-lived governments and Parliaments provides punctuation points for resetting or returning these powers. The civil service powers provided through the WM are not codified through legislation. The Constitutional Reform and

Governance Act 2010 reinforced neutrality through the Civil Service Code, but did not go further. If this is the case, what is the strategy to remove the role of SpADs and is it likely to be successful?

The exercise of power can suggest a misplaced belief in civil service competence (King and Crewe 2014). While the soft power exercised by the UK in its diplomatic role is frequently acknowledged (Pamment and Pamment 2016), this is also exercised internally through anticipatory policy generated through extended negotiations of international treaties. These preparations are undertaken through the strategic functions of the civil service (Dunleavy and Rhodes 1990; Smith 1999) and lack transparency. There is no dialogue about framing or methods of administering new powers that will be required. Soft power has been particularly important in changing public administration in Britain from 1970 onwards (Yi-Chong and Weller 2008; Morphet 2021a) and through membership of the EU 1972–2020 (Greer and Jarman 2011). While benefits of anticipatory domestic policy preparation have been removed after Brexit, delegated powers, such as those from the EU to the devolved administrations have been returned to Whitehall through Brexit implementation mechanisms (Morgan and Jones 2023; Brown Swan et al 2024).

The Westminster Model

The components of the constitution that comprise the WM are taken as constant (Headey 1975). However, in practice, they are fluid, not tightly drafted and can be invoked at any time, including when the civil service is under threat of change. The civil service has been combatting Government and Parliamentary Select Committee reports about its fitness for purpose and how it should change to meet current needs for 170 years. By invoking 'golden ageism', those who were heads of the home civil service – Warren Fisher (O'Halpin 1981; Greenaway 1983), Norman Brook (Theakston 1999; Kyle 2013) and Sir Edward Bridges (Bridges 1954; Chapman and O'Toole 2010), are regarded as archetypal mandarins (Fry 2000), all deflecting contemporaneous pressures for change using these mantras. In some cases, reforms that have reduced or changed civil service power have been reversed. These are points of punctuated equilibrium (Baumgartner et al 2018) with a civil service focus on restoration. The points of danger of such changes have included the publication of the Crossman diaries (Bogdanor 1977; Crossman and Howard 1991), the Fulton report (1968), joining the EU (Bulmer and Burch 2005), the Thatcher Next Steps approach (Hood 1990), Major's Citizen's Charter, the Blair government (Norton 2003; Bevir and Rhodes 2006), Lord Maude, who has had two attempts under different governments (Lodge 2014; Maude 2014; Diamond 2023b; Maude 2023) and the Johnsonian period (Durrant et al 2020; Ward and Ward 2023).

Others such as adviser to Cameron, Steve Hilton (Gamble 2011; Theakston 2012) and to Johnson, Dominic Cummings (Durrant et al 2020; Hayton 2022) have attempted to change the civil service (Pyper 2013; Rutter 2013; Stafford 2022). The civil service has withstood such attempts at reform as expressed by Turnbull (2005) (Weller and Haddon 2016) and Sir Richard Wilson (Cabinet Office 1999b; Wilson 1999). Despite reforms, little has had a significant effect on the operation of the more senior leadership culture and its use of power (Foster-Gilbert 2018). As Rhodes et al (2008) state, all retiring permanent secretaries reflect on the difficulties that they have had managing political change and pressures to maintain the civil service as it is.

Despite being criticised for being meaningless (Grube and Howard 2016; Richards and Smith 2016), the WM has been remarkably adaptable in its mechanisms to reassert the traditional power model. When each of the danger thresholds for change are reached, there appears to be a menu of action which is used as appropriate. This includes using the press and other media to undermine the source of change or the effects that the change might have on the British people (Bevir and Rhodes 2006). In some cases, this vilification can go on for over a decade as in the case of Blair (Burch and Holliday 2004; Garland 2021; Norton 2021).

The civil service can also rely on temporal space to revert to a previous position (Goetz and Meyer-Sahling 2013), using policy windows to restore the *status quo ante* (Birkland and DeYoung 2012). As Northcote Trevelyan (1854) stated in its first words, the ministers whom permanent civil servants advise, change from time to time – through the machinery of government, cabinet reshuffles and general elections. The emphasis here from the outset is on the differences between the permanent role of the civil service and the temporary roles of politicians. The changes proposed by Maude for the creation of ministerial teams in the period of the coalition government (Diamond 2018) in 2013 were swiftly reversed when a new Prime Minister took over in 2016. The civil service can also reconstruct the record through extended timescales in responding to independent inspectors' reports, inquiries and Select Committees.

While the relationships between the civil service and the executive have remained cordial is there only lip service paid to this? What criticisms have been made? Firstly, the civil service is seen as a 'Rolls Royce' policy machine but poor in implementation. However, how can a policy be successful if it cannot be implemented well (Mulgan 2003; Hyman 2005; Barber 2007)? Also when there are policy failures, where is blame attributed? The extent of agencification has led to blame being focused on the delivery layer of the civil service but it has now become clear that rather than having a detached relationship between minister, senior civil servants (SCS) and agencies, control exercised over agencies is greater than before while the operational experience of the SCS is less. Richards and Smith (2006) describe the relationship between ministers and civil servants as 'folklore' and Rhodes (2005) describes it as a legitimating myth rather than a reality. Together both sides wish to retain an elite power model. But who has control within it and why does this matter?

Given the changes in the fundamental basis of law following the UK's membership of the EU in 1972, Bevir (2008) argues that this marked a weakening of the civil service, reducing the power and role of Parliament (Baldini et al 2018) and of the executive (Slaughter and Burke-White 2006; Baratta 2014). The UK Parliament was not able to question the principles of EU legislation while UK citizens and organisations could hold the government to account for their failure to implement legislation. EU membership had influence on the WM including the application and implementation of the principle of subsidiarity (1992 and 2009) (Kersbergen and Verbeek 2004; van den Brink 2012), which required more power to be devolved to sub-national government even through these had no place in the UK constitution (Arribas and Bourdin 2012).

Multiple Government reforms but no change?

While the civil service might have feared change or losing control, Richards and Smith (2016) argue that the civil service has more independent responsibility than politicians because 'They are acting out of a sense of public duty and have a higher duty than ministers, being concerned with national, not sectional, interests' (p 503). Is this the case? As noted earlier, civil servants are not required to promote the public good. While a fluid and flexible approach to the WM is celebrated by former Permanent Secretaries, governments and Parliamentarians are not so sanguine about the performance and motivation of the civil service. Successive reports have been commissioned to discuss changes in training and skills or reinforce the relationships with ministers. However, as Weller and Haddon (2016) comment, there is very little discussion on what stimulates these reports or speeches on challenges to the civil service, nor how effective they are in promoting sustained change. Why are failures to promote change in the civil service not discussed further?

The UK civil service as a persistent political elite

The civil service is a persistent political elite which provides a lens through which past, current and future behaviour can be assessed. As Higley (2018) states, 'elites have enough power to manager hierarchies in their own interests' (p 25) and 'can be defined as individuals and small, relatively cohesive and stable groups with major decisional power' (p 27) where 'outcomes that are decisively affected by elites include the basic stability or instability of political regimes, the forms and workings of political institutions, and the main policies of governments' (p 27). However, there is also a need to understand not only how political elites hold but also maintain power. Do elites persist where there is a common enemy? Putnam (1975) argues that political elites need a degree of autonomy to be able to operate while Pakulski (2018) states that civil service elites have started to be regarded as more neutral and operational, defined as small networks that are 'lattices of leaders' (p 13).

It is this assumed neutral and administrative role that retains the attention of the civil service, (Farazmand 1999). Discussion on organisations focuses on their delivery and operation rather than who is developing the policies that they are implementing. It is this unseen and less accountable component of the civil service that determines its size, how policies and services are organised and the distribution internal and external resources (Farazmand 1999). Organisational elites are mutually interdependent, as is the case in the civil service and politicians performing functions maintaining 'invisibility shielding' (Domhoff and Dye 1987) while Wise (1994) argues that 'organizational effectiveness is "repeatedly sacrificed on the altar of interest protection and representation"' (p 85). Farazmand (1999) argues that with the increased concentration of power in large organisations, 'the inner circle strategic elites tend to centralize core-peripheral relationship and produce a much higher degree of organizational complexity' (pp 342–3). They can also protect their position by using techniques in elite interviews and research (Semenova 2018).

Elites influence others to change behaviours by using latent power in the way that arguments are presented or confrontation avoided (Keller 2018). Elites have powers of autonomy (Bottomore 1964) and can manage hierarchies in their own interests (Higley 2018) using networks with controlled entry. While the integration of an elite, including common aims, is an important component in their survival, there can also be a common enemy. Other aspects of survival include social homogeneity, recruitment patterns, personal interaction, value consensus, group solidarity and institutional context (Putnam 1976: 107). Political elites do not operate through confrontation but by using innovation, persuasion and soft power methods of control (Femia 2002). As Farazmand (1999) finds, much of the literature on organisations is on their delivery but far less attention is paid to those who are developing the policies that they are implementing – 'people do not downsize themselves; organizational elites do' (p 322). Elites can create organisations in their own interest and be less focused on their external administrative responsibilities (Moe 2005) and organisational effectiveness. The need to maintain control of the organisation gives elites power to shape their actions and outlooks, frequently overriding substantive interests and vague ideological principles (Wise 1994).

Are there constraints on political elite behaviour? Civil servants are permanent compared with politicians who are temporary, creating an advantage. While Fulton (1968) argued that recruitment from the same schools and universities created this elite, Theakston and Fry (1989) argue post-entry socialisation is more important; new civil servants in the fast stream soon understand what actions gain promotion (Headey 1972). There is also evidence of the cult of the individual civil servant as hero (Headey 1972; Barberis 1996b; Bailey and Lloyd 2017) with status being associated with proximity to these named individuals. Theakston and Fry found that between 1965 and 1986, 30 per cent of Permanent Secretaries had spent 26–30 years in the civil service before they assumed the role, with 40 per cent in one department only. There was also a pathway set from starting in a minister's office to spending time in the Core Executive and, despite the time spent in a department, loyalty to the civil service always supersedes that to a department (Nicholson 1967). Headey (1972) showed how the civil service foists its policies on ministers and uses its own discretion over the many policies which their ministers do not have time to consider. If ministers do not agree with the civil service advice then delay or obstructive tactics are used. Information can be withheld from ministers or underplayed by civil servants as demonstrated in the infected blood and Horizon inquiries (Dyer 2024). These processes also include bringing in external advice or mobilising interests in civil society. As Headey (1972) states, civil servants are responsible for 'answerability' rather than 'accountability' (p 41) with the view inside the civil service that reformers were using this as a mechanism to hide their own political failures.

Methods of maintaining power: operating the Core Executive

The Core Executive has been evolving since 1919 and in association with Cabinet Government (Burch and Holliday 2004). While the civil service is competitive between departments, the Core Executive is the main source of civil service power. This comprises three components: No 10 Downing Street, the Cabinet Office and the Treasury – with the Treasury being most dominant and the Cabinet Office least transparent. While the Core Executive can be viewed as a coherent whole externally, the relative power relationships mean that it can be undermined in the service of the Prime Minister and government if there are disagreements between its members. There appears to be a blindness to the view that the Core Executive operates without the growing number and influence of SpADs. If Prime Ministers do not consider that their levers of power are strong enough, they do not turn to the machinery of government as before, but appoint more SpADs. However, how does the civil service manage to maintain control, when its advice is no longer the primary source available? Have civil servants sought to retain control in other ways such as by silence or marginalising issues so that ministers are not alert to them?

Change in the Core Executive has been incremental and not disruptive. The Blair approach was to change its focus to delivery with more fundamental consideration of its role (Burch and Holliday 2004). However, the period of the Coalition government 2010–2015 moved from internal coordination to a review of bodies established to deliver policy within the state and extend their role of influence over them (Dommett and Flinders 2015). This reassertion of the Cabinet Office's centralisation of power was a response to the period of the previous governments where control had been shared with a range of bodies who now considered that they were micro-managed.

HM Treasury

It is impossible to work in the civil service and be unaware of the role and power of HM Treasury or be outside and not know of its idiosyncratic ways of exercising power in comparison with other organisations and countries. HM Treasury uses accounting practices unique to the UK that other countries fail to understand. These are short term and have major effects on all that the country does and can achieve. The power of the Treasury is also such that it can prevent any of the functional departments spending any of their allocated budgets (Beer 1955; Greenaway 1983) and can make or break prime ministers. The Prime Minister is the First Lord of the Treasury but this does not make the post holder responsible for the Treasury and its actions. While Blair was regarded as a strong Prime Minister by the SCS and not one who they would like to see in power again, in practice the domestic policy and expenditure in England was managed by his Chancellor, Gordon Brown. The Treasury had an iron grip on policy development and delivery through a range of means including spending reviews, star chambers for budgets and project changes. Since 2014, this grip has been gradually extended to the devolved administrations and local authorities in the UK through a project-by-project approval system that can include projects of the level of £60,000 (Morphet 2022).

The Treasury has been accused of exercising 'naked authoritarianism' (Chapman 1997: 161) with any meetings of minsters with their civil servants being regarded as perfunctory with decisions already made (Playfair 1965). The Treasury has its own agenda separate from the government (Wilkes and Westlake 2014; Urban et al 2024). Some Prime Ministers deal with this by trying to work with chancellors but in the main, have to seek accommodation. Any criticism of Treasury culture and behaviour is frequently characterised as a 'misunderstanding' (Playfair 1965), seldom made by politicians and those responsible for public organisations. The Treasury has the power to discriminate against those who have been critical.

It is difficult to undertake research on members of the SCS, particularly leading members in the Core Executive as they are practiced elite interviewees, and understand the presentation of arguments and positions in ways that do not necessarily represent the realities of the situation described (Rhodes et al 2008). When considering undertaking research in the Treasury, this is even more difficult because of the reign of fear that operates both within Whitehall and in the wider public sector. Any criticism can be associated with a loss of funding not just for a project but across a whole department (Burch and Holliday 2004).

The Treasury uses spending reviews (SRs) to exercise power over functional departments. SRs are rarely discussed apart from the competition for resources and who has been successful. However, they have a more fundamental structural role in the exercise of Treasury power. Firstly, they allow government priorities to be changed without other reasons being given and were useful for implementation of EU policies. Secondly, while SR focus is on projects funded for the review period, they have build-up and run-down periods either side and can be operational for 7 years, overlapping with previous reviews. SRs provide functional departments with the legitimation and resources that are critical for implementation of their projects which can be attractive career opportunities. They provide performative opportunities for rising members of the SCS rather than on mainstream issues that are the department's responsibilities. SRs take time and effort within departments and can detract and divert from the importance of the mainstream. They allow the Treasury to undertake performance reviews on previously funded initiatives, suggesting departments wishing to undertake new initiatives should stop others and fund them within existing budgets. This provides the Treasury with opportunities to reshape departmental budgets and priorities giving them the power over the administration of the government's agenda. As Thomas (2021) states, all government departments are 'outgunned' by the Treasury (p 7).

Cabinet Office

The Cabinet Office is the most opaque department dealing with issues before they enter the public domain. Chapman (1997) queries whether the growth of its role in managing the careers of the SCS and devolution means that it has come to challenge the Treasury in its influence in the Core Executive. However, others suggest that the centre of government is weak with the Cabinet Office at the heart of this failure (Urban et al 2024). Thomas (2021) argues that the Cabinet Office should be the main delivery engine for the Prime Minister's priorities, agreed and programmed at the beginning of their period in office. Further, Thomas argues that the Cabinet Secretary and Chief Operating Officer should have more control of the civil service across government in order to achieve these ends. While arguing that the Cabinet Office can realise coordination across departments, it is not strong enough to provide support to the Prime Minister in comparison with other countries such as Australia, Canada and Germany.

There are two issues to consider in examining the Cabinet Office. Firstly, does the Cabinet Office regard its principal role as advising the Prime Minister or of interpreting policy from a range of international and political sources? Second, does the Prime Minister regard the Cabinet Office as having primacy in this advice, given the increasing number of SpADs who also have a delivery and coordinating role? Until the Blair government, the Cabinet Office had evolved into an organisation that managed Cabinet Committees and senior civil servants' careers. Blair expanded their role to include a constitution secretariat, later adding Social Exclusion and the EU (Burch and Holiday 2004). The Institute for Government has argued that the Cabinet Office and the Prime Minister's Office should be combined to strengthen the centre of government (Urban et al 2024), although Dunleavey (2024) argues that this is not a realistic approach. It is also interesting to note how little research has been undertaken on the role of the Cabinet Office other than by 'insiders'.

No 10 Downing Street

How strong is the Prime Minister's office and role in directing decision making of government departments and other parts of the Core Executive? The Prime Minister is *primus inter pares* and has no executive power over the Cabinet or the civil service. Prime Ministers have used a range of methods to maintain power – through their personality (Heath, Thatcher), preparation and agreement with the Treasury (Blair and Cameron), the use of special advisers (Blair, Cameron, Johnson and Sunak), dismissing civil servants (Truss), but the overall level of control is weak. This is considered to be a contributing factor to the weakness of any government and frequent proposals to extend the size of the Prime Minister's office, create a Prime Minister's department or merge the Prime Minister's office with the Cabinet Office (Urban et al 2024) are suggested.

The power of the Cabinet Secretary in managing the delivery of a Prime Minister's priorities is also weak and they have no power over Whitehall (Thomas 2021). Simon Case, Cabinet Secretary for Johnson, Truss, Sunak and Starmer shared responsibilities for the departmental Permanent Secretaries with the Permanent Secretaries of the Treasury and the Cabinet Office who is also the government's Chief Operating Officer. This system can work if all three postholders are in alignment but there is capacity for coalitions between members of the triumvirate and departmental permanent secretaries. As there is no overall power for the Prime Minister, Permanent Secretaries regard their position as autonomous, only subject to Treasury rules.

Civil servants use a range of mechanisms to retain power in No 10 above all other parts of government. The combination of being Head of the Home Civil Service and Cabinet Secretary has been used most frequently. In some cases even more distinct roles have been added such as Head of Security when Sedwill held these roles under May. In some cases the Cabinet Secretary has sought to create the form of government with O'Donnell, then Cabinet Secretary, choosing the parties in the 2010 coalition government. There have also been attempts to split the role of Cabinet Secretary and Head of the Home Civil Service when occupied by Kerslake and Heywood but this was never likely to be successful. Responsibilities were reunified under Heywood, one of the civil service's 'heroic' figures (Bailey and Lloyd 2017). More recently there has been concern about the weakness of the Cabinet Secretary and Head of the Home Civil Service during the period of Johnson's government in 2019–22, failing to deal with procurement fast lanes and Partygate by an activist Prime Minister (IfG 2023a).

Some prime ministers have used strong internal appointments as head of their offices to improve their power across Whitehall. Mrs Thatcher had Charles Powell and Tony Blair appointed his brother Jonathan Powell. Thatcher and Blair had strong press secretaries – Bernard Ingham and Alistair Campbell, while later Prime Ministers had advisers – Steve Hilton for Cameron, Hill and Timothy for May and Cummings for Johnson. All resigned during their Prime Minister's term in office.

There is also a weakness in holding government departments to account by the Prime Minister. This was an issue that was tackled by Blair through the creation of the PMSU and PMDU together with the public service agreements for departments but these were all unloved by the civil service and were abolished as soon as the Labour government fell in 2010. These initiatives created a longer term approach to government and the achievement of its objectives but since 2010, there has been a return to short termism (Thomas 2021).

Methods of maintaining power: recruitment and promotion

Internal recruitment and promotion

The initial selection and recruitment of members of the SCS relies on finding a select group. Although not taking entrants as young as Jesuits, to be assured of a successful career in the SCS, joining the fast stream before 27 and having a clear idea about how to manage your career, particularly on entry are critical. Joining a ministerial team can be necessary for longer term success, as is a period in the Treasury (Ridley 1983).

Once inside the SCS, onward advancement is managed by the Cabinet Office. Most promotion is internal (NAO 2024a). Opportunities to apply for promotion will depend on good performance gradings by line managers at annual reviews and these assessments are based on conforming to expectations. Organisations relying on internal recruitment have compliant workforces and those who do not fit may find themselves managed out of the organisation or sent on less attractive career paths. Internal recruitment within the civil service is not based on evidence that it provides more effective officials or improves performance. It is not a Human Resources strategy but a longstanding culture. Internal recruitment and promotion also implies civil servants have less experience of external organisations. There has been some response to this criticism and SCS promotion now requires external experience organisations (Baxendale 2014).

Ridley (1983) described the civil service as a 'career service' with an assumption that the political dimension of administration makes it different from other sectors (Bunbury 1928) taking a lifetime's experience to know how to manage these administrative and political interfaces. Thatcher initially intended to reform the civil service (Fry 1984) but apart from agencification and some interventions in senior posts, it eluded her. As a career service, the loyalty and orientation of civil servants is to the service and not to their specific roles. Outside, people might specialise in types of activity moving between organisations in their careers. Civil servants have an internal career ladder, but those who enter in the lower grades find a pathway to the top challenging. The culture of the civil service has had a range of outcomes. It has provided continuity but based on the power of internal recruitment to generate conformity. There is no focus on how well policies have been administered and the evidence of civil service coverups in inquires such as that for infected blood (Wise 2024) demonstrates how internal cultures will act to protect its interests.

Manage external appointees both in and out of the job

Maintaining the power of the internal civil service culture has been achieved by restricting access to those who have wider experience and might be critical of what they see. In Northcote Trevelyan (1854) there had been some support for the later recruitment into the SCS but after 1919, dominated by Haldane and then Fisher, there was a clamp down on external appointments. During the Second World War, external appointees did not become members of the 'established' civil service but unestablished employees of government with no access to pensions or security of tenure. In the early 1960s, there was a programme to introduce 25 external mid-career appointees directly into SCS differing from other short term 'irregular' appointments. Responses to this scheme varied. While there were criticisms that this programme would endanger the morale of traditional entry SCS members, Sheriff (1972) found that the opposite was true. Those joining the SCS from outside were more alert to external job opportunities even where they considered it likely that they would remain. This created a mechanism to move them on if other opportunities were offered, allied with their performance through lack of interpretable feedback, promotion denied or slow in coming.

There have been some notable external appointees but they have not remained in post for long. During the period immediately before Blair, Michael Bichard was appointed as Permanent Secretary of the Department for Education after training in law and then experience as a local authority chief executive. Before becoming Permanent Secretary, Bichard was head of the Benefits Agency (Ribbins and Sherratt 2022). For his own development inside the civil service, he was constantly being focused on when he would return to local government (p 382). He remained as an outsider. This may also have been associated with his interest in management and he held the view that he was not regarded as an effective policy adviser (p 382). On being asked about his experience of entering the civil service after a career in local government, not least when Bichard's first two SCS posts were major institutional and service reforms including joining together the Department for Education and the Department of Employment, Bichard stated that the impact of his approach was more on the civil service than on him. He stated that 'I don't think you can lead an organisation if you are a prisoner of their culture' (Ribbins and Sherratt 2022: 385). Bichard also brought in a number of external appointees to help the merger, provide a new focus for the department and was more interested in delivery than on hierarchical gradings. Lord Kerslake had a similar background, trained in public accountancy, then as a chief executive in two local authorities, entering the civil service as Head of the Homes and Communities Agency before becoming Permanent Secretary of the Department for Communities and Local Government. He became the Head of the Home Civil Service 2011–14 but was not invited to Cabinet or appointed as Cabinet Secretary (Pyper 2013). While splitting these posts was not unusual, it indicated that a career outside the civil service was not regarded as providing sufficient experience for political interfaces. Kerslake gave up this role to a more traditional civil servant. Those who joined the civil service from senior local government roles in the Blair government also left after short periods of time (Toynbee 2023). While there were some reforms in recruitment, the evidence demonstrates the short time periods that outsiders spend in the SCS reflects a negative experience (NAO 2024a). How has this quick turnover of outside appointees been achieved? Firstly, many joining the SCS from other careers have been given fixed term contracts and, although part of the SCS, their roles have been focused on political priorities that can be removed once these have changed. Secondly, many external appointments were never absorbed into the mainstream management of any functional department and they found themselves on intermediate rather than mainstream grades – having no power over staff.

Where external candidates are appointed to the most senior roles, they frequently have a number 2 or deputy who is a traditional civil servant acting as a watcher, deflector and diverter. Some issues may never get to the top and be dealt with before the most senior but external appointee has seen them. Their word can be reinterpreted and given a different emphasis to that intended. The scale and size of most departments is enough to reduce the ability of many SCS staff to be informed across all issues, particularly those that do not appear to be so interesting politically. In order to terminate the contracts of external appointees, then issues can be raised which make their continuance difficult. The contracts and job descriptions, including accountabilities, can be changed and they may not be given security information as 'outsiders'. External appointees and their failure to absorb internal culture have seen their appointments described as 'disastrous' (Foster Gilbert 2018) by long serving civil servants without much explanation of why this is the case.

For more mainstream recruitment of perceived outsiders, that is, professionals as economists, lawyers or planners and statisticians, the SCS has ensured that the progression of those in these roles has remained separate from access to mainstream top jobs. Much of this concern is related to the position of professionals who have some specific technical and/or management training and by dint of their membership of a professional body, they have loyalties to the code of ethics provided by those bodies. If professionals do not adhere to their professional codes of conduct then they can be struck off these registers. However, being a member of the SCS requires a primary duty to the operation of the WM and any official with twin loyalties may be an official with divided loyalties. There have been attempts to open up the career pathways for progression in the SCS, to enable professionals to move to more senior posts but in practice this has not frequently occurred.

Maintaining power: creating a lattice of leverage

Over recruitment

Like some major management consultancies, the SCS overrecruits fast stream entrants and over time, its numbers are reduced through a range of mechanisms including secondment or encouragement to move into a job in an allied sector with a possible expectation of moving back. This has become a particularly attractive route for ambitious members of the SCS, who are aware that a period in the private sector can be helpful in their career advancement (IfG 2024) but not all find a way back.

What do these surplus former SCS members do when they find themselves outside? While given no promises about a return, they remain constantly hopeful. However, they are able to take jobs where organisations find their knowledge and networks inside the SCS advantageous and those remaining in the SCS find it helpful to have former colleagues in key or leading roles in the public, private and third sectors. Moving into a senior role in the City or in a major company can be financially advantageous for individual civil servants and may be a gateway to other appointments. For an organisation, candidates with SCS experience offer opportunities for networked access and understanding how decisions are made (Faccio 2006; Goldman et al 2009). While the expectations of obtaining such senior roles were primarily on retirement from the SCS, some have occurred earlier with some evidence that companies with good links to government achieve higher stock valuations (Gonzalez-Bailon et al 2013). Former SCS members have run trades unions, the National Trust, charities, become journalists, headed Oxbridge colleges, become VCs of Universities, head of the Local Government Association, lobbyists, academics and consultants. Providing some inside information to former SCS members, inviting them to ministerial discussions or asking them to serve as advisers all provide soft power's arm's length influence over many of the state's key organisations.

Revolving doors

The use of revolving doors between members of the SCS and external organisations has increased and Mulgan (2021) describes this as a better way for organisations to understand each other. In their research on officials who move from the SCS into external bodies, Andrews and Beynon (2024) argue that this practice may have public interest concerns by both civil servants dealing with potential employers in favourable ways and for businesses and organisations to cultivate members of the SCS. There is particular interest in appointing members of the SCS in parts of the private sector where they have had responsibilities for procurement. While members of the SCS dealing with procurement have lower status than their policy colleagues, an appointment to the private sector may be considered a reasonable payback. This activity is more apparent in the Ministry of Defence. Andrews and Benyon also found that there is more movement from the Cabinet Office and FCO which are associated with the Core Executive and policy formation. This suggests instrumental targeting of those engaged in early, central policy processes.

The facilitation of relationships between members of the SCS and outside interests is undertaken by the Whitehall and Industry Group (WIG) with the objectives of creating networks between the SCS and other sectors. WIG started in the 1980s as a Cabinet Office initiative with Marks & Spencer, as a secondment scheme to enable members of the SCS to obtain wider experience. It transferred to charitable status in 1997 and expanded its links with the not-for-profit sector. Now it has over 130 briefings each year together with leadership development programmes and recruitment of NEDs. The Cabinet Office also has an interchange programme to support secondments which are seen as secure ways of gaining experience of other sectors without losing seniority within the SCS. While offering opportunities to gain new skills, secondments also help secure promotion, although some had concerns about re-entry into their former departments (WIG 2022). However, as with other SCS training and development processes, there is no agreed evaluation of the experience gained by secondees and their responses in research are anecdotal (Barkworth 2004). For the host organisations, they value understanding how government works.

Public appointments

In March 2022, there were 4,476 public appointments, of which 58 per cent were made by Government Ministers and 42 per cent were appointments delegated by ministers to junior ministers and civil servants (Gill and Dalton 2022). Public appointments depend on assessment and recommendation by civil servants. Those seeking these roles understand they need to maintain good relations with the SCS. Until the mid-1990s, public appointments were made by government departments but this was called into question when there were accusations of sleaze and political patronage at the end of Major's government. The Office of the Commissioner for Public Appointments was established and supported through the Cabinet Office, although with inadequate staff (McTavish and Pyper 2007). In Scotland there is a separate Commissioner who is more independent and funded through the Scottish Parliament. Where civil servants are appointed to public bodies, this is within civil service rules as overseen by the First Civil Service Commissioner but with little control by ministers (Gill and Dalton 2022). When public appointments are to be made, departmental civil servants draw up specifications, which are approved by ministers and then sit on appointment panels. Appointments are undertaken within departments and not monitored by the Cabinet Office. The process can be fraught with disagreements between civil servants, advisers and ministers who contribute at each stage and appointments can be delayed by power struggles between the department and No 10 (Gill and Dalton 2022).

The extent of political involvement and patronage for public appointments is higher than formerly (Gill and Dalton 2022). Ministers' views on candidates may differ from civil servants who sit on panels to represent them. The twin features of politicisation and patronage have grown since the Johnson government where civil servants have been lobbied by SpADs to include Conservative party donors for these roles (Gill and Dalton 2022). More recently, the government has been operating a system of public appointments which has been used to control client organisations. The appointment of former senior politicians to chair major arts bodies such as the British Museum is an example, but there has also been a suggestion of conflict of interest in the appointment of Robbie Gibb to the BBC board whilst also being a part owner of the Jewish Chronicle and sometime adviser to GB news as well as being an ally of Boris Johnson. The role of the First Civil Service Commissioner was non-political for over 100 years until former MP and chair of the Vote Leave campaign, Baroness Stuart was appointed. This post is expected to safeguard civil service impartiality but, as a crown appointment, is not subject to scrutiny (Gill and Dalton 2022).

Honours

Honours are awarded by the sovereign and Prime Minister. The majority of honours are given to those who are in public service including current and former civil servants. The judgment on who receives an award is moderated by the civil service. In each department the process is led by the Permanent Secretary with an independent chair and advisers. To be considered for an honour, individuals are supported through 'write in' campaigns to civil servants to get their candidates on the list and it is often helped if these supporters have received honours. The public can nominate those they consider worthy of an honour, with each vetted by these departmental teams. Those who have caused problems, spoken out against the government or civil service will not receive an honour. There are those in society who crave these honours and shape their careers to improve their chances. Political honours can be supported by party donations.

In 2004, Sir Haydn Phillips, Permanent Secretary of the Department of Constitutional Affairs, published a review of the honours system. He made three recommendations including that its chairs should be independent, but the system should not be detached from the civil service. He also recommended that the process should continue to be led by Permanent Secretaries who are regarded as impartial by those advising on the system. External advisers are appointed for 3 years and can be renewed for another period. Philips found that in the nine sub-committees established to make nominations, 62 per cent of their membership was drawn from civil servants and it was recognised that, while their role is significant, there are other ways it could be run. Philips recommended retaining much of the system as operated by the civil service because it is seen to be impartial and objective.

Managing ministers

The SCS maintains control over access to ministers through the Private Office (Rhodes 2007). Blair, as Prime Minister, never had access to a mobile phone. All his communication was through his office and networks installed on his appointment. Other ministers speak about being cut off from friends and media with information provided in pre-digested formats. Access can be extended to selected journalists for placed stories, think tanks and advisers. When ministers attend meetings, answer questions in Parliament, or are interviewed, they are provided with briefings which include lines to take. Ministers have attempted to circumnavigate this issue through the appointment of SpADs. There were proposals for each minister to have a planning unit around them in the Fulton Report but this was never implemented. HM Government (2012) proposed that there should be SpADs included in a team of 20 around the minister appointed directly without any civil service veto (Lodge 2014). This was later dropped when May became Prime Minister.

Managing outside Whitehall

Gaslighting

Sowing confusion and undermining institutions is a method of government gaslighting the population or specific institutions within it (Cheung 2021). It can be associated with fake news, false statistics, wrong international comparisons and misappropriated outcomes. All of these have been used in the UK and there is an issue about the extent to which the civil service has been compliant. This may include agreeing government statements which are open electioneering as by the Treasury in 2024. It may be by failing to regulate or stop false communications, for example those used by the Conservative Party in the London mayoral elections 2024. While gaslighting is normally associated with authoritarian regimes (Cheung 2021), it can also be associated with authoritarian politicians within democratic systems and their interest in maintaining power. Over time their parties may shift the dial on what is acceptable communication behaviour as shown by Johnson when Prime Minister. Here gaslighting is extended to institutions of the state such as the judiciary and 'experts'.

Gaslighting is used to maintain power and control by destabilising and undermining others, as well as removing their ability to own their own narrative (Garrick and Buck 2022). It is less discussed in the way the civil service works with institutions it wishes make more compliant (Garrick and Buck 2022). There are two particular institutions where gaslighting has been used in the UK – in local government and in the role of the EU in the UK during its membership. There are a range of techniques that are used (Short 2023). Firstly those being gaslighted can be persistently undermined, belittled and ridiculed. Secondly, they can be blamed for problems and thirdly they can be set up for failure with schemes and initiatives that do not work. Gaslighting wears down the target over time so that it can become tired, lack confidence and assume that the blame attributed must in some way be true. They also become compliant in their behaviour, seeking to gain any scraps of benefit that may be available. The reduction of the powers and role of local government in England at the hands of the civil service has been consistent since the early 1990s and associated with the denigrating confusion introduced by government for local government reorganisation. In hindsight, it is clear that the civil service wanted to demonstrate a lack of competence in English local government as it introduced mechanisms to control the effects of EU subsidiarity principles introduced in the Maastricht Treaty 1992. Institutions such as Government Offices of the Regions (Spencer and Mawson 2000) and Regional Development Agencies were introduced to determine how EU policies and structural funds were to be applied rather than providing local government with powers of project selection (Danson and Lloyd 2012). When the EU Committee of the Regions was established in 1994, the government proposed to send their nominees as members rather than democratically elected local leaders. The members of the SCS who became directors of the government offices for the regions were intended to evolve into *prefets* with territorial control (Barter 2002).

The gaslighting operated for the UK–EU relationship was one of fear and silence. References to the role of EU policy and legislation were strongly discouraged by the SCS and those raising them were encouraged into silence by colleagues. Persistence in raising these issues could result in a loss of funding and wider institutional sanctions in a practical omerta. Anyone raising the issue was seen as being pro-EU and therefore in some way unpatriotic. Denigration of critics and a failure to engage in discussion suggested those criticising the civil service did not understand the issues. This stonewall approach is well known to those seeking to engage with civil servants but seldom discussed. It is also a useful 'tell' when working with those who hold the trust of civil servants when they use the same tactics.

Hiding in plain sight

One of the key ways in which the SCS maintain power is to hide important issues in plain sight. The most obvious way in which this is done was through the abolition of Departmental websites so it is no longer possible to easily access and view policy documents. These will be available through an online search if the correct title is known but such searches rely on having expectation that reports exist. This failure to provide departmental policies and websites has been overcome to some extent by the increasing role of the House of Commons Library. Here, the staff research matters for MPs and have access to information direct from departments which must respond to their requests. The reports and briefings published are now most frequently the only source of information on the derivation and management of a particular policy, how it has been changed and how effective it is in practice.

10

The Civil Service – Forwards or Back?

What is the need for change?

The maintenance of power by the Senior Civil Service (SCS), despite efforts of successive governments to implement long-lasting reform, is a constitutional issue. It unbalances the Westminster Model (WM) in more consistent and persistent ways than other tendencies such as prime ministerial presidentialism or by-passing Parliament (Freedman 2024a). Reversion to 'business as usual' for the SCS, whatever changes are implemented, is a serious issue that is never discussed. There is no accountability for poor implementation or evaluation of policy advice. If the British state is to thrive, there needs to be a full discussion of the persistence of SCS power and the lattice of leverage it exercises as discussed in Chapter 9. Reform of civil service culture as a self-maintaining elite is more challenging than ever recognised. The civil service is a closed organisation, led, but not managed, by culturally reinforcing elite 'heroes'. Within an internally focused organisation, recruitment will be in the image of existing senior staff. In response to Brexit and devolution, Permanent Secretaries have sought to increase their control over parts of their functions outsourced or peripheralised as mechanistic in the 1980s and 1990s for which they have financial but not operational responsibility.

There are expectations, that over time, powers lost to the SCS, through successive government reforms, can be regained and there seems little that a government can do to ensure that changes are culturally embedded. While the growing dissatisfaction with the delivery of policy has failed to be addressed by 'set piece' reform reviews, which are dropped when governments change, there are stages to longer lasting change which are not generally considered in these processes. While these civil service reviews make the case for change from the government's perspective, they do not make it from that of the country or make the case for change to civil servants.

In order to approach change in ways that appeal to the culture of the civil service, a number of issues need to be addressed. These issues have been considered in this book including the increasing role of political advisers, devolution, including subsequent attempts to recentralise the state and Brexit – all set in the context of major failures of policy administration. These issues require constitutional attention not short-term reform (Denham and Morphet 2024). Freedman (2024a), in his book *Failed State*, also points to the inability of governments to change civil service culture, exemplifying this through removing local authorities, as a key part of government and undermining of the role of parliament in refining legislation prior to its implementation. He cites the speeding news cycle, which is generated by social media rather than traditional news outlets of the press and terrestrial TV, with clickbait stories being more important than policy narrative. In identifying these challenges, Freedman also discusses the actions that could be taken to overcome them – including greater decentralisation and restoring the primacy of policy over short-term media responses. His proposed solutions to these issues are thoughtful and some are being taken up by the government (Freedman 2024b). However, his view about civil service reform rests on providing the SCS with more power and higher pay, bowing to the mantra that the SCS needs the 'brightest and the best' minds when his arguments demonstrate that the country needs a greater focus on those who have greater experience of policy administration. He does not consider, alongside others proposing reform such as the IfG, what will bring the SCS to recognise that they need to engage in cultural reform rather than the maintenance of power.

In considering the issues that are more foundational to the British constitution, which, up to now, the civil service has not been able to reverse, how can these be accommodated within the WM or which more formal constitutional changes could influence change of civil service cultural values? There are four issues to consider – devolution, the increased role of special advisers, Brexit and the contractual state.

Can the WM accommodate devolution?

The Conservative Government 2019–24 proposed civil service reforms, set in a 'Declaration on Government Reform' (Cabinet Office 2021) in the context of what had been learned from the management of the COVID-19 pandemic. The proposed reforms highlighted that the four nations of the UK handled the pandemic differently with little power in Whitehall to control the UK. It demonstrated that devolution made Whitehall primarily in charge of England only. While this had been identified as an issue, with action to return central powers through Brexit reforms, the public recognition of the limited range of powers for Whitehall within a national crisis was a wake-up moment. While the *de jure* powers of the devolved administration had been reduced, the *de facto* leadership role for their places had been cemented. It also demonstrated that the Mayors of Combined Authorities in England were on the same trajectory of public recognition and approval (Kippin and Morphet 2023). The WM does not recognise the sub-national state in the UK and it may require other changes to confirm to the civil service that they have to find a new cultural accommodation. This could be through the reform of the House of Lords based on the nations and regions – directly or indirectly elected, like those in the rest of the world. Prime Minister Starmer's new Council for the Nations and Regions introduced in July 2024 could become this new second chamber (Balls et al 2024), legitimating devolved administrations by recognising their role in leadership of the UK state. There are also more pragmatic solutions. The English Devolution White Paper (2024) on 'local first' as a practical embodiment of subsidiarity could change power relations although the civil service is already embedded in these new sub-regional structures of Mayoral Combined Authorities (Anderson 2024) so this might be only of limited effect.

A second and longer lasting change could be generated if the UK re-engages with the EU. At the point of Brexit, the strengthening and extension of subsidiarity in the EU Treaty was about to take more significant effect and would have had consequences in the UK's constitution for increased devolved decision making and funding. A case for further extensions of subsidiarity is being made by sub-national governments within the EU, who argue that their role at the local level, implementing EU objectives for economic growth, reducing economic disparities and improving conditions for EU citizens, including housing, is at the front line of fighting growing tides of populism. Subsidiarity is an embedded treaty principle and its practices and potential are also supported by other international institutions such as the World Bank, the OECD and IMF and appears likely to grow in importance. The EC is also gradually changing its focus away from silo polices to how they interact spatially within places. If the UK decides to re-engage, it will soon discover that EU policy processes are like a travelator. The UK could not engage at the point where it left the EU in 2020 but would need to align with policies as they are at the point of re-engagement. There could be considerable changes required in the way that subsidiarity is applied in the UK state to meet the EU's terms. This could have a significant effect on function and role of the civil service.

Can the WM accommodate SpADs?

The Committee for Standards in Public Life (CSPL) (2023) argued that deteriorating relationships have an influence on the effectiveness of government. In evidence to the Public Administration and Constitutional

Affairs Committee (PACAC), the CSPL described this 'democratic tension' inherent in the relationship between ministers and civil servants (Worlidge 2023). While relationships between the civil service and ministers can be difficult, not least when civil servants have to provide ministers with unwelcome advice on policy and its delivery, they are not accustomed to being openly criticised and attacked. The civil service has managed to ignore, incorporate and reverse reforms pressing it to increase its focus on the administration of policy. However, the growth in SpADs to make good these skills deficits threatens the WM in different ways. In government, there are now three parties in the marriage where there were two, and the inability of the civil service to remove SpADs has changed to a position of accommodation. How long can this position continue without formal recognition that change in the WM is needed? At the same time, the power of the Treasury over Departments and the SpADs within them remains unchallenged, shaping behaviours and reducing energy for change.

What will be the long-term consequences for the civil service of Brexit?

The loss of policy focus and competence during the UK's membership of the EU, when a transactional model was used, has yet to be understood and addressed. It is still possible for the Cabinet Office to use policy framing that was part of EU future preparations before the UK left but there is also a danger of failing to realise the speed with which EU policy can change and the dynamic influence of a regular re-set of the Commission members and the Multiannual Financial Framework processes that begin in 2025. The focus of the Labour Government, elected in 2024, to restore relations with the EU and to smooth the speed of regulatory alignment between the UK and the EU will encourage and enable re-engagement on a wide range of issues so the policy vacuum may only be a short one in practice.

How can the civil service be focused on administration within the contractual state?

The failure of the contractual state and the civil service's role in this is being increasingly foregrounded, as shown in this book, but what is most surprising is the non-attribution of blame. Each of the inquiries into the most recent round of failures – Windrush, the Post Office Horizon prosecutions, infected blood, border control, water quality, Grenfell – have all appeared to have little relationship with advice given by civil servants. In any other organisation there would be investigations into these failures which would have focused on decision making processes and reforms. In these cases, the successive rounds of inquiry have found that these administrative disasters have been compounded by failures to implement the recommendations of previous inquiries. Can the state continue to allow this level of failure and cost without examining more fundamentally how decisions are taken and changing the advice processes that make them? Freedman (2024a) recommends that these services should be taken back from arm's length or outsourced arrangements but there is still no guarantee that this would work, given the way in which SCS culture despises what are regarded as mechanistic and not cerebral tasks. Other options could be to decentralise some of them to the local state or increase the independence of regulators, reporting to parliament rather than ministers.

What are the possible tools for change?

If changes are needed, then what tools for maintained change are available? One would be to attempt cross-party consensus for reform but this can be undermined by changes in government. The second could be a Royal Commission or Inquiry but any major proposals can be undermined and vilified as Fulton demonstrated. Other options may include changing the focus of the constitution which would have, *inter alia*, effects on the way in which the civil service functions. This may be difficult to achieve although incremental constitutional reforms could have a role, including reforming the role of accounting officers (AOs) by changing their terms of reference from the Treasury to require them to work in a more joined up way across government and to make permanent secretaries, as AOs, responsible for the consequences of administrative expenditure decisions leaving policy expenditure decisions to ministers. Reform of the Treasury's grip, that has been in operation since its own memorandum of 1868, could be given a legal basis that could be examined and challenged in law.

Civil servants accepting the need for change in the civil service

The future of the civil service appears to be located in its past. The strength of its culture in maintaining its position and long-term view of its role remains unassailable despite many public criticisms by politicians but there is still no attribution for policy failure. While governments attempt to change the civil service's focus, recruitment and performance, no mechanism has been found that will cause the civil service to change in fundamental and permanent ways. Recruiting in its own image, maintaining an internal focus on organisation and powers (NAO 2024), the civil service has developed a range of strategies to retain the status quo. Over recruitment allows it to place fast streamers into think tanks, run government bodies, lead charities and serve on a myriad of bodies. It creates a sense of yearning in civil servants to return to their former jobs. For older, former civil servants, hanging on to their briefcases was a visible symbol of belonging to this elite. For others, understanding the importance of maintaining contacts through their new external positions but never being repatriated, not least as they are more useful in the roles that they are now performing and subsequently rewarded through appointments and/or honours.

What effective measures can be implemented to address this civil service culture in ways that prove more effective and long-lasting than measures taken hitherto? Like a piece of stretched elastic, reforms return to the original form once released. What could make the civil service accept the need and embrace reform to incorporate change?

There are some options. The first is to force reform through changing accountability between the civil service and the institution of government. The role of Parliamentary scrutiny could be extended to include greater transparency, more accountability of civil servants to Parliament, and/or a clearer requirement for officials to issue ministerial directions where they believe a decision is irregular, falls short of high standards of public conduct, is unlikely to be feasible, or does not represent the best use of public money. The civil service could also be given a public service obligation, shifting their accountability to the people. These measures would remove their primary accountability to the executive and may create difficulties in management.

Another approach could be for the civil service to recognise that its own position and credibility is under threat within the state. Should government decide to increase the accountability of the civil service for their client role in outsourced contracts and make named civil servants responsible for projects, this might change this internally focused culture. A further approach could be to end internal recruitment and make appointments open to public job markets. There would be strong opposition to both of these suggestions and ministers might feel fearful of suggesting them. But this fear of recommending change and seeing it through, provides one of the greatest cases for it to be undertaken and needs public discussion.

Do these proposals go far enough? The solutions suggested by the Cabinet Office in 2023 appear to be the same as those in Fulton (1968) and subsequently – wider recruitment from outside, including more specialist and professionals, but there is no consideration as to why these practices have not worked over the last 50 years. It was suggested that this failure to recruit related to the type of advertisements without considering the culture and the failure to retain external appointees (NAO 2024) – a topic addressed by Polly Toynbee (2023) in her piece after the death of Lord Kerslake.

Meanwhile, the civil service reforms proposed by the Conservative Government 2019–24 were lost at the point of the General Election and the incoming Labour Government has reverted to the more generic approaches to civil service reform that could have been stated by almost all previous governments since the 1960s:

> The government is also developing a strategic plan for a more efficient and effective civil service, including through improving skills and harnessing digital technology to drive better outcomes for public services. (HM Treasury 2024b: para 2.12)

> The civil service is a key enabler to support improved productivity across the UK's public services. This government is therefore taking forward work to deliver a civil service workforce plan and underpinning reform proposals for a more efficient and effective civil service, including bold options to improve skills, harness digital technology and drive better outcomes for public services. (HM Treasury 2024: para 2.98)

In making these bland statements, the Labour Government may be suggesting no great civil service reforms so it will be interesting to see whether the next failure of administration that is uncovered will generate a different government response or whether policies for devolution and EU re-engagement will be used to generate change in other ways. Sir Keir Starmer is unique among Prime Ministers in that he has been part of the SCS at the highest levels and participated in its operations in practice. His appointment and then dismissal of senior civil servant Sue Gray as an adviser in favour of his chief SpAD perhaps suggests a pathway of change that has yet to be revealed with a more subtle approach to long lasting civil service reform in the future. We will see …

References

Aberbach, J. D. and Rockman, B. A. (1994) 'Civil servants and politicians: neutral or responsive competence', *Governance*, 7: 461–9.

Agasisti, T., Arena, M., Catalano, G. and Erbacci, A. (2015) 'Defining spending reviews: a proposal for a taxonomy, with applications to Italy and the UK', *Public Money & Management*, 35(6): 423–30.

Ahrend, R., Farchy, E., Kaplanis, I. and Lembcke, A. C. (2014) *What Makes Cities More Productive? Evidence On The Role Of Urban Governance From Five OECD Countries*, Paris: OECD.

Aidt, T., Grey, F. and Savu, A. (2021) 'The meaningful votes: voting on Brexit in the British House of Commons', *Public Choice*, 186: 587–617.

Aitken, J. (1995) HM Treasury Press Release, 15 February, HM Treasury.

Alder, J. (1999) 'The structure of the UK Constitution: an overview', *Constitutional and Administrative Law*, London: Palgrave, pp 44–68.

Alesina, A. and Spolaore, E. (2005) *The Size of Nations*, Cambridge, MA: MIT Press.

Al-Jamal, D. and Cullingford, C. (2016) '"Sitting with Nellie"? Subject knowledge and the role of the mentor', in C. Cullingford (ed) *Mentoring in Education: An International Perspective*, London: Routledge, pp 135–52.

Allcock, T. and Campbell, M. L. (2021) 'The UK Dangerous Dogs Act: improved, but legally and ethically flawed', *Veterinary Record*, 189(3): e24, DOI: 10.1002/vetr.24

Allen, N. and Bara, J. (2021) 'Clear blue water? The 2019 party manifestos', *The Political Quarterly*, 92(3): 531–40.

Anderson, P. (2024) 'Making English devolution work: Mayoral Combined Authorities and inter-governmental relations', PSA Annual Conference, 27 March, University of Strathclyde.

Andrew, C. (2012) *The Defence of the Realm: The Authorized History of MI5*, London: Penguin.

Andrews, L. (2017) 'How can we demonstrate the public value of evidence-based policy making when government ministers declare that the people "have had enough of experts"?', *Palgrave Communications*, 3(1): 1–9.

Andrews, L. (2021) 'The forward march of devolution halted – and the limits of progressive unionism', *The Political Quarterly*, 92(3): 512–21.

Andrews, L. (2024) 'The ministerial role: activism and agency', in *Ministerial Leadership: Practice, Performance and Power*, Cham: Springer, pp 73–95.

Andrews, R. and Beynon, M. J. (2024) 'The revolving door in UK government departments: A configurational analysis', *Regulation & Governance*, 18(2): 590–611.

Apps, P. (2022) *Show Me the Bodies: How We Let Grenfell Happen*, London: Oneworld Publications.

Armstrong, K. A. (2018) 'Regulatory alignment and divergence after Brexit', *Journal of European Public Policy*, 25(8): 1099–117.

Armstrong R. (1985) 'The Duties and responsibilities of civil servants in relation to minsters', in G. Marshall (ed), *Ministerial Responsibilities*, Oxford: Oxford University Press, pp 140–5.

Armstrong W. (1970[1971]) 'The Civil Service Department and its tasks' in R. A. Chapman and A. Dunsire (eds) *Style in Administration: Readings in British Public Administration*, London: Allen & Unwin, pp 318–37.

Arribas, G. V. and Bourdin, D. (2012) 'What does the Lisbon Treaty change regarding subsidiarity within the EU institutional framework?', *EIPAScope*, 2012(2): 13–17.

Arshed, N. (2017) 'The origins of policy ideas: the importance of think tanks in the enterprise policy process in the UK', *Journal of Business Research*, 71: 74–83.

Aucoin, P. and Heintzman, R. (2000) 'The dialectics of accountability for performance in public management reform', *International Review of Administrative Sciences*, 66(1): 45–55.

Bachtler, J. and Mendez, C. (2020) 'Cohesion policy', *Policy-Making in the European Union* [online], Available from: https://strathprints.strath.ac.uk/75890/1/Bachtler_Mendez_OUP_2020_Cohesion_policy_doing_more_with.pdf

Bailey, J. and Lloyd, P. (2017) 'The introduction of design to policymaking: Policy Lab and the UK government', *Annual Review of Policy Design*, 5(1): 1–14.

Bailey, S. and Elliott, M. (2009) 'Taking local government seriously: democracy, autonomy and the constitution', *The Cambridge Law Journal*, 68(2): 436–72.

Baldini, G., Bressanelli, E. and Massetti, E. (2018) 'Who is in control? Brexit and the Westminster model', *The Political Quarterly*, 89(4): 537–44.

Balls, E. (2024) 'Britain's growing regional divides: Reviewing the regional economics, politics and policy-making of the UK since 1979', Harvard University [online], Available from: https://sites.harvard.edu/uk-regional-growth/

Balogh, T. (1959) 'The apotheosis of the dilettante', in H. Thomas (ed) *The Establishment: A Symposium*, London: Anthony Blond.

Bara, J. (2005).) 'A question of trust: Implementing party manifestos', *Parliamentary Affairs*, 58(3): 585–99.

Baratta, R. (2014) 'Complexity of EU law in the domestic implementing process', *Theory and Practice of Legislation*, 2: 293.

Barber, M. (2007) *Instruction to Deliver Fighting to Transform Britain's Public Services*, London: Methuen.

Barber, M. (2015) *How to Run a Government*, London: Allen Lane.

Barberis, J. P. (1989) *Permanent Secretaries in the British Civil Service: An Historical and Biographical Survey*, Manchester: The University of Manchester.

Barberis, P. (1996a) 'Introductory essay: Whitehall since the Fulton report', in P. Barberis (ed) *The Whitehall Reader*, Maidenhead: Open University Press pp 1–20.

Barberis, P. (1996b) *The Elite of the Elite: Permanent Secretaries in the British Higher Civil Service*, London: Dartmouth Publishing.

Barca, F. (2009) *Agenda for a Reformed Cohesion Policy*, Brussels: European Communities.

Barker, A. and Wilson, G. K. (1997) 'Whitehall's disobedient servants? Senior officials' potential resistance to ministers in British government departments', *British Journal of Political Science*, 27(2): 223–46.

Barkworth, R. (2004) 'Secondments: A review of current research: A background paper for IES research network members', Brighton: Institute for Employment Studies [online], Available from: https://www.employment-studies.co.uk/system/files/resources/files/mp66.pdf

Barlow, P. and Paun, A. (2013) *Civil Service Accountability to Parliament*, IfG.

Barratt, E. (2014) '"Modernizing" government – the case of the cooperatives of the civil service', *Management & Organizational History*, 9(2): 150–65.

Bartels, L. (2016) 'The UK's status in the WTO after Brexit' [online], Available from: https://papers.ssrn.com/sol3/papers.cfm?abstract_id=2841747

Barter, W. R. (2002) 'Regional government in England: reviewing the evidence base', in J. Tomaney and J. Mawson (eds) *England*, Bristol: Policy Press, pp 11–24.

Barwell, G. (2021) *Chief of Staff*, London: Atlantic Books.

Baumgartner F. and Leech, B. (2001) 'Interest niches and policy bandwagons: patterns of interest group involvement in national politics', *Journal of Politics*, 63(4): 1191–213.

Baumgartner, F. R., Jones, B. D. and Mortensen, P. B. (2018) 'Punctuated equilibrium theory: explaining stability and change in public policymaking', *Theories of the Policy Process*, 55–101.

Baxendale, C. (2014) *How to Best Attract, Induct and Retain Talent recruited into the Senior Civil Service* [online], Available from: https://www.civilservant.org.uk/library/2014-Baxendale_Report.pdf

Beer, S. (1955) 'Treasury control: the coordination of financial policy in Great Britain', *The American Political Science Review*, 49(1): 144–60.

Bell, E., Fourton, C. and Sowels, N. (2021) 'Introduction: public services in the UK: the ongoing challenges of delivery and public accountability', *Revue Française de Civilisation Britannique*, 26(2) [online], Available from: https://journals.openedition.org/rfcb/7803

Bennett, C. (1991) 'What is policy convergence and what causes it?', *British Journal of Political Science*, 21(2): 215–33.

Bennister, M. (2009) 'Tony Blair as prime minister', in T. Casey (ed) *The Blair Legacy: Politics, Policy, Governance, and Foreign Affairs*, London: Palgrave Macmillan, pp 165–77.

Benton, M. and Russell, M. (2013) 'Assessing the impact of parliamentary oversight committees: the select committees in the British House of Commons', *Parliamentary Affairs*, 66(4): 772–97.

Bevan, G. (2023) *How did Britain Come to This?* London: LSE Press.

Bevir, M. (2008) 'The Westminster model, governance and judicial reform', *Parliamentary Affairs*, 61(4): 559–77.

Bevir, M. and Rhodes, R. A. (2006) 'Prime ministers, presidentialism and Westminster smokescreens', *Political Studies*, 54(4): 671–90.

Bevir, M. and Rhodes, R. A. (2010) *Interpretive Political Science, Volume 4*, London: Routledge.

Bezes, P. (2007) 'Building Weberian bureaucracies in the era of New Public Management?' *International Reviews*, (2): 9–29.

Birkland, T. A. and DeYoung, S. E. (2012) 'Focusing events and policy windows', in E. Araral, S. Fritzen, M. Howlett, M. Ramesh and X. Wu (eds) *Routledge Handbook of Public Policy*, London: Routledge, pp 175–88.

Blackstone, T. and Plowden, W. (1988) *Inside the Think Tank: Advising the Cabinet, 1971–83*, London: Heinemann.

Blair, T. (2010) *A Journey*, London: Penguin.

Blick, A. (2014) 'Harold Wilson, Labour and the machinery of government', in G. O'Hara and H. Parr (eds) *The Wilson Governments 1964–1970 Reconsidered*, London: Routledge, pp 40–59.

Blick, A. and Hennessy, P. (2019) 'Good chaps no more', *Safeguarding the Constitution in Stressful Times* [online], Available from: https://consoc.org.uk/wp-content/uploads/2019/11/FINAL-Blick-Hennessy-Good-Chaps-No-More.pdf

Blunkett, D. (2006) *The Blunkett Tapes: My life in the Bear Pit*, London: Bloomsbury.

Bogdanor, V. (1977) 'The Crossman diaries', *Political Studies*, 25(1): 110–21.

Bogdanor, V. (1997) 'Ministerial accountability', *Parliamentary Affairs*, 50(1): 71–84.

Bostock, D. (2002) 'Coreper revisited', *Journal of Common Market Studies*, 40(2): 215–34.

Bottomore, T. (1964) *Elites and Society*, New Jersey: Basic Books.

Bovaird, T. (2015) 'Marketing in public sector organizations', in *Public Management and Governance*, London: Routledge, pp 76–89.

Bovaird, T. and Russell, K. (2007) 'Civil service reform in the UK, 1999–2005: revolutionary failure or evolutionary success?', *Public Administration*, 85(2): 301–28.

Boyle, E. (1965) 'Minister or Civil Servant? I. Minister', *Public Administration*, 43(3): 251–9.

Boys-Smith, S. W. (1968) *The Relations Between the British Treasury and the Departments of the Central Government in the Nineteenth Century*, Doctoral dissertation, University of British Columbia.

Brans, M. and Vancoppenolle, D. (2005) 'Policy-making reforms and civil service systems: an exploration of agendas and consequences', in M. Painter and J. Pierre (eds) *Challenges to State Policy Capacity: Global Trends and Comparative Perspectives*, London: Palgrave Macmillan, pp 164–84.

Bray, J. (1979) *Decision in Government*, London: Victor Gollancz.

Brenner, N. (2019) *New Urban Spaces: Urban Theory and the Scale Question*, Oxford: Oxford University Press.

Bridges, E. (1950[1971]) 'Portrait of a profession' in R. A. Chapman and A. Dunsire (eds) *Style in Administration: Readings in British Public Administration*, London: Allen & Unwin, pp 44–60.

Bridges, E. (1954) 'The reforms of 1854 in retrospect', *The Political Quarterly*, 25(4): 316–23.

Bristow, G. (2001) 'Bypassing Barnett: the comprehensive spending review and public expenditure in Wales', *Economic Affairs*, 21(3): 44–7.

Brown, A. (2020) 'All power to 10 Downing Street: Johnson's first major reshuffle and the perils of presidentialism', *British Policy and Politics at LSE*, 1–3.

BrownSwan, C., Anderson, P. and Sijstermans, J. 2024 'Politics and the Pandemic: The UK Covid-19 Inquiry and Devolution', *The Political Quarterly*.

Bryson, J. M., Crosby, B. C. and Bloomberg, L. (2014) 'Public value governance: Moving beyond traditional public administration and the new public management', *Public Administration Review*, 74(4): 445–56.

Bullock, H., Mountford, J. and Stanley, R. (2001) *Better Policy-Making*, London: Centre for Management and Policy Studies.

Bulmer, S. (2013) 'Politics in time meets the politics of time: historical institutionalism and the EU timescape', in K. Goetz and J.-H. Meyer-Sahling (eds) *The EU Timescape*, London: Routledge, pp 128–45.

Bulmer, S. and Burch, M. (2005) 'The Europeanization of UK Government: from Quiet Revolution to Explicit Step-Change?', *Public Administration*, 83(4): 861–90.

Bunbury, H. (1928) 'Efficiency as an alternative to control', *Public Administration*, VI: 96–105.

Burch, M. and Holliday, I. (2004) 'The Blair government and the core executive', *Government and Opposition*, 39(1): 1–21.

Burnham, J. and Pyper, R. (2008) *Britain's Modernised Civil Service*, London: Macmillan International Higher Education.

Butcher, T. (1991) 'The Thatcher era and the civil service: the legacy of the 1980s', *Teaching Public Administration*, 11(2): 12–21.

Butcher, T. (1995) 'The Major Government and Whitehall: the civil service at the crossroads', *Teaching Public Administration*, 15(1): 19–31.

Butler, R. (2004) *Review of Intelligence on Weapons of Mass Destruction*, London: The Stationery Office.

Cabinet Office (1970) *The Reorganisation of Central Government*, Cm 4505, London: HMSO.

Cabinet Office (1994) *The Civil Service: Continuity and Change*, Cm 2627, London: HMSO.

Cabinet Office (1999a) *Modernising Government*, Cm 4310, London: HMSO.

Cabinet Office (1999b) *Reform of the Civil Service: The Wilson Report*, London: HMSO.

Cabinet Office (2003) *The Government's Response to the Ninth Report of the Committee on Standards in Public Life*, Cm 5964, London: HMSO.

Cabinet Office (2012) *Reforms to Increase Accountability at the Very Top of the Civil Service* [online], Available from: https://www.gov.uk/government/news/reforms-to-increase-accountability-at-the-very-top-of-the-civil-service

Cabinet Office (2015) *Introduction to Devolution: Devolution and You* [online], Available from: https://assets.publishing.service.gov.uk/media/5c37319aed915d731281fe13/IntroductionToDevolution.pdf

Cabinet Office (2021) *Declaration on Government Reform* [online], Available from: https://www.gov.uk/government/publications/declaration-on-government-reform

Cabinet Office and DLUHC (2022) *Review of Intergovernmental Relations* [online], Available from: https://www.gov.uk/government/publications/the-review-of-intergovernmental-relations/review-of-intergovernmental-relations-html

Cabinet Office, Civil Service and DLUHC (2023) *Devolution: Guidance for Civil Servants* [online], Available from: https://www.gov.uk/government/publications/devolution-guidance-for-civil-servants/devolution-guidance-for-civil-servants

Cairney, P. (2011) *The Scottish Political System Since Devolution*, Exeter: Imprint Academic.

Cairney, P. and Kippin, S. (2023) *Politics and Policy Making in the UK*, Bristol: Policy Press.

Cambridge Dictionary (2024) [online], Available from: https://dictionary.cambridge.org/dictionary/english/administration

Campbell, Colin and Wilson, Graham (1995) *The End of Whitehall: A Comparative Perspective*. Cambridge, MA: Blackwell

Cassese, S. (1999) '3 Italy's Senior Civil Service: An Ossified', *Bureaucratic Elites in Western European States: A Comparative Analysis of Top Officials*, 55.

Castle, B. (1973) 'Mandarin Power', Sunday Times, 10 June.

Cavari, A., Rosenthal, M. and Shpaizman, I. (2023) 'Reevaluating the policy success of private members bills', *Research & Politics*, 10(2), DOI: 10.1177/20531680231181750

Cave, J. and Gibson, S. (2024) 'Assessing the impacts of primary and secondary legislation – a Real Options approach to rules for making rules', M-RCBG Associate Working Paper Series [online], Available from: https://dash.harvard.edu/bitstream/handle/1/37377675/Final_AWP_223.pdf?sequence=1

Cawood, I. (2016) 'Conclusion Joseph Chamberlain: his reputation and legacy', in I. Cawood and C. Upton (eds) *Joseph Chamberlain: International Statesman, National Leader, Local* Icon, London: Palgrave Macmillan UK.

Chapman, L. (1978) *Your Disobedient Servant*, London: Chatto and Windus.

Chapman, R. A. (1988) *Ethics in the British Civil Service*, London: Routledge.

Chapman, R. A. (1991) 'New arrangements for recruitment to the British Civil Service: cause for concern', *Public Policy and Administration*, 6(3): 1–6.

Chapman, R. (1997) *The Treasury in Public Policy-Making*, London: Routledge.

Chapman, R. A. (2000) 'Recruitment to the civil service fast stream development programme', *Public Policy and Administration*, 15(1): 3–14.

Chapman, R. (2004) *The Civil Service Commission, 1855/1991: A Bureau Biography*, London: Taylor Francis

Chapman, R. A. (2005) 'The Proposed UK Civil Service Act: a legal framework for enhancing ethics and integrity?', *Teaching Public Administration*, 25(1): 31–44.

Chapman R. and Dunsire, A.(eds) (1971) *Style in Administration: Readings in British Public Administration*, Allen and Unwin for the Royal Institute of Public Administration.

Chapman, R. A. and O'Toole, B. J. (1995) 'The role of the civil service: A traditional view in a period of change', *Public Policy and Administration*, 10(2): 3–20.

Chapman, R. A. and O'Toole, B. J. (2010) 'Leadership in the British civil service: an interpretation', *Public Policy and Administration*, 25(2): 123–36.

Cheung, A. Y. (2021) 'Legal gaslighting', *University of Toronto Law Journal*, 72(1): 50–80.

Christensen, T. and Lægreid, P. (2006) 'Agencification and regulatory reforms', in T. Christensen and P. Lægreid (eds) *Autonomy and Regulation: Coping with Agencies in the Modern State*, Cheltenham: Edward Elgar.

Christoph, J. B. (1975) 'A comparative view: Administrative secrecy in Britain', *Public Administration Review*, 35(1): 23–32.

Christoph, J. B. (1984) 'Rubbing up or running down? Dilemmas of civil service reform in Britain', in D. T. Studlar and J. L. Waltman (eds) *Dilemmas of Change in British Politics*, London: Palgrave Macmillan, pp 48–68.

Christoph, J. R. (1975) 'High civil servants and the politics of consensualism in Great Britain', in M. Dogan (ed) *The Mandarins of Western Europe*, London: John Wiley, pp 25–62.

Cliffe, J. (2022) 'Liz Truss and the rise of the libertarian right', *New Statesman*, 28 September.

Clifford, B. and Morphet, J. (2015) 'A policy on the move? Spatial planning and state actors in the post-devolutionary UK and Ireland', *The Geographical Journal*, 181(1): 16–25.

Clifford, B. and Morphet, J. (2023) *Major Infrastructure Planning and Delivery: Exploring Nationally Significant Infrastructure Projects (NSIPs) in England and Wales*, London: UCL Press.

Clift, B. (2023) *The Office for Budget Responsibility and the Politics of Technocratic Economic Governance*, Oxford: Oxford University Press.

Coats, D. and Passmore, E. (2008) *Public Value: The Next Steps in Public Service Reform*, London: Work Foundation, pp 1–65.

Cockfield, A. (1994) *The European Union: Creating the Single Market*, London: John Wiley and Sons.

Cole, A. (2012) 'Serving the nation: devolution and the civil service in Wales', *The British Journal of Politics and International Relations*, 14(3): 458–76.

Common, R. (2004) 'Organisational learning in a political environment: improving policy-making in UK government', *Policy Studies*, 25(1): 35–49.

Committee on Standards in Public Life (CSPL) (2023) *Response from the Committee on Standards in Public Life to the PACAC inquiry on Civil Service Leadership and Reform*.

Coombes, R. (2023) 'Food tsar resigns, saying that voters are "fed up" with broken food system', *BMJ*, 380: 673.

Cooper, C. A. (2020) 'Politics and the permanency of permanent secretaries: testing the vitality of the Westminster administrative tradition, 1949–2014', *British Politics*, 15(3): 311–25.

Corbett, J., Grube, D. C., Lovell, H. C. and Scott, R. J. (2020) *Institutional Memory as Storytelling: How Networked Government Remembers*, Cambridge: Cambridge University Press.

Corry, D. (2024) *Tales of the Unelected*, London: Bridge House.

Coyle, D. and Sensier, M. (2019) 'The imperial treasury: appraisal methodology and regional economic performance in the UK', *Regional Studies*, 54(3): 283–95.

Craven, R. (2020) 'The legal and social construction of value in government procurement markets', *Journal of Law and Society*, 47(1): 29–59.

Crossman, R. and Howard, A. (1991) *The Crossman Diaries*, London: Mandarin.

Cushion, S., Morani, M., Kyriakidou, M. and Soo, N. (2022) '(Mis)understanding the coronavirus and how it was handled in the UK: an analysis of public knowledge and the information environment', *Journalism Studies*, 23(5–6): 703–21.

Czischke, D. (2014) *Social Housing in Europe*, London: John Wiley & Sons.

Dahl, R. A. (1969) *Modern Political Analysis* (2nd edn) London: Yale University Press.

Dahlström, C., Peters, B. G. and Pierre, J. (eds) (2011) *Steering from the Centre: Strengthening Political Control in Western Democracies*, Toronto: University of Toronto Press.

Daintith, T. and Page A. (1999) *The Executive in the Constitution Structure, Autonomy and Internal Control*, Oxford: Oxford University Press.

Danson, M. and Lloyd, G. (2012) 'Devolution, institutions, and organisations: changing models of regional development agencies', *Environment and Planning C: Government and Policy*, 30(1): 78–94.

Dávid-Barrett, E. and Fazekas, M. (2020) 'Grand corruption and government change: an analysis of partisan favoritism in public procurement', *European Journal on Criminal Policy and Research*, 26(4): 411–30.

Davidson, S. and Elstub, S. (2014) 'Deliberative and participatory democracy in the UK', *The British Journal of Politics and International Relations*, 16(3): 367–85.

Davies, M. R. (1998) 'Civil servants, managerialism and democracy', *International Review of Administrative Sciences*, 64(1): 119–29.

Davis, A. (2018) *Reckless Opportunists: Elites at the end of the establishment*, Manchester: Manchester University Press.

Davis, G., Weller, P., Eggins, S. and Carswell, E. (1999) 'What drives machinery of government change? Australia, Canada and the United Kingdom, 1950–1997', *Public Administration*, 77(1): 7–50.

Davis, J. M. (2009) *Prime Ministers & Civil Service Reform 1960–74* (Doctoral dissertation), https://core.ac.uk/reader/30695613

Dawar, K. (2018) 'Legal issues of economic disintegration: government procurement and BREXIT', *Legal Issues of Economic Integration*, 45(2): 121–39.

Dawson, M. (2001) 'Leadership for the 21st century in the UK civil service', *International Review of Administrative Sciences*, 67(2): 263–71.

De Bièvre, D. (2013) 'The EU regulatory trade agenda and the quest for WTO enforcement', in J. Peterson and A. Young (eds) *The European Union and the New Trade Politics*, London: Routledge, pp 57–72.

Dehousse, R. (2013) 'The politics of delegation in the European Union', *Les Cahiers Europeens de Sciences Po*, 4 [online], Available from: https://sciencespo.hal.science/hal-02405022/file/n-4-2013-dehousse.pdf

De Lemos, T., Betts, M., Eaton, D. and De Almeida, L. T. (2000) 'From concessions to project finance and the private finance initiative', *Journal of Project Finance*, 6(3): 19–37.

Denham, A. and Garnett, M. (1998) 'Think tanks, British politics and the "climate of opinion"', in D. Stone, A. Denham and M. Garnett (eds) *Think Tanks Across Nations*, Manchester: Manchester University Press, pp 21–41.

Denham, J. and Morphet, J. (2024) 'Centralised by design: Anglocentric constitutionalism, accountability and the failure of english devolution', *The Political Quarterly*.

Derlien, H-U (1995) 'Public administration in Germany: political and societal relations', in J. Pierre (ed) *Bureaucracy in the Modern State: An Introduction to Comparative Public Administration*, Cheltenham: Edward Elgar, pp 64–91.

Diamond, P. (2018) *The End of Whitehall? Government by Permanent Campaign*, Cham: Springer.

Diamond, P. (2021) 'Destroying one public service Bargain without making another: A comment on Lowe and Pemberton, *The Official History of the British Civil Service, Volume II: 1982–1997*', *The Political Quarterly*, 92(1): 95–100.

Diamond, P. (2022) 'A Prime Minister's department might strengthen accountability and capacity in British government, but can also have serious repercussions', British Politics and Policy at LSE [blog], Available from: https://blogs.lse.ac.uk/politicsandpolicy/prime-ministers-department/

Diamond, P. (2023a) 'Post-Brexit challenges to the UK machinery of government in an "Age of Fiasco": the dangers of muddling through?', *Journal of European Public Policy*, 30(11): 2251–74.

Diamond, P. (2023b) 'Core executive politics in the Cameron era, 2010–16: the dynamics of Whitehall reform', *Government and Opposition*, 58(3): 516–34.

Diamond, P. and Richardson, J. (2023) 'The Brexit omnishambles and the law of large solutions', *Journal of European Public Policy*, 30(11): 2235–50.

Dibb, G. and Jung, C. (2024) 'Rock bottom: Low investment in the UK Economy', IPPR [online], Available from: https://www.ippr.org/articles/rock-bottom

Dicey, A. V. (1885) *Law of the Constitution*, Oxford: Oxford University Press.

DLUHC (2022) *Levelling Up the United Kingdom*, Cm 604, London: HMSO.

Doherty, L. and Sayegh, A. (2022) 'How to design and institutionalize spending reviews', *IMF How To Notes*, 2022(4) [online], Available from: https://www.imf.org/en/Publications/Fiscal-Affairs-Department-How-To-Notes/Issues/2022/09/20/How-to-Design-and-Institutionalize-Spending-Reviews-523364

Doig, A. (2003) 'Political corruption in the United Kingdom', in M. J. Bull and J. L. Newell (eds) *Corruption in Contemporary Politics*, London: Palgrave Macmillan, pp 178–90.

Dolezal, M., Ennser-Jedenastik, L., Müller, W. C., Praprotnik, K. and Winkler, A. K. (2018) 'Beyond salience and position taking: how political parties communicate through their manifestos', *Party Politics*, 24(3): 240–52.

Dolowitz, D. P. and Marsh, D. (1996) 'Who learns what from whom: a review of the policy transfer literature', *Political Studies*, 44(2): 343–57.

Dolowitz, D. P. and Marsh, D. (2000) 'Learning from abroad: the role of policy transfer in contemporary policy-making', *Governance*, 13(1): 5–23.

Domhoff, G. W. and Dye, T. R. (1987) *Power Elites and Organizations*, London: Sage.

Dommett, K. and Flinders, M. (2015) 'The centre strikes back: meta-governance, delegation, and the core executive in the United Kingdom, 2010–14', *Public Administration*, 93(1): 1–16.

Dowding, K. (1995) *The Civil Service*, London: Routledge.

Dowding, K. (2003) 'The civil service', in J. Hollowell (ed) *Britain Since 1945*, Oxford: Blackwell, pp 179–93.

Draca, M., Green, C. and Homroy, S. (2023) 'Financing UK democracy: a stocktake of 20 years of political donations disclosure', *Fiscal Studies*, 44(4): 433–49.

Drechsler, W. and Kattel, R. (2020) 'Debate: The developed civil servant – providing agility and stability at the same time', *Public Money & Management*, 40(8): 549–51.

Dudley, G. and Gamble, A. (2023) 'Brexit and UK policy-making: an overview', *Journal of European Public Policy*, 30(11): 2573–97.

Du Gay, P. (2000) 'Entrepreneurial governance and public management: the anti-bureaucrat's Paul du Gay', *New Managerialism, New Welfare?*, 69(2.1): 62.

Du Gay, P. (2006) 'Machinery of government and standards in public service: teaching new dogs old tricks: Texts reviewed', *Economy and Society*, 35(1): 148–67.

Dunleavy, P. (1991) *Democratic Bureaucracy and Public Choice*, London: Harvester Press.

Dunleavy, P. (2024) 'Restructuring UK government at the centre – why the IfG Commission's naïve plan will not work', *The Political Quarterly* [online], Available from: https://eprints.lse.ac.uk/123456/3/Restructuring_UK_government_at_the_centre_-_Why_the_IFG_Commission_s_na_ve_plan_will_not_work.pdf

Dunleavy, P. and Rhodes, R. A. (1990) 'Core executive studies in Britain', *Public Administration*, 68(1): 3–28.

Dunlop, A. 2021 *The Dunlop Review into UK Government Union Capability*, Cabinet Office.

Durrant, T. and Haddon, C. (2022) *Reinforcing Ethical Standards in Government*, London: Institute for Government.

Durrant, T., Blacklaws, N. and Zodgekar, K. (2020) *Special Advisers and the Johnson Government*, London: Institute for Government.

Durrant, T., Pannell, J. and Haddon, C. (2021) *Updating the Ministerial Code*, London: Institute for Government.

Durrant, T., Lilly, A. and Tingay, P. (2022) 'WhatsApp in government: How ministers and officials should use messaging apps–and how they shouldn't', Institute for Government [online], Available from: https://www.instituteforgovernment.org.uk/publication/whatsapp-government

Department Work and Pensions and BEIS Committees publish report on Carillion (2018) House of Commons

Dyer, C. (2024) 'Infected blood scandal: "Chilling" cover up hid truth for decades, public inquiry finds', *BMJ*, 385: q1139.

Eckersley, P. M. and Ferry, L. (2011) 'Budgeting and governing for deficit reduction in the UK public sector: Act one, 'The Comprehensive Spending Review', *Journal of Finance and Management in Public Services*, 14–23 [online], Available from: https://eprints.whiterose.ac.uk/110923/1/l_ferry_and_p_eckersley.pdf

Ehlermann, C. D. and Goyette, M. (2006) 'The interface between EU state aid control and the WTO disciplines on subsidies', *European State Aid Law Quarterly*, 5(4): 695–718.

Einfeld, C. (2019) 'Nudge and evidence based policy: fertile ground', *Evidence & Policy*, 15(4): 509–24.

Eleftheriadis, P. (2017) 'Constitutional illegitimacy over Brexit', *The Political Quarterly*, 88(2): 182–8.

Elliott, I. C. (2020) 'The implementation of a strategic state in a small country setting – the case of the "Scottish Approach"', *Public Money & Management*, 40(4): 285–93.

Elliott, I. C., Bottom, K. A., Carmichael, P., Liddle, J., Martin, S. and Pyper, R. (2022) 'The fragmentation of public administration: differentiated and decentered governance in the (dis) United Kingdom', *Public Administration*, 100(1): 98–115.

Elstub, S., Carrick, J., Farrell, D. M. and Mockler, P. (2021) 'The scope of climate assemblies: lessons from the climate assembly UK', *Sustainability*, 13(20): 11272.

Emerson, M., Blockmans, S., Peers, S. and Wriglesworth, M. (2014) 'British Balance of Competence Reviews, Part II: Again, a huge contradiction between the evidence and Eurosceptic populism', *EPIN Papers*, 40.

Erridge, A. (2000) 'Public procurement', *Public Policy and Administration*, 15(4): 14–24.

Evans, A. (2018) 'Planning for Brexit: the case of the 1975 referendum', *The Political Quarterly*, 89(1): 127–33.

Ewen, S. (2023) *Before Grenfell: Fire, Safety and Deregulation in Twentieth-Century Britain*, London: University of London Press.

Fabian Society (1964) *The Administrators* (Fabian Tract 355), London: The Fabian Society.

Faccio, M. (2006) 'Politically connected firms', *American Economic Review*, 96(1): 369–86.

Fahy, N., Hervey, T., Greer, S., Jarman, H., Stuckler, D., Galsworthy, M. and McKee, M. (2017) 'How will Brexit affect health and health services in the UK? Evaluating three possible scenarios', *The Lancet*, 390(10107): 2110–8.

Falconer, P. K. and Ross, K. (1999) 'Citizen's charters and public service provision: lessons from the UK experience', *International Review of Administrative Sciences*, 65(3): 339–51.

Farazmand, A. (1999) 'The elite question: Toward a normative elite theory of organization', *Administration & Society*, 31(3): 321–60.

Faulkner, D. (2014) *Servant of the Crown: A Civil Servant's Story of Criminal Justice and Public Service Reform*, Hook, Hampshire: Waterside Press.

Femia, J. V. (2002) *Against the Masses. Varieties of Anti-Democratic Thought since the French Revolution*, Oxford: Oxford University Press.

Finlayson, A. (2011) 'Cameron, culture and the creative class: The Big Society and the post-bureaucratic age', *Political Quarterly*, 82(s1): 35–47.

Fitz, J. and Halpin, D. (2013) 'Ministers and mandarins: educational research in elite settings', in *Researching the Powerful in Education*, London: Routledge, pp 44–62.

Fleming, S. and Parker G. (2024) 'Rachel Reeves to seek "improved" UK-EU trade terms if Labour wins election', *Financial Times*, [online], 16 June, Available from: https://www.ft.com/content/d0a1f720-24a7-4cbb-80ce-da9e96c592f8

Fletcher, T., Malik, M. and Lord Sedwill (2024) 'The World in 2040: renewing the UK's approach to international affairs', UCL Policy Lab [online], Available from: https://www.ucl.ac.uk/policy-lab/sites/policy_lab/files/the_world_in_2040-_renewing_the_uks_approach_to_international_affairs.pdf

Flinders, M. (2011) 'Daring to be a Daniel: the pathology of politicized accountability in a monitory democracy', *Administration & Society*, 43(5), 595–619.

Flinders, M., Judge, D., Rhodes, R. A. W. and Vatter, A. (2022) '"Stretched but not snapped": a response to Russell and Serban on retiring the "Westminster model"', *Government and Opposition*, 57(2): 353–69.

Foley, M. (2004) 'Presidential attribution as an agency of prime ministerial critique in a parliamentary democracy: the case of Tony Blair', *The British Journal of Politics and International Relations*, 6(3): 292–311.

Foster, C. D. and Plowden F. J. (1996) *The State Under Stress*, Maidenhead: Open University Press.

Foster-Gilbert, C. (ed) (2018) *The Power of Civil Servants: David Normington and Peter Hennessey*, London: Haus Publishing.

Fournier, P. (2011) *When Citizens Decide: Lessons From Citizen Assemblies on Electoral Reform*, Oxford: Oxford University Press.

Frame, I. (2022) 'The ends and means of banking: the Royal Bank of Scotland after the 2008 crisis', *Journal of Corporate Law Studies*, 22(2): 931–70.

Freedland, M. (2001) 'The marketization of public services', *Citizenship, Markets and the State*, 90–110.

Freedman, S. (2024a) *Failed State Why Nothing Works and How We Fix It*, London: Macmillan.

Freedman, S. (2024b) *Public Service Reform and Devolution. Labour Together* [online], Available from: https://www.labourtogether.uk/all-reports/public-service-reform-and-devolution

Freeguard, G., Davies, O., Tingay, P. and Savur S. (2017) *Ministerial Directions*, London: Institute for Government.

Friedman, M. (1974) *Free Markets for Free Men*, Chicago, IL: Graduate School of Business, University of Chicago.

Fry, G. K. (1984) 'The development of the Thatcher Government's "Grand Strategy" for the civil service: a public policy perspective', *Public Administration*, 62(3), 322–35.

Fry, G. K. (1995) 'The Fulton Committee's Management Consultancy Group: The blocks of Civil Service Work examined, *Public Policy and Administration*, 10(3): 88–90.

(2000) 'Three giants of the inter-war British Higher Civil Service: Sir Maurice Hankey, Sir Warren Fisher and Sir Horace Wilson', in K. Theakston (ed) Bureaucrats and Leadership, London: Palgrave Macmillan UK, pp 39–67.

Fulton Committee (1968) *Committee on the Civil Service*, Report (Cmnd 3638), London: HMSO.

Gains, F. (1999) 'Implementing privatization policies in "next steps" agencies', *Public Administration*, 77: 4713–30.

Gains, F. (2003) 'Executive agencies in government: the impact of bureaucratic networks on policy outcomes', *Journal of Public Policy*, 23(1): 55–79.

Gains, F. and John, P. (2010) 'What do bureaucrats like doing? Bureaucratic preferences in response to institutional reform', *Public Administration Review*, 70(3): 455–63.

Gallas, A. (2016) *The Thatcherite Offensive*, London: Brill.

Galván Labrador, A. and Zografos, C. (2023) 'Empowerment and disempowerment in climate assemblies: The French citizens' convention on climate', *Environmental Policy and Governance* [online], Available from: https://onlinelibrary.wiley.com/doi/pdfdirect/10.1002/eet.2093

Gamble, A. (1989) 'Privatization, Thatcherism, and the British state', *Journal of Law & Society*, 16: 1.

Gamble, A. (1990) 'Theories of British politics', *Political Studies*, 38(3): 404–20.

Gamble, A. (2011) 'Project Cameron', *Public Policy Research*, 18(3): 173–8.

Gamble, A. (2015) 'Austerity as statecraft', *Parliamentary Affairs*, 68(1): 42–57.

Gamble, A. (2021) 'Taking back control: the political implications of Brexit' in *The Politics and Economics of Brexit*, London: Routledge, pp 127–44.

Gandon, A. (2023) 'Civil Unrest: a portrait of the Civil Service through Brexit, the pandemic and political turbulence', Reform [online], Available from: https://reform.uk/wp-content/uploads/2023/10/Civil-unrest.pdf

Garland, R. (2021) *Government Communications and the Crisis of Trust: From Political Spin to Post-truth*, London: Macmillan.

Garrick, J. and Buck, M. (2022) *The Psychosocial Impacts of Whistleblower Retaliation: Shattering Employee Resilience and the Workplace Promise*, Cham: Springer International Publishing.

Gaussen, S. (2019) 'The UK supreme court finds that Boris Johnson's prorogation of parliament was unlawful', *Bar News: The Journal of the NSW Bar Association*, 24–25.

Gay, O. (2009) *Special Advisers*, London: House of Commons Library, Standard Note SN/PC/03813.

Gentleman, A. (2019) *The Windrush Betrayal: Exposing the Hostile Environment*, London: Faber & Faber.

Gerodimos, R. (2004) 'The UK BSE crisis as a failure of government', *Public Administration*, 82(4): 911–29.

Gerson, D. (2020) 'Leadership for a high performing civil service: towards senior civil service systems in OECD countries', *OECD Working papers on Public Governance* [online], Available from: https://www.oecd.org/en/publications/2020/09/leadership-for-a-high-performing-civil-service_8125d0d5.html

Gibson, L. and Cowie, G. (2024) *A Shift in Approach? Assimilated law reform and the change of government*, Research Briefing House of Commons.

Giddens, A. (2013) *The Third Way and its Critics*, London: John Wiley & Sons.

Gill, M. and Dalton, G. (2022) *Reforming Public Appointments*, London: Institute for Government.

Gill, M., Clyne, R. and Dalton, G. (2021) *The Appointment and Conduct of Departmental NEDs*, London: Institute for Government

Goetz, K. H. (2011) 'The development and current features of the German civil service system', in F. M. van der Meer (ed) *Civil Service Systems in Western Europe* (2nd edn), Cheltenham: Edward Elgar Publishing.

Goetz, K. H. and Meyer-Sahling, J. H. (2013) 'Political time in the EU: dimensions, perspectives, theories', in K. H. Goetz and J. H. Meyer-Sahling (eds) *The EU Timescape*, London: Routledge, pp 1–22.

Goldman, E., Rocholl, J. and So, J. (2009) 'Do politically connected boards affect firm value?', *Review of Financial Studies*, 22(6): 2331–60.

González-Bailon, S., Jennings, W. and Lodge, M. (2013) 'Politics in the boardroom: corporate pay, networks and recruitment of former parliamentarians, ministers and civil servants in Britain', *Political Studies*, 61(4): 850–73.

Gorton, V., McVie, S. and Murray, K. (2022) 'Partygate raises important questions about rules, guidance and compliance during COVID' LSE COVID-19 [Blog], Available from: https://blogs.lse.ac.uk/covid19/2022/05/06/partygate-raises-important-questions-about-rules-guidance-and-compliance-during-covid/

Goslin, R. C. (1979) 'Development and training of senior administrators in the UK civil service: a review of issues and trends', *International Review of Administrative Sciences*, 45(1): 6–20.

Gouldner, A. W. (1958) 'Cosmopolitans and locals: toward an analysis of latent social roles', *Administrative Science Quarterly*, II: 444–80.

Graham, J. W. (1986) 'Principled organizational dissent: A theoretical essay', *Research in Organizational Behavior*, 8: 1–52.

Grandia, J. and Meehan, J. (2017) 'Public procurement as a policy tool: using procurement to reach desired outcomes in society', *International Journal of Public Sector Management*, 30(4): 302–9.

Gray, S. (2022) *Findings of the Second Permanent Secretary's Investigation into Alleged Gatherings on Government Premises during Covid Restrictions.* No 10 Downing Street.

Gray, S. (2024) 'Labour would introduce citizens' assemblies, Sue Gray says' *Civil Service World*, [online], 19 February, Available from: https://www.civilserviceworld.com/professions/article/labour-plans-citizens-assemblies-sue-gray

Greenaway, J. R. (1983) 'Warren Fisher and the transformation of the British Treasury, 1919–1939', *Journal of British Studies*, 23(1): 125–42.

Greer, S. L. (2007) 'Conclusion: what might we do', in S. L. Greer and D. Roland (eds) *Developing Policy, Diverging Values. The Values of the United Kingdom's National Health Services*, London: Nuffield Trust, pp 87–102.

Greer, S. L. and Jarman, H. (2000) 'The British civil service system', in H. A. G. M. Bekke and F. M. van der Meer, *Civil Service Systems in Western Europe*, Cheltenham: Edward Elgar, pp 13–36.

Greer, S. and Jarman, H. (2007) 'What Whitehall? The rise of the client dominated department', paper presented at the American Political Science Association Annual Meeting, Chicago, September.

Greer, S. L. and Rauscher, S. (2011) 'When does market-making make markets? EU health services policy at work in the United Kingdom and Germany', *JCMS: Journal of Common Market Studies*, 49(4): 797–822.

Greer, S. L., Falkenbach, M., Jarman, H., Löblová, O., Rozenblum, S., Williams, N. and Wismar, M. (2021) 'Centralisation and decentralisation in a crisis: how credit and blame shape governance', *Eurohealth*, 27(1): 36–40.

Grey, A. and Jenkins, B. (1983) 'The state of policy analysis and evaluation in government', in A. Grey and B. Jenkins (eds) *Policy Analysis and Evaluation in British Government*, London: Royal Institute of Public Administration, pp 11–16.

Grimshaw, D., Vincent, S. and Willmott, H. (2002) 'Going privately: partnership and outsourcing in UK public services', *Public Administration*, 80(3): 475–502.

Grube, D. C. (2017) 'Civil servants, political history, and the interpretation of traditions', *The Historical Journal*, 60(1): 173–96.

Grube, D. C. and Howard, C. (2016) 'Is the Westminster system broken beyond repair?', *Governance*, 29(4): 467–81.

Grube, D. C. and Killick, A. (2023) 'Groupthink, polythink and the challenges of decision-making in cabinet government', *Parliamentary Affairs*, 76(1): 211–31.

Guttsman, W. L.(ed) (1969) *The English Ruling Class*, London: Weidenfeld and Nicholson.

Haddon, C. (2012) *Reforming the Civil Service: The Efficiency Unit in the Early 1980s and the 1987 Next Steps Report*, London: Institute for Government.

Hajikazemi, S., Aaltonen, K., Ahola, T., Aarseth, W. and Andersen, B. (2020) 'Normalising deviance in construction project organizations: a case study on the collapse of Carillion', *Construction Management and Economics*, 38(12): 1122–38.

Haldane (1918) *Report on the Machinery of Government*, Cd 9230, London: HMSO.

Halligan, J. (2021) 'Politicization of public services in comparative perspective', in *Oxford Research Encyclopedia of Politics*, Oxford: Oxford University Press.

Halpin, D. (2011) 'Explaining policy bandwagons: organized interest mobilization and cascades of attention', *Governance*, 24(2): 205–30.

Hambleton, R. and Howard, J. (2013) 'Place-based leadership and public service innovation', *Local Government Studies*, 39(1): 47–70.

Hanretty, C. (2021) 'The pork barrel politics of the Towns Fund', *The Political Quarterly*, 92(1): 7–13.

Harmel, R., Tan, A. C., Janda, K. and Smith, J. M. (2018) 'Manifestos and the "two faces" of parties: Addressing both members and voters with one document'. Party Politics, 24(3): 278–88.

Harris, B. (2013) 'The Scots, the Westminster parliament, and the British state in the eighteenth century', in J. Hoppit (ed) *Parliaments, Nations and Identities in Britain and Ireland, 1660–1850*, Manchester: Manchester University Press, pp 124–45.

Harris, C. (1925) 'Decentralization', *Public Administration*, III: 117–33.

Hay, C. (2003) 'Macroeconomic policy coordination and membership of the Single European Currency: Another case of British exceptionalism?', *The Political Quarterly*, 74(1): 91–100.

Hayton, R. (2022) 'Can the Conservative Party survive Boris Johnson?', *Political Insight*, 13(1): 18–19.

Hazell, R. and Yong, B. (2012) *The Politics of Coalition: How the Conservative-Liberal Democrat Government Works*, London: Bloomsbury Publishing.

Hazell, R. and Reid, F. (2018) 'Private Members' bills', in C. Leston-Bandeira and L. Thompson (eds) *Exploring Parliament*, Oxford: Oxford University Press, pp 122–30.

Headey, B. (1972) 'The Civil Service as an elite in Britain and Germany', *International Review of Administrative Sciences*, 38(1): 41–8.

Headey, B. (1975) 'A typology of ministers: implications for minister civil servant relationships in Britain', in M. Dogan (ed) *The Mandarins of Western Europe*, London: John Wiley, pp 63–86.

Hechter, M. (2017) *Internal Colonialism: The Celtic Fringe in British National Development*, London: Routledge.

Heclo, H. and Wildavsky, A. (1974) *The Private Government of Public Money*, London: Macmillan.

Heenan, D. (2021) 'Cross-border cooperation health in Ireland', *Irish Studies in International Affairs*, *32*(2): 117–36.

Hennessey P. (1986) *Cabinet*, Oxford: Basil Blackwell.

Hennessy P. (1989) *Whitehall*, London: Secker and Warburg.

Hennessey P. (1996) *Muddling Through*, London: Gollancz.

Hennessy, P. (2005) 'Rulers and servants of the state: The Blair style of government 1997–2004', *Parliamentary Affairs*, 58(1): 6–16.

Hesletine M. (1987) *Where There is a Will*, London: Penguin.

Herman, V. and Alt, J. E. (1975) 'Introduction' in V. Herman and J. E. Alt *Cabinet Studies: A Reader*, London: Macmillan, pp xi–xxvi.

Hewitt, G. (2020) 'The Windrush scandal: an insider's reflection', *Caribbean Quarterly*, 66(1): 108–28.

Heywood, P. and Dobson, R. (2019) 'Clean but compromised: corruption in the UK public administration', *DPCE Online*, 38(1) [online], Available from: https://www.iris.unina.it/retrieve/893ed6c0-744b-4400-9f0e-2cd3e0d800b8/%282019%29%20Corruzione%20contratti%20pubblici%20%28Cina%2C%20Giappone%29.pdf

Heywood, S. (2021) *What Does Jeremey Think?* London: HarperCollins.

Hickson, K. (2005) *The IMF Crisis of 1976 and British Politics*, London: Bloomsbury Publishing.

Higley, J. (2018) 'Continuities and discontinuities in elite theory', in H. Best and J. Higley (eds) *The Palgrave Handbook of Political Elites*, London: Palgrave Macmillan, pp 25–39.

HM Government (1970) *The Reorganisation of Central Government*, Cmnd 4506, London: HMSO.

HM Government (1999) *Modernising Government White Paper*.

HM Government (2012) *The Civil Service Reform Plan*.

HM Government (2023) *Independent Review of Governance and Accountability in the Civil Service: The Rt Hon Lord Maude of Horsham* [online], Available from: https://www.gov.uk/government/publications/review-of-governance-and-accountability/independent-review-of-governance-and-accountability-in-the-civil-service-the-rt-hon-lord-maude-of-horsham-html

HM Treasury (1991) *Competing for Quality*, London: HMSO.

HM Treasury (1937–38) '5 Epitome of the Reports from the Committees of Public Accounts, 1857–1937', Parliamentary Papers, 22: 20–1.

HM Treasury (2022) *The Green Book*, Gov.uk [online], Available from: https://www.gov.uk/government/publications/the-green-book-appraisal-and-evaluation-in-central-government/the-green-book-2020

HM Treasury (2023) *Managing Public Money*, Gov.uk [online], Available from: https://www.gov.uk/government/publications/managing-public-money

HM Treasury (2024a) *Annex to the Memorandum of Understanding for the 'Trailblazer' Single Settlements with Greater Manchester and West Midlands Combined Authorities* [online], Available from: https://assets.publishing.service.gov.uk/media/65e71b503f69457ff10360e2/Annex_to_the_Memorandum_of_Understanding_for_the__Trailblazer__Single_Settlements_with_Greater_Manchester_and_West_Midlands_Combined_Authorities.pdf

HM Treasury (2024b) *Autumn Budget 2024 Fixing the Foundations to Deliver Change*.

Hodkinson, S. (2018) 'Grenfell foretold: a very neoliberal tragedy', *Social Policy Review*, 30: 5–26.

Hogwood, B. W. (1997) 'The machinery of government, 1979–97', *Political Studies*, 45(4): 704–15.

Hogwood, B. W. (2008) 'Public employment in Britain: From working in to working for the public sector?', *The State at Work*, 19–39.

Hood, C. (1990) 'De-Sir Humphreyfying the Westminster model of bureaucracy: a new style of governance?', *Governance*, 3(2): 205–14.

Hood, C. (1995) '"Deprivileging" the UK civil service in the 1980s: dream or reality?', in J. Pierre (ed) *Bureaucracy in the Modern State: An Introduction to Comparative Public Administration*, Cheltenham: Edward Elgar, pp 92–117.

Hood, C. (2011) *The Blame Game: Spin, Bureaucracy and Self-preservation in Government*, Oxford: Princeton.

Hood, C. and Lodge, M. (2006) *The Politics of Public Service Bargains*, Oxford: Oxford University Press.

Hood, C., Baldwin, R. and Rothstein, H. (2000) 'Assessing the Dangerous Dogs Act: when does a regulatory law fail?', *Public Law*, Summer 2000: 282–305.

Hood, C., Lodge, M. and Clifford, C. (2002) 'Civil service policy-making competencies in the German BMWi and British DTI: a comparative analysis based on six case studies', *The Smith Institute*, 67 [online], Available from: https://www.civilservant.org.uk/library/2001-CARR-CivilServicePolicymakingMainReport.pdf

Horton, S. (1996) 'The civil service', in *Managing the New Public Services*, London: Palgrave, pp 155–76.

Horton, S. (2000) 'Competency management in the British civil service', *International Journal of Public Sector Management*, 13(4): 354–68.

Horton, S. (2006) 'The public service ethos in the British civil service: an historical institutional analysis', *Public Policy and Administration*, 21(1): 32–48.

House of Commons (2018) *Citizens' Assembly on Social Care* [online], Available from: https://publications.parliament.uk/pa/cm201719/cmselect/cmcomloc/citizens-assembly-report.pdf

House of Commons Home Affairs Committee (2024) 'House of Commons Oral evidence: One-off session with the former Inspector of Borders and Immigration', HC 596 Tuesday 27 February, Home Affairs Committee.

Houston, D. J., Aitalieva, N. R., Morelock, A. L. and Shults, C. A. (2016) 'Citizen trust in civil servants: a cross-national examination', *International Journal of Public Administration*, 39(14): 1203–14.

Hunt, G. (2013) 'Civil servants and whistle-blowing: loyal neutrality and/or democratic ideal?', in C. Neuhold, S. Vanhoonacker and L. Verhey (eds) *Civil Servants and Politics: A Delicate Balance*, London: Palgrave Macmillan, pp 45–67.

Hyman, P. (2005) *1 out of 10: from Downing Street Vision to Classroom Reality*, London: Random House.

Immervoll, H. and Richardson, L. (2011) 'Redistribution policy and inequality reduction in OECD countries: what has changed in two decades?' OECD Social, Employment and Migration Working Papers [online], Available from: https://www.oecd-ilibrary.org/social-issues-migration-health/redistribution-policy-and-inequality-reduction-in-oecd-countries_5kg5dlkhjq0x-en

Institute for Government (2023a) 'Civil service staff numbers' [online], Available from: https://www.instituteforgovernment.org.uk/explainer/civil-service-staff-numbers#:~:text=As%20of%20September%202023%2C%20there,servants%20than%20a%20year%20ago

Institute for Government (2023b) 'Whitehall Monitor 2023 (Part 1): The size, cost and make-up of the civil service' [online], Available from: https://www.instituteforgovernment.org.uk/publication/whitehall-monitor-2023/size-cost-make-civil-service

Institute for Government (2024) Power with Purpose Final report of the Commission on the Centre of Government. London: IfG.

Institute for Fiscal Studies (IFS) (2024) 'The £600 billion problem awaiting the next government', IFS Zooms In Podcast, [online], 25 April, Available from: https://ifs.org.uk/articles/ps600-billion-problem-awaiting-next-government

Jakobi, A. P. (2012) 'International organisations and policy diffusion: the global norm of lifelong learning', *Journal of International Relations and Development*, 15: 31–64.

James, O. (2003) *The Executive Agency Revolution in Whitehall*, Basingstoke: Palgrave Macmillan.

James, O. (2004) 'The UK core executive's use of public service agreements as a tool of governance', *Public Administration*, 82(2): 397–419.

James, O. and Lodge, M. (2003) 'The limitations of "policy transfer" and "lesson drawing" for public policy research', *Political Studies Review*, 1: 173–93.

James, S. (1986) 'The central policy review staff, 1970–1983', *Political Studies*, 34(3): 423–40.

Janik, M. T. (1986) 'A US perspective on the GATT Agreement on Government Procurement', George Washington Journal of International Law & Economics, 20: 491.

Jarman, H. and Greer, S. L. (2010) 'In the eye of the storm: civil servants and managers in the UK Department of Health', *Social Policy & Administration*, 44(2): 172–92.

Jeffery, C. (2009) 'Devolution in the United Kingdom: problems of a piecemeal approach to constitutional change', *Publius: The Journal of Federalism*, 39(2): 289–313.

Jenkins R. (1975) *On Being a Minister in Cabinet Studies: A Reader*, V. Hermann and J. Alt (eds) London: Macmillan, pp 210–20.

Jennings, W., Bevan, S. and John, P. (2011) 'The agenda of British government: the speech from the throne, 1911–2008', *Political Studies*, 59(1): 74–98.

Jones, K. (1994) *An Economist among Mandarins: A Biography of Robert Hall (1901–1988)*, Cambridge: Cambridge University Press.

Kassim, H. (2001) '1 Representing the United Kingdom in Brussels: the fine art of positive co-ordination 53', *The National Co-ordination of EU Policy*, 47.

Kavanagh, D. and Richards, D. (2001) 'Departmentalism and joined-up government', *Parliamentary Affairs*, 54(1): 1–18.

Kavanagh, D. and Richards, D. (2003) 'Prime ministers, ministers and civil servants in Britain', in D. L. Weakliem (ed) *Elite Configurations at the Apex of Power*, Leiden: Brill, pp 175–95.

Kaye, S. and Powell, R. (2024) 'Devolve by default; decentralisation and a redefined Whitehall', Reform [online], Available from: https://reform.uk/publications/devolve-by-default/

HMSP, M. (2002) 'Plurinational democracy in a post-sovereign order', *Northern Ireland Legal Quarterly*, 53(4).

Keating, M. (2021) *Fractured Unions: Brexit and the Territorial Constitution*, [online], Available from: https://papers.ssrn.com/sol3/papers.cfm?abstract_id=3952189

Keating, M. and Cairney, P. (2006) 'A new elite? Politicians and civil servants in Scotland after devolution', *Parliamentary Affairs*, 59(1): 43–59.

Keating, M., Cairney, P. and Hepburn, E. (2009).) 'Territorial policy communities and devolution in the UK', *Cambridge Journal of Regions, Economy and Society*, 2(1): 51–66.

Keating, M., Cairney, P. and Hepburn, E. (2012) 'Policy convergence, transfer and learning in the UK under devolution', *Regional & Federal Studies*, 22(3): 289–307.

Keller, F. B. (2018) 'Analyses of elite networks', in H. Best and J. Higley (eds) *The Palgrave Handbook of Political Elites*, London: Palgrave Macmillan, pp 135–52.

Kelly, G., Mulgan, G. and Muers, S. (2002) *Creating Public Value*, London: Cabinet Office.

Kelso, A. (2017) 'The politics of parliamentary procedure: an analysis of Queen's Speech debates in the House of Commons', *British Politics*, 12: 267–88.

Kersbergen, K. V. and Verbeek, B. (2004) 'Subsidiarity as a principle of governance in the European Union', *Comparative European Politics*, 2: 142–62.

King, A. and Crewe, I. (2014) *The Blunders of Our Governments*, London: One World Publishing.

Kingdon, J. W. and Stano, E. (1984) *Agendas, Alternatives, and Public Policies*, Boston: Little, Brown.

Kippin, S. and Morphet, J. (2023) 'Coordination, agenda-setting, and future planning: the role of Combined Authorities during the COVID-19 Pandemic', *International Review of Public Policy*.

Kirby, J. (2019) 'AV Dicey and English constitutionalism', *History of European Ideas*, 45(1): 33–46.

Koch, R. (2020) *Green Public Procurement under WTO Law: Experience of the EU and Prospects for Switzerland*, Quebec: Dokumen.

Koop, C. and Lodge, M. (2020) 'British economic regulators in an age of politicisation: from the responsible to the responsive regulatory state?', *Journal of European Public Policy*, 27(11): 1612–35.

Knox, C. and Carmichael, P. (2024) 'Local government in Northern Ireland: partnerships, minimalism and marginalisation', *Local Government Studies*, 1–23.

Krugman, P. (1991) 'Increasing returns and economic geography', *Journal of Political Economy*, 99(3): 483–99.

Kuper, S. (2022) *Chums: Updated*, London: Profile Books.

K. Kyle, (1999) 'The Mandarin's Mandarin: Sir Norman Brook, Secretary of the Cabinet', *Contemporary British History*, 13(2): 64–78.

Labour Party (2024) *Change: The Labour Party Manifesto* [online], Available from: https://labour.org.uk/change/

Lane, J. E. (2020) 'The principal–agent approach and public administration', in *Oxford Research Encyclopedia of Politics*, Oxford: Oxford University Press.

Larik, J. (2020) 'Brexit, the EU-UK Withdrawal Agreement, and global treaty (re-) negotiations', *American Journal of International Law*, 114(3): 443–62.

Lee, C. K. and Strang, D. (2006) 'The international diffusion of public sector downsizing: network emulation and theory-driven learning', *International Organization*, 60(Fall): 883–909.

Le Grand, J. and Robinson, R. (eds) (2018) *Privatisation and the Welfare State*, London: Routledge.

Leitch, S. (2006) *Skills in the UK: the Long Term Challenge*.

Leston-Bandeira, C. (2019) 'Parliamentary petitions and public engagement: an empirical analysis of the role of e-petitions', *Policy & Politics*, 47(3): 415–36.

Levinson, S. (2022) 'Confronting the modern executive: four perspectives', *Perspectives on Politics*, 20(2): 646–52.

Levitt, R. and Solesbury, W. (2006) 'Outsiders in Whitehall', *Public Money and Management*, 26(1): 10–12.

Levitt, R. and Solesbury, W. (2013) 'New development: policy tsars – Whitehall's expert advisers revealed', *Public Money & Management*, 33(1): 77–80.

Lidington, D. (2020) *Minsters Reflect David Lidington*, IfG.

Lijphart, A. (1984) *Democracies: Patterns of Majoritarian and Consensus Government in Twenty-One Countries*, London: Yale University Press.

Lijphart, A. (1999) *Patterns of Democracy: Government forms and performance in thirty-six countries*. Yale University Press.

Linde, C. (2015) 'Memory in narrative', *The International Encyclopedia of Language and Social Interaction*, London: Wiley-Blackwell.

Ling, T. (2002) 'Delivering joined–up government in the UK: dimensions, issues and problems', *Public Administration*, 80(4): 615–42.

Lloyd, L. (2019) *The Brexit Effect*, London: Institute for Government.

Locock, L. (2000) 'The changing nature of rationing in the UK National Health Service', *Public Administration*, 78(1): 91–109.

Lodge, G. (2014) 'The civil service reform plan one year on, and the international evidence', *The Political Quarterly*, 85(1): 81–3.

Lodge, G., Kalitowski, S., Pearce N. and Muir, R. (2013) *Accountability and Responsiveness in the Senior Civil Service: Lessons from Overseas*, IPPR report, London: The Cabinet Office.

Løgreid, P. and Wise, L. R. (2007) 'Reforming human resource management in civil service systems: recruitment, mobility, and representativeness', in J. C. N. Raadschelders, T. A. J. Toonen and F. M. Van der Meer (eds) *The Civil Service in the 21st Century: Comparative Perspectives*, London: Palgrave Macmillan UK, pp 169–82.

Lowe R. (2005) 'Grit in the oyster or sand in the machine? The evolving role of special advisers in British government', *Twentieth Century British History*, 16(4): 497–505.

Lowe, R. (2011) *The Official History of the British Civil Service*, London: Routledge.

Lowe, R. and Pemberton, H. (2020) *The Official History of the British Civil Service: Reforming the Civil Service, Volume II: The Thatcher and Major Revolutions, 1982–97*, London: Routledge.

Ludlow, J. (2005) 'The Queen's Speech 2005: how government laws are initiated in the United Kingdom', *Commonwealth Law Bulletin*, 31(2): 61–7.

Lynch, P., Whitaker, R. and Cygan, A. (2019) *Brexit and Democracy: The Role of Parliaments in the UK and the European Union*, Cham: Springer.

Lynn, J. and Jay, A. (1988) *The Complete Yes Minister*, London: BBC Books.

Lynn, J. and Jay, A. (1989) *The Complete Yes Prime Minister*, London: BBC Books.

Mabbett, D. (2021) 'Rolling out the pork barrel', *The Political Quarterly*, 92(2): 169–71.

Mackenzie, W. J. M. and Grove, J. W. (1957) *Central Administration in Britain* Harlow: Longman.

MacKinnon, D. (2015) 'Devolution, state restructuring and policy divergence in the UK', *The Geographical Journal*, 181(1): 47–56.

Maddox, B. and Thomas, A. (2021) *The Answers to Dominic Cummings' Critique: 10 Essential Reforms to Government*, London: Institute for Government.

Mahmod, N. A. K. (1995) *The Constitutional Status of Civil Servants in the United Kingdom*, Aberdeen: University of Aberdeen.

Majone, G. (1997) 'From the positive to the regulatory state: causes and consequences of changes in the mode of governance', *Journal of Public Policy*, 17(2): 139–67.

Majone, G. (2001) 'Nonmajoritarian institutions and the limits of democratic governance: a political transaction-cost approach', *Journal of Institutional and Theoretical Economics*, 157(1): 57–78.

Margetts, H. (2006) 'E-government in Britain – A decade on', *Parliamentary Affairs*, 59(2): 250–65.

Marquand, D. (1981) 'Club government: the crisis of the Labour Party in national perspective', *Government & Opposition*, 16: 19–36.

Marsh, D. (1991) 'Privatization under Mrs. Thatcher: A review of the literature', *Public Administration*, 69(4): 459–80.

Marsh, D. (2011) 'The new orthodoxy: the differentiated polity model', *Public Administration*, 89(1): 32–48.

Marsh, D. (2023) 'Britain's failed attempt at monetary and fiscal exceptionalism', *The Economists' Voice*, 20(1) [online], Available from: https://www.degruyter.com/document/doi/10.1515/ev-2023-0021/html

Marsh, D. and Sharman, J. C. (2009) 'Policy diffusion and policy transfer', *Policy Studies*, 30(3): 269–88.

Marsh, H. and Marsh, D. (2002) 'Tories in the killing fields? The fate of private members' bills in the 1997 parliament', *Journal of Legislative Studies*, 8(1): 91–112.

Marsh, P. (1994) *Joseph Chamberlain – Entrepreneur in Politics*, London: Yale University Press.

Marston, G. and Watts, R. (2003) 'Tampering with the evidence: a critical appraisal of evidence-based policy-making', The Drawing Board: An Australian Review of Public Affairs, 3(3): 143–63.

Martin, C. (2024) *The Union and the State: Contested Visions of the UK's Future*, London: Institute for Government.

Martin, S. (2022) 'Has devolution delivered?' Welsh Centre for Public Policy [online], Available from: https://www.wcpp.org.uk/commentary/has-devolution-delivered/

Mason, R. (2023) 'One of Tories' biggest ever donors profited from £135m of NHS contracts', *The Guardian*, [online] 20 September, Available from: https://www.theguardian.com/politics/2023/sep/20/one-of-tories-biggest-ever-donors-frank-hester-profited-from-135m-of-nhs-contracts

Matthews, F. (2021) 'The value of "between-election" political participation: do parliamentary e-petitions matter to political elites?', *The British Journal of Politics and International Relations*, 23(3): 410–29.

Maude F. (2014) 'A changing game', *RSA Journal*, 160(5560): 16–19.

Maude F. (2023) *Independent Review of Governance and Accountability in the Civil Service*, London: HM Government

Mawson, J. and Spencer, K. (2014) 'The origins and operation of the Government Offices for the English regions', in J. Bradbury and J. Mawson (eds) *British Regionalism and Devolution*, London: Routledge, pp 158–79.

McCrudden, C. (ed) (2022) *The Law and Practice of the Ireland-Northern Ireland Protocol*, Cambridge: Cambridge University Press.

McGowan, L. (2023) 'State aid policy in the United Kingdom post-Brexit: a case of de-Europeanisation as orbiting Europeanisation', *Journal of European Public Policy*, 30(11): 2372–96.

McGrath, C. (2002) 'Policy making in political memoirs – the case of the poll tax', *Journal of Public Affairs*, 2(2): 71–84.

McKay, A. M. and Wozniak, A. (2020) 'Opaque: an empirical evaluation of lobbying transparency in the UK', *Interest Groups & Advocacy*, 9(1): 102–18.

McLean, J. and Tushnet, M. (2013) 'Administrative bureaucracy', in M. Tushnet, T. Fleiner and C. Saunders (ed) *Routledge Handbook of Constitutional Law*, 121–30.

McTavish, D. and Pyper, R. (2007) 'Monitoring the public appointments process in the UK: issues and themes surrounding the use of semi-independent commissioners', *Public Management Review*, 9(1): 145–53.

Meggitt-Smith, B. (2022) 'Partnering with agents: how the covid-19 pandemic changed relations between the UK government and public service contractors', *The Political Quarterly*, 93(2): 244–52.

Meyer-Sahling, J. H., Sass Mikkelsen, K. and Schuster, C. (2018) *How to Improve the Quality of Public Administration in Europe? Lessons from and for civil service reform* [online], Available from: https://meyer-sahling.net/wp-content/uploads/2018-Meyer-Sahling-Mikkelsen-Schuster-EUPACK.pdf

Michelson, N. (2023) 'The revolving door of former civil servants and firm value: a comprehensive approach', *European Journal of Political Economy*, 79(September): 102421.

Moe, T. M. (2005) 'Power and political institutions', *Perspectives on Politics*, 3(2): 215–33.

Monaghan, C. (2022) 'A question of justiciability: did the Prime Minister misdirect himself as to the meaning of bullying within the ministerial code? R (FDA) v The Prime Minister and Minister for the Civil Service [2021] EWHC 3279 (Admin)', *Judicial Review*, 27(3): 264–70.

Moore M. (1995) *Creating Public Value: Strategic Management in Government*, Cambridge, MA: Harvard University Press.

Morgan, K. and Jones, R. W. (2023) 'Brexit and the death of devolution', *The Political Quarterly*, 94(4): 625–33.

Moriue, S. (2020) 'Support for private members' bills in the United Kingdom and Japan', *Statute Law Review*, 41(3): 304–19.

Morphet, J. (2013) *How Europe Shapes British Public Policy*, Bristol: Policy Press.

Morphet, J. (2018) *Changing Contexts in Spatial Planning: New Directions in Policies and Practices*, London: Routledge.

Morphet, J. (2021a) *Outsourcing in the UK: Policies, Practices and Outcomes*, Bristol: Policy Press.

Morphet, J. (2021b) *The Impact of COVID-19 on Devolution: Recentralising the British State Beyond Brexit?*, Bristol: Policy Press.

Morphet, J. (2022) 'Deals and devolution: The role of local authority deals in undermining devolved decision making', *Local Economy*, 37(7): 622–38.

Morphet, J. and Clifford, B. (2018) 'Who else would we speak to?' National Policy Networks in post-devolution Britain: The case of spatial planning', *Public Policy and Administration*, 33(1): 3–21.

Morphet, J. and Denham, J. (2023) 'Trailblazer devolution deals: The next oxymoron in the policy litany of sub-national governance in England?', *Local Economy*, 38(8): 755–72.

Morris, R. K. (2011) 'The application of the Habitats Directive in the UK: compliance or gold plating?', *Land Use Policy*, 28(1): 361–69.

Mulgan, G. (2003) 'Joined up government in the United Kingdom: Past, present and future', *Canberra Bulletin of Public Administration*, 105: 25–9.

Nairne, P. (1980) 'The civil service 'mandarins and ministers' in Barberis, P. (ed) *The Whitehall Reader: the UK's Administrative Machine in Action*, Open University Press, pp 79–85.

Nash, C. and Smith, A. (2020) 'Developments in rail regulation in Britain', in M. Finger and J. Montero (eds) *Handbook on Railway Regulation*, Cheltenham: Edward Elgar Publishing, pp 45–6.

NAO (2013) *Integration across Government*, London: NAO.

NAO (2015) *Confirmed Impacts: Helping to Ensure an Effective Strategic Centre of Government*, London: NAO.

NAO (2016) *Financial Sustainability of Local Authorities: Capital Expenditure and Resourcing*, London: NAO.

NAO (2020) *Investigation into Government Procurement During the COVID-19 Pandemic*, London: NAO.

NAO (2021) *The Local Government Finance System in England: Overview and Challenges*, London: NAO.

NAO (2022) *The Equipment Plan 2022 to 2032*, London: NAO.

NAO (2023) *Civil Service Workforce: Recruitment, Pay and Performance Management*, London: NAO

NAO (2024a) *Investigation into Asylum Accommodation*, London: NAO

NAO (2024b) *Civil Service Leadership Capability*, London: NAO.

NAO (2024c) *Progress with the Merger of the FCO and DFID*, London: NAO.

Nesvetailova, A., Palan, R., Pagliari, S., Grahl, J., Murphy, R., Kaminska, I. and Christiansen, J. (2017) 'A Singapore on the Thames? Post-Brexit deregulation in the UK', CITYPERC Working Paper No. 2017–06.

Nicholson, M. (1967) *The System*, London: Hodder & Stoughton.

Nickson, S., Mullens-Burgess E. and Thomas, A. (2020) *Moving out Making a Success of Civil Service Relocation*, Institute for Government.

Nolan, M. P. (1995) *Standards in Public Life: First Report of the Committee on Standards in Public Life* (Chairman The Rt Hon. The Lord Nolan), London: HMSO.

Norris, E., Haddon, C., Worllidge, J., Owen, J. and Paxton, B. (2024) *Preparing for Government: How the Official Opposition Should Ready Itself for Power*, London: Institute for Government.

Norton, P. (2003) 'The presidentialisation of British politics', *Government and Opposition*, 38(2): 274–8.

Norton, P. (2007) 'Tony Blair and the constitution', *British Politics*, 2: 269–81.

Norton, P. (2021) 'Ministers, departments and civil servants', in B. Jones, P. Norton and I. Hertner (eds) *Politics UK*, London: Routledge, pp 504–26.

O'Flynn, J. (2007) 'From new public management to public value: paradigmatic change and managerial implications', *Australian Journal of Public Administration*, 66(3): 353–66.

O'Halpin, E. (1981) 'Sir Warren Fisher and the coalition, 1919–1922', *The Historical Journal*, 24(4): 907–27.

Oliver, T. (2015) 'To be or not to be in Europe: is that the question? Britain's European question and an in/out referendum', *International Affairs*, 91(1): 77–91.

O'Malley, E. (2024) 'Citizens' Assembly has to take its share of the blame for the wishy-washy referendums', *Irish Independent*, 17 March.

Osborne, D. and Gaebler, T. (1992) *Reinventing Government: How the Entrepreneurial Spirit is Transforming the Public Sector*, New York: Perseus Books.

O'Toole, B. J. (1989) 'The "next steps" and control of the civil service: a historical perspective', *Public Policy and Administration*, 4(1): 41–52.

Northcote, S. H. and Trevelyan, C. E. (1854) *Report on the Organisation of the Permanent Civil Service Together with a Letter from Rev. B. Jowett*, London: HMSO.

Page, E. C. (1985) 'Laws as an instrument of policy: A study in central-local government relations', *Journal of Public Policy*, 5(2): 241–65.

Page, E. C. (2007) 'Middle level bureaucrats: policy, discretion and control' in J. Raadschelders, T. Toonen and F. Van der Meer (eds) *Civil Service in the 21st Century: Comparative Perspectives*, London: Palgrave, pp 152–68.

Page, E. (2010) 'Has the Whitehall model survived?', *International Review of Administrative Sciences*, 76(3): 407–23.

Page, E. (2012) 'New life at the top: special advisers in British government', *Parliamentary Affairs*, 65(4): 715–32.

Page, E. C. and Wouters, L. (1995) 'The Europeanisation of the national bureaucracies', in J. Pierre (ed) *Bureaucracy in the Modern State: An Introduction to Comparative Public Administration*, Cheltenham: Edward Elgar, pp 185–204.

Page, E. C. and Jenkins, B. (2005) *Policy Bureaucracy: Government with a Cast of Thousands*, Oxford: Oxford University Press

Page, E. C. and Wright, V. (eds) (1999) *Bureaucratic Elites in Western European States: A Comparative Analysis of Top Officials*, Oxford: Oxford University Press.

Painter, C. (2008) 'A government department in meltdown: Crisis at the Home Office', *Public Money and Management*, 28(5): 275–82.

Painter, C. (2013) 'The UK Coalition government: constructing public service reform narratives', *Public Policy and Administration*, 28(1): 3–20.

Pakulski, J. (2018) 'The development of elite theory' in H. Best and J. Higley (eds) *The Palgrave Handbook of Political Elites*, London: Palgrave Macmillan, pp 9–16.

Parry, R. (2003) *The Home Civil Service after Devolution*, Devolution Policy Paper, Swindon: Economic and Social Research Council.

Parry, R. (2008) 'Changing UK governance under devolution', *Public Policy Administration*, 23: 114–20.

Pamment, J. (2016) *British Public Diplomacy and Soft Power: Diplomatic Influence and the Digital Revolution*, London: Palgrave Macmillan.

Parker, D. (2009) *The Official History of Privatisation. Vol. I: The Formative Years 1970–1987*, London: Routledge.

Parker, D. (2013) *The Official History of Privatisation. Vol. II: Popular Capitalism, 1987–97*, London: Routledge.

Parris, H. (1969) *Constitutional Bureaucracy*, London: Allen & Unwin.

Parry, R. (2012) 'The civil service and Intergovernmental Relations in the Post-devolution UK', *The British Journal of Politics and International Relations*, 14(2): 285–302.

Parston, G. (1989) 'The Ibbs Report: redefining the bottom line of the NHS?', *Journal of Management in Medicine*, 4(1): 34–7.

Part, A. (1990) The Making of a Mandarin, London: Andre Deutsch.

Pautz, H. (2014) 'British think-tanks and their collaborative and communicative networks', *Politics*, 34(4): 345–61.

Pautz, H. (2017) 'Managing the crisis? Think-tanks and the British response to global financial crisis and great recession', *Critical Policy Studies*, 11(2): 191–210.

Peers, S. (2022) 'So close, yet so far: the EU/UK trade and cooperation agreement', *Common Market Law Review*, 59(1): 49–80.

Perri 6 (2004) 'Joined-up government in the western world in comparative perspective: A preliminary literature review and exploration'. *Journal of Public Administration Research and Theory: J-PART*, 14(1): 103–38.

Peters, B. G. (1995) 'Bureaucracy in a divided regime: the United States', in J. Pierre (ed) *Bureaucracy in the Modern State: An Introduction to Comparative Public Administration*, Cheltenham: Edward Elgar, pp 18–38.

Peters, B. G. (1997) 'Shouldn't row, can't steer: what's a Government to do?', *Public Policy and Administration*, 12(2): 51–61.

Peters, B. G. (2006) 'Concepts and theories of horizontal policy management', Handbook of Public Policy, 1(1): 115–38.

Peters, B. G. (2013) 'Politicisation: What is it and why should we care?'. In C. Neuhold, S. Vanhoonacker and L. Verhey (eds) *Civil Servants and Politics: A Delicate Balance*, London: Palgrave Macmillan, pp 12–24.

Peters, B. G. and Pierre, J. (2004) 'Politicization of the civil service: concepts, causes, consequences', in G. Peters and J. Pierre (eds) *The Politicization of the Civil Service in Comparative Perspective*, London: Routledge, pp 13–25.

Peterson, D. J. (1979) 'The Trade Agreement Act of 1979: the agreement on government procurement', *George Washington Journal of International Law and Economics*, 14: 321.

Pierre, J. (1995a) 'Comparative public administration: the state of the art', in J. Pierre (ed) *Bureaucracy in the Modern State: An Introduction to Comparative Public Administration*, Cheltenham: Edward Elgar, pp 1–17.

Pierre J. (1995b) 'Governing the welfare state: public administration, the state and society in Sweden', in J. Pierre (ed) *Bureaucracy in the Modern State: An Introduction to Comparative Public Administration*, Cheltenham: Edward Elgar, pp 140–60.

Pierre J. (1995c) 'Conclusions: a framework of comparative public administration', in J. Pierre (ed) *Bureaucracy in the Modern State: An Introduction to Comparative Public Administration*, Cheltenham: Edward Elgar, pp 205–18.

Playfair, E. (1965) 'Minister or civil servant: II civil servant', *Public Administration*, 43(3): 260–8.

Plowden, E. (1989) *An Industrialist in the Treasury*, London: Andre Deutsch.

Plowden, W. (ed) (1987) *Advising the Rulers*, Oxford: Basil Blackwell.

Plowden W. (1994) 'Relationships between advisors and departmental civil servants', in W. Plowden (ed) *Ministers and Mandarins*, Institute for Public Policy Research, pp 170–4.

Polidano, C. (1999) 'The bureaucrat who fell under a bus: ministerial responsibility, executive agencies and the Derek Lewis affair in Britain', *Governance*, 12(2): 201–29.

Pollitt, C. (1994) 'The citizen's charter: a preliminary analysis', *Public Money & Management*, 14(2): 9–14.

Pollitt, C. (2003) 'Joined-up government: a survey', *Political Studies Review*, 1(1): 34–49.

Pollitt, C. (2009) 'Bureaucracies remember, post-bureaucratic organizations forget?', *Public Administration*, 87(2): 198–218.

Pollitt, C. and Bouckaert, G. (2011) *Public Management Reform* (3rd edn), Oxford: Oxford University Press.

Polsby, N. W. (2001) 'Legitimacy in British policy-making: functional alternatives to the civil service', *The British Journal of Politics and International Relations*, 3(1): 5–35.

Ponting, C. (1985) *The Right to Know: The Inside Story of the Belgrano Affair*. London: Sphere.

Post Office Horizon IT Inquiry (2024) [online], Available from: https://www.postofficehorizoninquiry.org.uk/

Poulsen, L. (2017) 'British foreign investment policy post-Brexit: treaty obligations vs. bottom-up reforms', Working Paper, UCL European Institute [online], 6 July, Available from: https://papers.ssrn.com/sol3/papers.cfm?abstract_id=3001782

Prodi, R. (2010) *Europe 2020: A European Strategy for Smart, Sustainable and Inclusive Growth*, Brussels: European Commission.

Public Accounts Committee (PAC) (2021) *Government's Delivery Through Arm's-length Bodies Eighteenth Report of Session 2021–22*, London: Public Accounts Committee, House of Commons.

Public Administration Select Committee (PASC) (2002) 'These unfortunate events: Lessons of recent events at the former DTLR', HC Paper 303, Session 2001–02.

Public Accounts Select Committee (PASC) 2015 Developing Civil Service Skills: a unified approach HC Paper 112, Session 2014-2015.

Putnam, R. D. (1973) 'The political attitudes of senior civil servants in Western Europe: A preliminary report', *British Journal of Political Science*, 3(3): 257–90.

Putnam, R. (1975) 'The political attitudes of senior civil servants in Britain, Germany and Italy' in M. Dogan (ed) *The Mandarins of Western Europe*, London: John Wiley, pp 87–127.

Putnam, R. (1976) *The Comparative Study of Political Elites*, Prentice-Hall.

Pyper R. (1995) *The British Civil Service*, Brighton: Harvester Press.

Pyper, R. (2013) 'The UK coalition and the civil service: A half-term report', *Public Policy and Administration*, 28(4): 364–82.

Pyper, R. (2020) 'Debate: The British civil service – contextualizing development challenges', *Public Money & Management*, 40(8): 555–7.

Raadschelders, J. C. and Rutgers, M. R. (1999) 'The waxing and waning of the state and its study: changes and challenges in the study of Public Administration', in *The Modern State and its Study*, London: Edward Elgar Publishing, pp 17–13.

Raadschelders, J. and Van der Meer, F. M. (2014) 'Administrative elites in the Netherlands from 1980 to 2011: making the invisible visible', *International Review of Administrative Sciences*, 80(4): 726–45.

Raadschelders, J., Toonen, T. and Van der Meer F. M. (2007) 'Civil servants in the enabling framework state in the 21st century', in J. Raadschelders, T. Toonen and F. Van der Meer (eds) *The Civil Service in the 21st Century: Comparative Perspectives*, London: Palgrave Macmillan, pp 299–314.

Rawlings, R. (2001) 'Quasi-legislative devolution: powers and principles', *Northern Ireland Legal Quarterly*, 52–54.

Renwick, A. (2017) 'Citizens' assemblies: a better way of doing democracy?', *Political Insight*, 8(3): 24–27.

Renwick, A., Dobrianska, N., Kelly, C. J. and Kincaid, C. (2023) 'Public attitudes to referendums on Irish unification in Northern Ireland: evidence from an online consultation', *Irish Political Studies*, 38(4): 413–37.

Renwick, A., Allan, S., Jennings, W., Mckee, R., Russell, M. and Smith, G. (2018) 'What kind of Brexit do voters want? Lessons from the Citizens' Assembly on Brexit', *The Political Quarterly*, 89(4): 649–58.

Rhodes, R. A. W. (2001) 'United Kingdom: everybody but us' in R. A. W. Rhodes and P. Weller (eds) *The Changing World of Top Officials*, Maidenhead: Open University Press, pp 111–51.

Rhodes, R. A. W. (2005) 'Is Westminster dead in Westminster (and why should we care)?', Inaugural lecture in the ANZSOG-ANU Public Lecture Series, The Shine Dome, Academy of Science, Canberra, 23.

Rhodes, R. A. W. (2007) 'The everyday life of a minister: a confessional and impressionist tale' in R. A. W. Rhodes, P. t'Hart and M. Noordegraaf (eds) *Observing Government Elites*, London: Palgrave, pp 21–50.

Rhodes, R. A. W. (2022) 'Court politics in an age of austerity: David Cameron's Court, 2010–2016', in K. Kolltveit and R. Shaw (eds) *Core Executives in a Comparative Perspective: Governing in Complex Times*, Cham: Springer International Publishing, pp 79–121.

Rhodes, R. A. W., t'Hart, P. and Noordegraaf, M. (2007) 'Being there' in R. A. W. Rhodes, P. t'Hart and M. Noordegraaf (eds) *Observing Government Elites*, London: Palgrave.

Rhodes, R. A., Wanna, J. and Weller, P. (2008) 'Reinventing Westminster: how public executives reframe their world', *Policy & Politics*, 36(4): 461–79.

Rhodes, R. A. W., Carmichael, P., McMillan, J. and Massey, A. (2003) 'Decentralizing the civil service. McGraw-Hill Education (UK)' in R. A. W. Rhodes, P. t'Hart and M. Noordegraaf (eds) *Observing Government Elites*, London: Palgrave, pp 1–20.

Ribbins, P. and Sherratt, B. (2022) 'Portrait of an "outsider" as permanent secretary in Whitehall: the life and times of Michael Bichard – an unmandarin like mandarin?', *Journal of Educational Administration and History*, 54(4): 375–96.

Richards, D. (1997) *The Civil Service under the Conservatives 1979–1997 Whitehall's Political Poodles?* Liverpool: Liverpool University Press.

Richards, D. and Smith, M. (2002) *Governance and Public Policy in the UK*, Oxford: Oxford University Press.

Richards, D. and Smith, M. (2006) 'Central control and policy implementation in the UK: A case study of the Prime Minister's Delivery Unit', *Journal of Comparative Policy Analysis*, 8(4): 325–45.

Richards, D. and Richards, D. (2008) 'Labour and the civil service: From managerialism to a reconstituted Westminster model', *New Labour and the Civil Service: Reconstituting the Westminster Model*, 95–140.

Richards, D. and Smith, M. J. (2016) 'The Westminster model and the "indivisibility of the political and administrative elite": A convenient myth whose time is up?', *Governance*, 29(4): 499–516.

Richards, D. and Diamond, P. (2023) 'What does Dominic Raab's resignation tell us about the current state of minister-civil servant relations?', Mile End Institute [Blog], Queen Mary University of London [online], Available from: https://www.qmul.ac.uk/mei/news-and-opinion/items/what-does-dominic-raabs-resignation-tell-us-about-the-current-state-of-minister-civil-servant-relations.html

Richardson, J. J. and Jordan, A. G. (1979) *Governing Under Pressure*, London: Martin Robertson.

Richardson, J. (2018) British Policy-making and the Need for a Post-Brexit Policy Style, Cham: Springer.

Rickard, E. and Ozieranski, P. (2021) 'A hidden web of policy influence: The pharmaceutical industry's engagement with UK's All-Party Parliamentary Groups', *PLoS One*, 16(6).

Riddell, P. (2019) *15 Minutes of Power: The Uncertain Life of British Ministers*. London: Profile Books.

Riddell, P., Gruhn, Z. and Carolan, L. (2012) *The Challenge of Being a Minister*, London: Institute for Government.

Ridley, F. F. (1983) 'Career service: a comparative perspective on civil service promotion', *Public Administration*, 61(2): 179–96.

Riggs, F. W. (1994) 'Bureaucracy and the constitution', *Public Administration Review*, 54(1): 65–72.

Robinson, G., Burke, L. and Millings, M. (2016) 'Criminal justice identities in transition: the case of devolved probation services in England and Wales', *British Journal of Criminology*, 56(1): 161–78.

Robinson, M. (2014) 'Spending reviews', *OECD Journal on Budgeting*, 13(2): 81–122.

Robinson, N. (2014) 'Michael Gove: battling "The Blob"', BBC News [online] 3 February, Available from: https://www.bbc.co.uk/news/uk-politics-26008962

Rohr, J. A. (2002) *Civil Servants and Their Constitutions*, Lawrence, KS: University Press of Kansas.

Roscoe, P. (2023) *How to Build a Stock Exchange*, Bristol: Bristol University Press.

Rose, R. (1975) *The Problem of Party Government*, London: Macmillan.

Rose, R. (1987) 'Steering the ship of state: one tiler but two pairs of hands', *British Journal of Political Science*, 17: 409–33.

Rose, R. (1993) *Lesson-Drawing in Public Policy: A Guide to Learning Across Time and Space*, Vol 91, Chatham: Chatham House Publishers.

Ross, S., Fenney, D., Thorstensen-Woll, C. and Buck, D. (2021) *Directors of Public Health and the Covid-19 Pandemic*, London: The King's Fund.

Rosson, W. (1971) 'The reorganization of central government', *Political Quarterly*, 42(1): 87–90.

Rouban, L. (1995) 'Public administration at the crossroads: the end of French specificity', in J. Pierre (ed) *Bureaucracy in the Modern State: An Introduction to Comparative Public Administration*, Cheltenham: Edward Elgar, pp 39–63.

Rouban, L. (ed) (1999) *Citizens and the New Governance: Beyond new public management,* Vol. 10, IOS Press [online], Available from: https://www.researchgate.net/profile/Calliope-Spanou/publication/272892087_Citizens_and_the_quality_of_public_administration_in_Greece_in_Luc_Rouban_ed_Citizens_and_the_New_Governance_IIAS_IIAP_ENA_IOS_Press_Amsterdam_1999_29-40/links/55ef131608ae199d47bff8cc/Citizens-and-the-quality-of-public-administration-in-Greece-in-Luc-Rouban-ed-Citizens-and-the-New-Governance-IIAS-IIAP-ENA-IOS-Press-Amsterdam-1999-29-40.pdf

Runciman, W. G. (ed) (2004) *Hutton and Butler: Lifting the Lid on the Workings of Power* (Vol 3), Oxford: Oxford University Press.

Russell, M. and Serban, R. (2021) 'The muddle of the "Westminster model": A concept stretched beyond repair', *Government and Opposition*, 56(4): 744–64.

Rutter, J. (2013) 'A better formula: will civil service reform improve Whitehall's use of expert advice?', in R. Doubleday and J. Wilsdon (eds) *Future Directions for Scientific Advice* [online], Available from: https://www.csap.cam.ac.uk/media/uploads/files/1/fdsaw.pdf#page=39

Rutter, J. (2022) *Relationship Breakdown: Civil Service-Ministerial Relations – Time for a Reset*, London: Institute for Government.

Samuels, A. (2022) 'Going postal: the Post Office Horizon scandal', *Solicitors Journal*, 165: 43.

Sanders, A. and Richards, D. (2022) 'The gendered dynamics of "partygate": leadership and hypermasculinity at the centre of Johnson's administration', British Politics and Policy at LSE [Blog], Available from: https://blogs.lse.ac.uk/politicsandpolicy/gendered-dynamics-partygate/

Sanders, D. (2023) 'One man's damage: the consequences of Boris Johnson's assault on the British Political System', *The Political Quarterly* [online], Available from: https://politicalquarterly.org.uk/blog/the-consequences-of-boris-johnsons-assault-on-the-british-political-system/

Sanderson, I. (2002) 'Evaluation, policy learning and evidence-based policy making', *Public Administration*, 80(1): 1–22.

Sandford, M. (2023) 'Muscular unionism': the British political tradition strikes back?', *Political Studies*, 72(3): 1160–77.

Sandford M. (2023b) *Trailblazer Devolution Deals*, Research Briefing House of Commons Library.

Sargeant, J, Coulter, S., Pannell, J., McKee, R. and Hynes, M. (2023) *Review of the UK Constitution Final Report.* London: The Bennett Institute and Institute for Government.

Sasse, T. and Norris, E. (2019) *Moving On: The Cost of High Staff Turnover in the Civil Service*, London: Institute for Government.

Sausman, C. and Locke, R. (2004) 'The British civil service: examining the question of politicisation' in G. Peters and J. Pierre (eds) *The Politicization of the Civil Service in Comparative Perspective*, London: Routledge, pp 111–24.

Sauter, W. (2008) 'Services of general economic interest and universal service in EU law', TILEC Discussion Paper No. 2008-017, *European Law Review*, 2 [online], Available from: https://papers.ssrn.com/sol3/papers.cfm?abstract_id=1136105

Savoie, D. J. (1999) *Governing From the Centre: The Concentration of Power in Canadian Politics*, Toronto: University of Toronto Press.

Self, P. (1965) *Bureaucracy or Management?*, London: Bell and Son.

Selvon, S. (1956) *The Lonely Londoners*, London: Allan Wingate.

Scott, A. (2009) 'The evolution of competition law and policy in the United Kingdom', LSE Working Papers, Law Department [online], Available from: https://eprints.lse.ac.uk/24564/1/WPS2009-09_Scott.pdf

Scott, C. (2000) 'Services of general interest in EC law: Matching values to regulatory technique in the public and privatised sectors', *European Law Journal*, 6(4): 310–25.

Seddon, P. (2023) 'Calling us the Blob is insulting, says top civil servant', BBC News [online] 12 July, Available from: https://www.bbc.co.uk/news/uk-politics-66174373

Semenova, E. (2018) 'Research methods for studying elites', in H. Best and J. Higley (eds) *The Palgrave Handbook of Political Elites*, London: Palgrave Macmillan, pp 71–7.

Semple, A. (2012) 'Reform of the EU procurement directives and WTO GPA: forward steps for sustainability?' [online], Available from: https://web.archive.org/web/20200321122717id_/http://ippa.org/jopp/download/vol12/Book/Chapter%204_Semple.pdf

Sharifi, S. and Bovaird, T. (1995) 'The financial management initiative in the UK public sector: the symbolic role of performance reporting', *International Journal of Public Administration*, 18(2–3): 467–90.

Shergold, P. (2015) *Learning from Failure: Why Large Government Policy Initiatives Have Gone so Badly Wrong in the Past and How the Chances of Success in the Future can be Improved*, University of Western Sydney.

Sheriff, P. E. (1972) 'Outsiders in a closed career: the example of the British civil service', *Public Administration*, 50(4).

Shipman, T. (2016) *All Out War: The Full Story of How Brexit Sank Britain's Political Class*, Glasgow: William Collins.

Shore, C. and Thedval, R. (2023) 'Researching the Eurocrats: from networks and attitudes', in M. Segers and S. Van Hecke (eds) *Cambridge History of the European Union*, Cambridge: Cambridge University Press, pp 471–93.

Short, J. L. (2023) 'Regulatory managerialism as gaslighting government', *Law and Contemporary Problems*, 86(3).

Sian, S. and Smyth, S. (2022) 'Supreme emergencies and public accountability: the case of procurement in the UK during the Covid-19 pandemic', *Accounting, Auditing & Accountability Journal*, 35(1): 146–57.

Simon, D. (1984) A Regional Perspective on the Humber Bridge: Empirical and Theoretical Issues, Leeds: University of Leeds [online], Available from: https://eprints.whiterose.ac.uk/2358/1/ITS370_WP181_uploadable.pdf

Slaughter, A. M. and Burke-White, W. (2006) 'The future of international law is domestic (or, the European way of law)', *Harvard International Law Journal*, 47: 327.

Slessor, T. (2002) *Ministries of Deception: Cover-ups in Whitehall*, White Lion Publishing.

Smith, B. C. (1988) *Bureaucracy and Political Power*, Hemel Hempstead: Wheatsheaf Books.

Smith, M. J. (1999) *The Core Executive in Britain*, New York: St. Martin's Press.

Smith, M. and Richards, D. (2020) 'From constitutionalism to idealism: conceptual approaches to analysing Whitehall', *The Routledge Handbook of British Politics and Society*.

Smith, P. (1991) 'Lessons from the British poll tax disaster', *National Tax Journal*, 44(4): 421–36.

Smith, T. and Young A. (1996) *The Fixers: Crisis Management in British Politics*, London: Dartmouth Publishing.

Smithson, R., Richardson, E., Roberts, J., Walshe, K., Wenzel, L., Robertson, R., ... and Proudlove, N. (2018) *Impact of the Care Quality Commission on Provider Performance: Room for Improvement?*, The King's Fund [online], Available from: https://www.kingsfund.org.uk/insight-and-analysis/reports/impact-cqc-provider-performance

Sotiropoulos, D. A. (1999) 'A description of the Greek higher civil service', *Bureaucratic Elites in Western European States: A Comparative Analysis of Top Officials*.

Sowa, J. E., and Selden, S. C. (2003) 'Administrative discretion and active representation: an expansion of the theory of representative bureaucracy', *Public Administration Review*, 63(6): 701–10.

Spencer, K. and Mawson, J. (2000) 'Transforming regional government offices in England: a new Whitehall agenda', in R. A. W. Rhodes (ed) *Transforming British Government: Volume 2: Changing Roles and Relationships*, London: Palgrave Macmillan, pp 223–36.

Stafford, M. (2022) 'The Prime Minister's team: how British Leaders have run Downing Street', *Political Insight*, 13(4): 11–13.

Stark, A. (2019) 'Explaining institutional amnesia in government', *Governance*, 32(1): 143–58.

Stead, A. D. (2017) *Regulation and Efficiency in UK Public Utilities*, Doctoral Dissertation, University of Hull.

Steinberg, S. S. and Austern, D. T. (1990) *Government, Ethics and managers A Guide to Solving ethical Dilemmas in the Public Sector*, New York: Quorum.

Stevens, A. (2011) 'Telling policy stories: an ethnographic study of the use of evidence in policy-making in the UK', *Journal of Social Policy*, 40(2): 237–55.

Stewart, J. and Walsh, K. (1992) 'Change in the management of public services', *Public Administration*, 70(4): 499–518.

Stokes, D. (2016) *Influences on Relationships Between Ministers and Civil Servants in British Government: A Study Based on The Perceptions of Former Ministers*. Doctoral Thesis, University of Chester [online], Available from: https://chesterrep.openrepository.com/bitstream/handle/10034/621539/Post%20viva%20-%20FOR%20FINAL%20SUBMISSION%20-%20JUNE%202016.pdf?sequence=1

Stone, D. and Garnett, M. (1998) 'Introduction: think tanks, policy advice and governance'.

Syal, R. (2020) 'Dominic Cummings calls for "weirdos and misfits" for No 10 jobs', *The Guardian* [online] 2 January, Available from: https://www.theguardian.com/politics/2020/jan/02/dominic-cummings-calls-for-weirdos-and-misfits-for-no-10-jobs

Talbot, C. and Wiggan, J. (2010) 'The public value of the National Audit Office', *International Journal of Public Sector Management*, 23(1): 54–70.

Taylor, R. (2014) 'The Heath government, industrial policy and the "new capitalism"', In *The Heath Government 1970–74*, London: Routledge, pp 139–59.

Thain, C. (2010) 'Budget reform in the United Kingdom: the rocky road to "controlled discretion"', *The Reality of Budgetary Reform in OECD Countries: Trajectories and Consequences*, Cheltenham: Edward Elgar, pp 35–64.

Thain, C. and Wright, M. (1995) *The Treasury and Whitehall: The Planning and Control of Public Expenditure 1976–1993*, Oxford: Clarendon Press.

Theakston, K. (1986) 'The use and abuse of junior ministers: increasing political influence in Whitehall', *Political Quarterly*, 57(1).

Theakston, K. (1995) *The Civil Service since 1945*, Oxford: Blackwell.

Theakston, K. (1999) *Leadership in Whitehall*, London: Macmillan.

Theakston, K. (2000) 'Permanent secretaries: comparative biography and leadership in Whitehall', R. A. W. Rhodes (ed) *Transforming British Government: Volume 2: Changing Roles and Relationships*, London: Palgrave Macmillan, pp 125–45.

Theakston, K. (2012) 'David Cameron as prime minister', in T. Heppell and D. Seawright (eds) *Cameron and the Conservatives: The Transition to Coalition Government*, London: Palgrave Macmillan, pp 194–208.

Theakston, K. and Fry, G. K. (1989) 'Britain's administrative elite: permanent secretaries 1900–1986', *Public Administration*, 67(2): 129–47.

Theakston, K. and Connelly, P. (2018) *William Armstrong and British Policy Making*, London: Palgrave Macmillan.

Thelen, K. (2009) 'Institutional change in advanced political economies', *British Journal of Industrial Relations*, 47(3): 471–98.

Thijs, N., Hammerschmid, G. and Palaric, E. (2017) *A Comparative Overview of Public Administration Characteristics and Performance in EU 28*, Brussels: European Commission.

Thomas, A. (2021) *The Heart of the Problem: A Weak Centre is Undermining the UK Government*, London: Institute for Government.

Thomas, A. (2022) *After Boris Johnson: What Now for the Civil Service?* London: Institute for Government.

Thomas, P. (2015) 'Reaching across the aisle: explaining the rise of all-party parliamentary groups in the United Kingdom', in *UK Political Studies Association 65th Annual Conference*, Sheffield, pp 763–77.

Thomas, R. (2008) 'Transposing European Union law in the United Kingdom: administrative rule–making, scrutiny and better regulation', *European Public Law*, 14(2).

Thompson, B. (1987) 'Ministers and mandarins and select committees', *The Modern Law Review*, 50(4): 492–505.

Towns, A. E. (2012) 'Norms and social hierarchies: Understanding international policy diffusion "from below"', *International Organization*, 66(2): 179–209.

Toynbee, P. (2023) 'We laid Bob Kerslake to rest this week. Think of him – and give the civil service the respect it deserves', *The Guardian* [online] 27 July, Available from: https://www.theguardian.com/commentisfree/2023/jul/27/bob-kerslake-civil-service-whitehall

Transparency International (2021) 'House of cards' [online], Available from: https://www.transparency.org.uk/house-of-cards-UK-housing-policy-influence-Conservative-party-donations-lobbying-press-release

Transparency International (2024) 'Concerns of corruption at all time high as UK falls to its lowest ever score of global corruption perceptions index' [online] 30 January, Available from: https://www.transparency.org.uk/concerns-corruption-all-time-high-uk-falls-its-lowest-ever-score-global-corruption-perceptions-index

Tribe F. (1949[1971]) Efficiency in the Public Services in R. A. Chapman and A. Dunsire (eds) *Style in Administration: Readings in British Public Administration*, London: Allen & Unwin, pp 146–60.

Trollope, A. (1865) 'The civil service', *Fortnightly*, 2: 613–26.

Tryggvadottir, Á. (2022) 'OECD best practices for spending reviews', *OECD Journal on Budgeting*, 22(1).

Turner, D., Weinberg, N, Elsden, E. and Bals E. (2023) 'Why hasn't UK regional policy worked? The views of leading practitioners', Harvard Kennedy School [online], Available from: https://www.hks.harvard.edu/sites/default/files/centers/mrcbg/files/Final_AWP_216_2.pdf

UK in a Changing Europe (2024) 'Brexit and the state 2024' [online], Available from: https://ukandeu.ac.uk/reports/brexit-and-the-state/

Ungoed-James, J. (2024) 'Tories accused of "colonizing" state by granting public roles to allies', *The Observer* [online] 2 June, Available from: https://www.theguardian.com/politics/article/2024/jun/02/tories-accused-of-colonising-state-by-granting-public-roles-to-allies

Urban, J. (2024) 'I am a big fan of more SpADS', X.com [online] 22 May, Available from: x.com/JordanUrban10/status/1793220266283114648

Urban, J. and Thomas, A. (2023) *Revamping Government Reform*, London: Institute for Government.

Urban, J., Thomas A. and Clyne R. (2024) *Power with Purpose: Final Report of the Commission on the Centre of Government. Why the Centre of Government Has Failed Successive Prime Ministers – and Seven Recommendations for Radical Reform*, London: Institute for Government.

van den Brink, T. (2012) 'The substance of subsidiarity: the interpretation and meaning of the principle after Lisbon', in M. Trybus and L. Rubini (eds) *The Treaty of Lisbon and the Future of EU Law and Policy*, Cheltenham: Edward Elgar Publishing.

Van Der Meer, F. M. (2011) 'Civil service systems in Western Europe: an introduction', in F. M. Van Der Meer, *Civil Service Systems in Western Europe* (2nd edn), Cheltenham: Edward Elgar, pp 1–12.

Van Der Meer, F. M. and Dijkstra, G. (2011) 'Civil service systems in Western Europe: variations and similarities' in F. M. Van Der Meer, *Civil Service Systems in Western Europe* (2nd edn), Cheltenham: Edward Elgar, pp 271–85.

Van Dorpe, K. and Horton, S. (2011) 'The public service bargain in the United Kingdom: The Whitehall model in decline?', *Public Policy and Administration*, 26(2): 233–52.

Vicary, S., Stone, K., McCusker, P., Davidson, G. and Spencer-Lane, T. (2020) '"It's about how much we can do, and not how little we can get away with": Coronavirus-related legislative changes for social care in the United Kingdom', *International Journal of Law and Psychiatry*, 72: 101601.

Vinten, G. (2003) 'Whistleblowing: the UK experience. Part 1', *Management Decision*, 41(9): 935–43.

Volden, C. (2002) 'A formal model of the politics of delegation in a separation of powers system', *American Journal of Political Science*, 111–33.

Wackerbauer, J. (2007) 'Regulation and privatisation of the public water supply in England, France and Germany', *Competition and Regulation in Network Industries*, 8(2): 101–16.

Walker, R. (2023) 'Boris Johnson: the moral case for government resignations in July 2022', *British Politics*, 18(1): 60–80.

Walsh, C. D. and Elkink, J. A. (2021) 'The dissatisfied and the engaged: citizen support for citizens' assemblies and their willingness to participate', *Irish Political Studies*, 36(4): 647–66.

Ward, J. (2020) 'The British state and the recentralisation of power: from Brexit to COVID-19', LSE British Politics and Policy [Blog], Available from: https://blogs.lse.ac.uk/politicsandpolicy/centralisation-of-power-brexit-covid19/

Ward, J. and Ward, B. (2023) 'From Brexit to COVID-19: the Johnson government, executive centralisation and authoritarian populism', *Political Studies*, 71(4): 1171–89.

Ward, N. and Lowe, P. (2007) 'Blairite modernisation and countryside policy', *The Political Quarterly*, 78(3): 412–21.

Warner, N. (1984) 'Raynerism in practice: anatomy of a Rayner scrutiny', *Public Administration*, 62(1): 7–22.

Warner, S., Richards, D., Coyle, D. and Smith, M. J. (2021) 'English devolution and the Covid-19 pandemic: governing dilemmas in the shadow of the treasury', *The Political Quarterly*, 92(2): 321–30.

Weller, P. and Haddon, C. (2016) 'Westminster traditions: Continuity and change', *Governance*, 29(4): 483–98.

Wettenhall, R. (2011) 'Organisational amnesia: a serious public sector reform issue', *International Journal of Public Sector Management*, 24(1): 80–96.

White, A. and Dunleavy, P. (2010) 'Making and breaking Whitehall departments: a guide to machinery of government changes', LSE e-print [online], Available from: https://eprints.lse.ac.uk/27949/1/Making_and_breaking_Whitehall_departments_%28LSERO%29.pdf

White, L. A. (2020) 'Do international organizations influence domestic policy outcomes in OECD countries?', in R. Nieuwenhuis and W. Van Lancker (eds) *The Palgrave Handbook of Family Policy*, Cham: Palgrave Macmillan, pp 69–86.

Whitehall and Industry Group (WIG) (2002) Attachments and Secondments Research Project.

Whitham, B. (2023) 'The UK in the world: from "internal colonialism" to "global Britain"'. Paper prepared for presentation in the 'Colonial Legacies' lecture series of the Foreign, Commonwealth and Development Office (FCDO), [online], 20 December 2023, Available from: https://eprints.soas.ac.uk/41199/1/The%20UK%20in%20the%20World%20From%20Internal%20Colonialism%20to%20Global%20Britain.pdf

Wiborg, S. (2015) 'Privatizing education: free school policy in Sweden and England', *Comparative Education Review*, 59(3): 473–97.

Wilkes, G. (2014) *The Unelected Lynchpin: Why Government Needs Special Advisers*, London: Institute for Government.

Wilkes, G. and Westlake, S. (2014) *The End of the Treasury*, London: NESTA.

Wilkes, G., Bartrum, O. and Clyne, R. (2024) *Treasury 'Orthodoxy'*, London: Institute for Government.

Wilkins, P. (2002) 'Accountability and joined-up government', *Australian Journal of Public Administration*, 61(1): 114–19.

Williams, S. (1980) 'The decisionmakers', in W. Plowden (ed) *Policy and Practice: The Experience of Government*, London: Royal Institute of Public Administration.

Williams, W. (1983) 'British policy analysis: some preliminary observations from the US', in A. Grey and B. Jenkins (eds) *Policy Analysis and Evaluation in British Government*, London: Royal Institute of Public Administration, pp 17–24.

Willman, J. (1994) 'The civil service' in D. Kavanagh and A. Seldon (eds) *The Major Effect*, London: Macmillan, pp 64–82.

Wilson, G. (2004) 'Organise your life the Downing Street way', BBC [online], Available from: http://news.bbc.co.uk/1/hi/magazine/3746191.stm

Wilson, R. (1999) 'The civil service in the new millennium', speech at City University, London.

Wilson, R. (2002) 'Portrait of a profession revisited', *Political Quarterly*, 73(4): 381–91.

Wise, C. (1994) 'The public service configuration problem: designing public organizations in a pluralistic public service', in A. Farazmand (ed) *Modern Organizations: Administrative Theory in Contemporary Society*, Westport, CT: Praeger, pp 81–103.

Wolff, S. and Piquet, A. (2022) 'Post-Brexit Europeanization: re-thinking the continuum of British policies, polity, and politics trajectories', *Comparative European Politics*, 20: 513–26.

Wood, G. T., Onali, E., Grosman, A. and Haider, Z. A. (2023) 'A very British state capitalism: variegation, political connections and bailouts during the COVID-19 crisis', *Environment and Planning A: Economy and Space*, 55(3): 673–96.

Woodhouse, D. (2004) 'The constitutional and political implications of a United Kingdom Supreme Court', *Legal Studies*, 24(1–2): 134–55.

Woodhouse, D. (2013) 'Civil servants and politicians: a very British relationship', in C. Neuhold and S. Vanhoonacker (eds) *Civil Servants and Politics: A Delicate Balance*, London: Palgrave Macmillan, pp 71–89.

Work and Pensions and BEIS Select Committees (2018) *Report on Carillion* [online], Available from: https://committees.parliament.uk/committee/164/work-and-pensions-committee/news/97606/work-and-pensions-and-beis-committees-publish-report-on-carillion/

Worlidge J. (2023) 'Strained Whitehall relationships need a long-term fix', London: Institute for Government [online] 15 August, Available from: https://www.instituteforgovernment.org.uk/comment/strained-whitehall-relationships-need-long-term-fix

Wright, G., Stojanovic, A. and Klemperer, D. (2020) *Influencing the EU after Brexit*, London: Institute for Government.

Wright, T. and Gamble, A. (1998) 'Commentary: and so to England', *The Political Quarterly*, 69(1): 1–3.

Yi-Chong, X. and Weller, P. (2008) '"To be, but not to be seen": exploring the impact of international civil servants', *Public Administration*, 86(1): 35–51.

Yong, B. and Hazell, R. (2014) *Special Advisers: Who They Are, What They Do and Why They Matter*, London: Bloomsbury Publishing.

Zhelyazkova, A. (2013) 'Complying with EU directives' requirements: the link between EU decision-making and the correct transposition of EU provisions', *Journal of European Public Policy*, 20(5): 702–21.

Index

A

accountability 7, 14, 28, 35, 61–63, 66–67, 71, 80, 82, 88, 102–103, 138–141, 146, 155, 168, 173
  ministerial accountability 31, 33, 35
accountants 13
accounting officers 23, 26, 29, 101, 138–140, 172
agenda setting 122
agencies 1–2, 5, 7, 21, 23–24, 27–28, 34, 36–37, 40, 60–61, 63, 67, 70, 73, 76–77, 82–83, 89, 100, 131, 134, 137, 139, 144, 146, 152, 167
agencification 4, 13, 18, 22, 27, 34–36, 63–64, 98, 145, 152, 160
agriculture 118, 123
air quality 47
Aitken, Jonathan 14
All Party Parliamentary Groups (APPG) 49–50, 66
Armstrong, Robert viii, 9, 31–32, 47, 96, 117, 139
  Armstrong Memorandum 9, 15
asylum seekers 36, 75–76, 78, 121
austerity 14, 22, 45, 60, 72, 75, 90, 101, 125
Australia 5, 28, 57, 118–119, 121, 158
Austria 6, 25

B

Barber, Michael 66, 68–69, 76
Barnett Formula 103–104
Barwell, Gavin 94
behaviours 19, 47, 72, 87, 95–97, 147–148, 153–156, 166–167, 171
behavioural insights see also nudge 59
Bevin, Ernest 123
Bichard, Michael 161
Blair, Tony 11, 16, 18–19, 22–23, 26, 33, 38, 40, 44–46, 56–57, 60–62, 64–68, 70, 74, 80, 93–94, 98, 103, 135, 152, 166
blob 12, 84, 134
Blunkett, David 84
borders 21, 36, 69, 111, 118, 137, 171
Boyle, Edward 52–53, 92

bribery 148
Bridges, Edward viii, 9, 31, 52, 66, 92, 144, 150–151
Brown, George 10, 17
Brown, Gordon 23, 26, 61–62, 74, 94, 106–107, 135, 156
building control 53, 143
bullying 95, 148
Bunbury, H. 33, 39, 67–68, 132, 160
Butler, Robin 46
by-election 47

C

Cabinet Committees 158
Cabinet Office 16, 21, 24, 32, 35, 38, 53, 65, 73, 106, 108, 110, 113, 116, 123–124, 126, 136, 140, 155–159, 163–164, 171, 173
Cabinet Secretary 15, 22–23, 30, 32, 38, 46, 68, 79–80, 88, 97, 136, 138, 157–159, 161
Campbell, Alistair 94, 159
Canada 50, 118, 158
capability reviews 38
Cardiff 108
Care Quality Commission 131
career planning 17
Carillon 29, 77, 141, 147
Cameron, David 11, 42, 54, 62, 84, 93–94, 125, 152, 158–159
Casey, Louise 62, 90
Castle, Barbara 40, 47, 85–86
centralisation 34, 64, 100, 102–103, 156
Central Policy Review Staff (CPRS) 56, 67, 131
Centre for Policy Studies 49
Chamberlain, Joseph 12
Chancellor of the Exchequer 19, 23, 30, 62, 93, 143, 156
Chapman, Leslie 95
chief executive 30, 32, 62, 79, 88, 161
chief operating officer 157–158
Chilcot Inquiry 46
citizen 5, 21, 28, 36, 44, 95, 108, 134, 153, 170

citizen's assemblies 50–51
Citizen's Charter 18, 27–28, 131, 151
civil service code 96, 148, 151
Civil Service College 17, 135
Civil Service Commission 22, 36, 164–165
client function 29, 36, 77–78, 132, 140, 164, 173
clientelist 4, 58, 107
club government 90
Coalition government 4, 14, 22–23, 45, 51, 60, 94, 106, 152, 156, 159
cohesion (EU) 72, 107, 112, 116–117, 128–129
colonial 98–99, 117
Colonial Office 99
combined authority 100, 103, 107, 113, 170
Commonwealth 43, 99, 124
competency framework 37, 67
competition 5–8, 16, 18, 24–29, 32–34, 52, 57, 62, 80, 83, 89, 92, 94, 105, 119, 128, 136, 140, 145–147, 157
Competition Act 1989 26
Conservative Party 84, 87, 109, 125, 164, 166
constitutional bureaucracy 63, 76
contract management viii, 29, 77, 140
contractors 27, 35, 87, 91, 132, 138, 140–141, 147
construction 24–27, 29
core executive 14, 16, 21, 23–24, 27, 32–34, 38–39, 42–44, 52–53, 60, 64–65, 108, 116, 118, 122–123, 126–127, 145–146, 155–158, 163
Cornwall 99
coroners 47, 132
corruption 47, 72, 146–148
COVID-19 19, 32, 37, 46–47, 73, 80, 87, 95–96, 101, 108–109, 113, 115, 125, 136, 138, 144, 169
crisis management 69
crony capitalism 147
Crosby, Lynton 94
Crossman, Richard 40, 80, 85, 151
Cummings, Dominic 11–12, 54–55, 85, 90, 93–94, 152, 159
Customer 4, 6, 16, 27, 135

D

Davies, David 125
Dawes, Melanie 88
deals 71, 100–101, 107, 112–113, 118
decentralisation 7, 92, 102, 169, 172
delegation 98, 101–103, 105, 108, 113–114
deliberative assemblies 15, 50–51, 122
deliverology 68
demand management 70
democratic deficit 102
Department of Work and Pensions (DWP) 21, 36

depoliticisation 4–5, 7
deprivileging 18, 84, 89, 112
Devolved Administrations (DAs) 19, 22, 40–41, 63, 75, 100, 151, 156, 170
devolution 101–106, 108–113
Dicey 9
Dilnot, Andrew 55
disasters 47, 109, 171
diversity 35, 27
donors 41, 49, 52, 119, 127, 148, 164
driving licences 24, 27, 36, 111, 113
Dunlop Review 101, 108
dynamic alignment 57, 116–117, 125

E

East India Company 98
economic growth 71, 118, 170
Eddington, Rod 62
education 3, 19, 28, 57, 68, 103, 105, 109, 111, 121, 123, 161
effectiveness 13–14, 18, 27, 56–58, 60, 80, 82–83, 121, 134–135, 148, 154, 170
efficiency 4, 13–14, 17–18, 27–29, 41, 44, 68, 76, 134
elites 4, 49, 153–154
England 9, 19, 21–22, 41, 57, 75–76, 100–106, 109, 112–113, 144–145, 156, 167, 169
energy 34, 36, 43, 117, 142, 144
enforcers 93
ethics 15, 83, 87, 147–148, 162
Ethnicity 71
European Investment Bank (EIB) 142
exceptionalism viii, 32, 99, 122, 142, 144
experts 3, 10, 51, 54, 59, 65, 86, 92, 122, 124, 126, 134–135, 166

F

Fabian Society 17
Falklands War 14, 95
fast Lane 80, 87, 95, 138, 159
fast stream 16, 29–30, 82–83, 123, 134, 144, 147, 155, 159, 162, 177
Financial Management Initiative (FMI) 13, 61, 82
financial services 115, 117, 125
Finland 3, 5
First Division Association (FDA) 32–33
fiscal policy 71
Fisher, Warren viii, 16, 54, 92, 150–151, 160
France 2–9, 19–20, 25, 50, 76, 121
fraud 33, 95, 146, 148
freedom of information 96
free schools 29
Fulton Report 10, 17–19, 24, 30, 49, 61. 64, 79, 81, 131, 135, 144, 148, 151, 155, 166, 172–173

INDEX

G

gateway reviews 133
gender 71
General Agreement on Tariffs and Trade (GATT) 6, 24, 27
  Government Procurement Agreement (GPA) 6–7, 13, 18–20, 24–29, 32, 44, 63, 71, 75–77, 98, 140
general election 4, 43, 45, 58, 60, 64, 68, 73, 103, 108, 115, 118, 152, 173
generalists 13, 17, 30, 41, 65, 136
Germany 4–7, 19–20, 25, 89, 137, 158
Gershon, Peter 133
Ghosh, Helen 88
gold plating 43
Good Friday Agreement 100, 107
Goodman, Arnold 17
Gore Commission 8
Goschen Formula 103
Gove, Michael 41, 84
Government Offices for the Regions (GoR) 71, 92, 167
Government Procurement Agreement (GPA) see General Agreement on Tariffs and Trade (GATT)
Grace Commission 8
grades 31, 35, 37, 39, 114, 138, 144, 160, 162
Green Book 56, 133, 141
Grenfell Tower 53, 143, 171
Gray, Sue 51, 90, 96–97, 108, 174
Greece 3–4, 7

H

Hailsham, Lord 10
Haldane Report viii, 9, 16, 40–41, 64, 67, 74, 92, 98, 130, 150, 160
Hartlepool 47
health 12, 28, 50, 68, 70, 87, 96, 111, 122–123, 126, 143
  NHS 28, 24, 47, 69–70, 79, 95
  public health 34, 109, 138
Heath, Edward 18, 44, 56, 67, 74, 98, 146, 158
Heseltine, Michael 82, 89
Heywood, Jeremy viii, 18, 22, 135, 159
Hill, Fiona 85, 94, 159
Hilton, Steve 11, 42, 54, 84, 90, 94, 152, 159
His Majesty's Revenues and Customs (HMRC) 21, 23, 36
HM Treasury Memorandum 67, 139, 143
Home Secretary 23, 30, 36, 55, 82, 95, 137
honours system 31, 68, 94, 165
housing 23. 25. 28, 34, 34, 47, 49, 58, 70, 74–75, 101, 121, 142, 170
hospitality 91

hostile environment 29, 36
human rights 48, 96

I

ideology 3, 7, 26, 41, 44, 56, 91, 99, 96, 117, 120–121, 127, 148
Ibbs Report 13
incremental change 17, 69, 125, 133, 156, 172
Indian Civil Service 98
infected blood 46, 82, 155, 160, 171
infrastructure 43, 62, 71, 78, 127, 139, 142–145
Ingham, Bernard 159
inquiries 31, 132, 148, 150, 152, 155, 171–172
integration 128, 146, 154
International Financia Reporting Standard (IFRS) 145
International Monetary Fund (IMF) 25, 117, 127–128, 170
Institute of Economic Affairs (IEA) 49
Institute for Fiscal Studies (IFS) 50, 139
Institute for Government (IfG) 10, 22, 36, 53, 64, 82, 147, 159, 162, 169
institutional memory 33, 41, 56, 130, 133–134, 143, 148
Ireland 50–51, 100, 111, 118
Italy 3

J

Javid, Savid 93
Johnson, Boris 9–11, 19, 22, 47, 54, 79–80, 85, 87, 93–94, 96–97, 101, 109, 118, 125, 128, 140, 147, 151–152, 158–159, 164–166
Joined Up Government (JUG) 33, 172
Joseph, Keith 25

K

Kerslake, Bob 22, 159, 161, 173
King's Speech 45, 72–73

L

Labour Party 44, 50, 100, 103, 108, 118
Lamont, Norman 93
Langstaff Inquiry 46
lattice of leverage 30, 154, 162, 168
lawyers 142, 162
leadership 2, 8, 17, 38–39, 41–43, 53, 83, 88, 97, 102, 108, 152, 164, 170
levelling up 34, 47, 57, 72, 101, 112, 129
Levido, Isaac 94
Lewis, Derek 21, 82
lines to take 89, 166
Lisbon Treaty 42–43, 106–107
Lloyd George, David 9
lobbying 41–42, 49, 52, 55, 61, 63, 93, 112, 163

local government 23, 28, 34, 54, 61, 65, 69, 91, 106–107, 109, 112–113, 135, 143, 145–14, 161, 163, 166–167

M

Maastricht Treaty 42–43, 107, 167
machinery of government (MoG) 9, 23, 46, 64, 73, 98, 101, 115, 125, 127, 150, 155
Major, John 14, 18, 26–28, 30, 44, 67, 73–74, 93, 135, 151, 164
management consultants 27, 30, 32, 135
management skills 13, 17, 41
Manchester 25, 109, 113
mandarin 151
market making 28
market testing 28, 40
Maude, Francis 35, 41, 54, 62, 97, 131, 139, 150–152
May, Theresa 36, 85, 94, 101, 108, 111, 125, 159, 166
McSweeney, Morgan 94
MINIS 82
ministerial code 53, 83
ministerial direction 86–87, 96, 138, 140, 173
Ministry of Defence (MoD) 77, 163
Modernising Government White Paper 37–38, 59
monarchy 94
Mulgan, Geoff 11, 90, 152, 163
muscular unionism 101, 106, 109

N

National Audit Office (NAO) 15, 24, 37–39, 41, 54, 61, 72, 77–78, 80, 82, 87, 90–92, 95, 130–131, 138–139
National Institute for Clinical excellence (NICE) 70
National Rail 141
National School of Government 135
National Trust 88, 163
Neo-liberalism 5, 7
Netherlands 5–6, 19–20, 25, 28, 89
new public management (NPM) 15, 27–29
new towns 71
New Zealand 5, 57, 118, 121
Next Steps Agencies 26, 28, 34, 36, 67, 76, 89, 100, 131, 134, 151
Nolan Committee on Standards in Public Life 39, 91, 147
non-executive director (NED) 62–63, 90, 164
Normington, David 54
North Atlantic Treaty Organisation (NATO) 117
Northcote Trevelyan Report viii, 8, 10, 15–16, 47, 54–55, 64, 85, 92, 98, 140, 150, 152, 160

Northern Ireland 99, 101, 103–104, 106–107, 109–111, 116
Nudge see also behavioural insights 59

O

Ockenden Inquiry 46
O'Donnell, Gus viii, 38, 136, 159
OECD 6, 19, 57, 71, 75, 102, 116–117, 120, 121–122, 127–128, 145, 170
Office for Budget Responsibility (OBR) 24, 80
Ofsted 131
orbital Europeanism 127–128
Osmotherly rules 139–140
outsourced 22, 27, 29, 61, 75, 77, 100, 132, 168, 172–173
Oxbridge 30, 79, 110, 163

P

partygate 19, 90, 95–97, 136–137, 159
Parliament
  House of Commons 19, 48, 51, 53, 72, 137, 159, 141, 167
  House of Lords 10, 45, 50, 3, 65, 72, 100, 170
  Members' ballots 48
  Parliamentary Question (PQ) 31
passports 21, 24, 27, 36, 146
Patel, Priti 83
patronage 85, 164
payroll 27, 78
performance management 17, 38, 131
performance objectives 35
performance related pay (PRP) 39
personnel 32, 61
petitions 50
Plowden, Edwin 17, 90, 123
policy
  agenda 3, 55, 59
  bandwagons 51
  communities 42, 58, 122
  convergence 57, 105, 110, 122–123
  copying 56–57
  design 61, 68, 135–136
  diffusion 121–123
  divergence 105, 111
  evidence based 58
  lab 136
  network 58, 134
  transfer 28, 56–57, 112, 121–122
  tsars 54, 62, 65, 83
  windows 51, 61, 152
politicisation 1, 3, 4, 7, 10–11, 49, 55, 90–91, 147–148, 164
poll tax 66, 137
Ponting, Clive 14, 95, 139
post code lottery 105
Post Office 21, 29, 46–47, 82, 90, 142, 171

INDEX

Powell, Charles 159
Powell, Jonathan 94, 159
power hoarding 10, 109
presidentialism ix, 9, 22, 80, 90, 168
Prescott, John 74
Prime Minister
  PMDU 38, 62, 66, 68–69, 159
  PMSU 38, 63, 68, 159
prison service 21–222, 24, 27, 36, 82, 161
Private finance initiative (PFI) 26
private office 30, 93–94, 165
private secretary 79, 94
private sector 6–8, 12–14, 19, 24, 24–26, 28–29, 32, 50, 54, 61, 63, 67–68, 74, 77–78, 91, 138, 144–145, 147, 162–163
privatisation 25, 29, 44
probation service 22, 27, 29, 36
procurement (see also General Procurement Agreement) viii, 25, 27, 44, 61, 63, 77, 80, 87, 95, 117, 120, 130, 117, 120, 138, 141, 145, 147, 159, 163
professionals 1, 30, 34, 95, 162, 173
project boards 133
project management 39, 133
Public Accounts Select Committee (PASC) 15, 78, 81, 94, 139
public appointments 90, 164
public bodies 12, 27–29, 36, 164
public discourse 14, 51, 115, 131
public interest 5, 13–15, 24, 26, 95, 131, 141, 163
public involvement 6
public service agreements (PSA) 18, 38, 61, 69, 84, 159
public service bargain 62, 90
public service ethos 4, 6, 14
public service obligation 2, 5, 173
public value 2, 4–5, 12, 15–16, 18, 31
punctuated equilibrium 98, 148, 151

Q

quangos 103–104
Queen Elizabeth II 96, 111

R

railways 24, 29, 36, 141, 143
Rayner Scrutinies 13, 17, 26, 54, 62, 90
recentralising 106
redistribution 71–72
Rees-Mogg, Jacob 48, 85
referendum 19, 22, 37, 51, 63, 100, 103, 106, 108, 112, 115, 117–118, 123–126, 131, 134, 143
refugees 76, 87
refuse collection 28
regions 71, 115, 167, 170
regulators 24, 26, 35, 88–89, 172
revolving doors 147, 163

Ridley, Nicholas 25, 50, 159–160
risk 41, 69, 78, 87, 131–133, 140–142, 144, 147
Rose, Stuart 62
Royal Bank of Scotland (RBS) 141–142
Royal Commissions 46, 54, 172
Rural Payments Agency 27, 36
Rwanda 96, 121

S

Salisbury Convention 45, 72
Scandinavia 20
Scotland 51, 96, 99, 101, 103–106, 109–112, 164
scrutiny 14–15, 31, 47, 78, 165, 173
secondment 147, 162–164
Sedwill, Mark 159
Select Committees 9, 15, 31, 39, 46, 75, 79, 89, 130–131, 139, 141, 144, 151–152
senior responsible owner (SRO) 133, 139
scientific civil service 34
Sewel Convention 108
Shared Prosperity Fund 72, 112
Sharp, Evelyn 85
short termism 33, 64, 74, 90, 127, 133, 137, 143–145, 156, 160
Single Market (EU) 6, 43, 77, 108, 118, 120, 142
skills 2, 6, 10, 13, 16–17, 38–41, 55, 61, 67, 81–82, 91, 93, 121, 124, 136, 153, 164, 171, 174
socialisation 30, 39, 155
social care 51, 55, 70
social exclusion 62, 158
social media 15, 47, 58, 169
social value 15–16, 26, 77
sofa government 18, 45–46
soft power 31, 118, 122, 151, 154, 163
specialists 7, 17, 30–31, 39, 41, 53, 62, 93
specification 4, 6, 28–29, 77–78, 132, 140–141, 164
spending reviews 33, 74, 127, 156–157
stakeholders 133, 135
Starmer, Keir 85, 94, 158, 170, 174
steering not rowing 8, 27
stocktakes 69
subsidiarity 43, 99, 101–102, 106–107, 153, 167, 170
Sunak, Rishi 15, 45, 47, 57, 94, 109, 119, 158
Sweden 4–5, 8, 25, 28, 57
Syria 76

T

targets 18, 29, 36, 62, 67–69, 78, 83–84, 101, 107, 119, 132
Thatcher, Margaret 11, 54–14, 17–18, 24, 26, 28, 44, 50, 54–56, 60–62, 64, 66, 79, 81–82, 84–85, 89, 93, 98, 119, 123, 131, 137, 151, 158–160

think tank ix, 27, 30, 41–42, 49–50, 58, 66, 76, 81, 87, 91, 93, 119, 122, 127, 137, 148, 166, 172
Timothy, Nick 85, 94, 159
Total Place 71, 146
track and trace 29, 138
training and development 6–7, 16, 19, 31, 38–41, 65, 133, 142, 144, 153, 161–162, 164
transparency 27–28, 31, 56, 74, 91, 124, 126, 151, 173
transparency International 49, 72, 147
transport 25, 68, 70, 115–116, 121, 123, 126–127, 142–144
treaties 42–43, 98, 105, 115, 118, 120–121, 127, 151
tribunals 36, 132
Truss, Liz 11, 48, 55, 79–80, 85, 93, 109, 117, 119–120, 125, 136, 142–143, 158
trust 5, 80, 92, 105–106, 124–125, 163, 167
Tufton Street 49
Turnbull, Andrew 152

U

Ukraine 46, 76
UKREP 123
unintended consequences 98

United States 2–3, 5, 8, 18, 24, 26, 54, 57, 89, 117
utilities 6, 25–27

V

Volcker Commission 8

W

Wales 99–101, 103–104, 106, 109–110
water 24–25, 29, 82, 144, 171
welfare state 2, 7, 9, 24, 28, 70, 84, 89, 106
World Economic Forum 117, 123, 128
WhatsApp 87
Whistleblower 14, 95
Whitehall and Industry Group (WiG) 163–164
White, Sharon 88
Whole Government Accounts (WGA) 145
Wilson, Harold 17–18, 85, 126, 143, 146
Wilson, Richard 68, 152
Windrush 29, 36, 78, 82, 99, 132, 171
World Trade Organisation (WTO) 6, 27, 29, 63, 71, 77, 98, 115, 117, 119–120, 127, 129

Y

Yes Minister 12, 86–87

www.ingramcontent.com/pod-product-compliance
Lightning Source LLC
Chambersburg PA
CBHW051540020426
42333CB00016B/2015